FORGOTTEN ISLAND

The WWII Story of One Sailor's Survival
on Japanese-Occupied Guam

JOHN J. DOMAGALSKI

A KNOX PRESS BOOK
An Imprint of Permuted Press
ISBN: 979-8-88845-280-6
ISBN (eBook): 979-8-88845-281-3

Forgotten Island:
The WWII Story of One Sailor's Survival on Japanese-Occupied Guam
© 2024 by John J. Domagalski
All Rights Reserved

Cover art by Jim Villaflores

Permuted Press, LLC
New York • Nashville
permutedpress.com

Published in the United States of America
1 2 3 4 5 6 7 8 9 10

To Edward Domagalski

US Army—Korean War

TABLE OF CONTENTS

WHEN AMERICA "INVADED" AN UNKNOWN ISLAND

CAPTAIN HENRY GLASS UNDERSTOOD HIS orders were to remain sealed until he was at sea. The fifty-four-year-old veteran American naval officer was in command of the protected cruiser USS *Charleston*. The warship departed Honolulu, Hawaiian Territory on June 4, 1898 sailing in a westerly direction. The vessel was a powerful warship in terms of turn-of-the-century naval technology. Her eight-inch and six-inch guns were supplemented with an assortment of smaller-caliber weapons. Armor plating protected critical areas of the ship, such as her conning tower and gun shields.

The cruiser was escorting three transports—*City of Peking*, *Australia*, and *City of Sydney*. All three were loaded with troops. A little more than a month passed since the American Asiatic Squadron, a group of warships operating in the Far East under the command of Commodore George Dewey, destroyed the Spanish Pacific Squadron during the Battle of Manila Bay. The decisive naval battle took place in the opening days of the Spanish-American War. Control of the Spanish colony of the Philippines was ready to be taken by the

Americans—as soon as soldiers from the United States could arrive to start the occupation.

Glass called some of his sailors aboard *Charleston* to the quarter deck after the last view of the Hawaiian shoreline faded from the horizon. He ripped open the envelope containing orders from Secretary of the Navy John Long. The ships were directed to sail to Manila, Philippines. The lengthy voyage across the vast Pacific Ocean spanned over 5,000 miles. Glass was ordered to report to Dewey upon his arrival. The troops aboard the transports were to enforce the American control of the archipelago.

The confidential orders from Secretary Long contained an additional mission. "On your way, you are hereby directed to stop at the Spanish Island of Guam. You will use such force as may be necessary to capture the port of Guam, making prisoners of the governor and other officials and any armed force that may be there."[1] Long further directed all fortifications and Spanish naval vessels in the immediate vicinity to be destroyed. He noted the operations around Guam were to be brief; the main mission was to deliver the troops to the Philippines.

Glass immediately set a course for Guam. The island was a little more than halfway between Honolulu and Manila. The mission quickly sent sailors into *Charleston*'s library to scrutinize charts and encyclopedias for information about their new destination.[2] They learned it was the largest and most populated island of the Marianas, a chain comprising fifteen islands spanning a north-south arch in the middle of the Pacific and was associated with Spain for centuries.

The island of Guam was discovered by Ferdinand Magellan on March 6, 1521.[3] The famous Portuguese explorer, sailing under the

Spanish flag, left Europe on September 20, 1519 with five ships on a voyage to circumnavigate the world.[4] The explorer traveled south through the Atlantic making various stops before rounding the bottom of South America to enter the Pacific. Magellan then sailed on a northwesterly course across the vast ocean discovering various island groups during the voyage.

The sailors were exhausted, hungry, and looking for provisions when they arrived at Guam. Magellan formally claimed the island for Spain. The arrival of the explorer and his ships marked the beginning of centuries of Spanish involvement with the island.

The European sailors quickly came in contact with the indigenous population of Guam—the Chamorro people. The Chamorros are thought to have arrived in the Mariana Islands from Asia many centuries earlier. Magellan was reported to have been greatly impressed with the rigging among the native boats to the point of labeling the new lands "Islas de los Velas Latinas" or Island of the Lateen Sails.[5] The explorer continued his voyage west, eventually making landfall in the Philippines, where he later met with death.

The Chamorros subsequently lived largely undisturbed on Guam for over a hundred years. Although ships occasionally stopped at the island, there was no direct rule from Spain.[6] The process of transforming the island into a Spanish colony began in 1668 when a group of Jesuit priests and soldiers arrived to create a permanent settlement on the island. Spanish traders and additional missionaries followed. Guam and the nearby islands were renamed the Marianas in honor of Queen Maria of Spain.[7] She was reported to have taken a personal interest in converting the Chamorro residents to Catholicism.[8]

Tensions steadily rose as the Spanish began force-teaching the Chamorros Christianity and sought to establish rule over their subjects. The new rulers implemented the standard Spanish colonial policy of enslavement, forced labor, and the killing of those not accepting the new authority.[9] The persecution was serious enough to start an armed revolution.

More than two decades of fighting between the rulers and their subjects followed, with superior Spanish firepower eventually winning the conflict. The islanders were further ravaged by a variety of diseases introduced by the Europeans. The Spanish later transported other Chamorros from the northern Marianas to Guam for resettlement in new villages, often under the observant eye of a Spanish priest, and banned the use of offshore canoes to prevent their escaping.[10] Various island customs and traditions slowly changed, and the Chamorro language gradually blended with Spanish.

A governor-general for Guam was eventually appointed by the Spanish Crown in Europe with two larger Spanish colonies to the east and west—Mexico and the Philippines—holding variable amounts of sway over Guam and the Marianas at various times over the next century. The grip of the Spanish authoritarian rule loosed considerably by the middle of the 1800s with Spain maintaining a lazy control over Guam.[11] Spain's hegemony over the Marianas became progressively weaker as the century progressed, resulting in more local involvement.

The Spanish empire was reaching its twilight as the nineteenth century progressed. The nation's once powerful naval forces were diminished and the global geography under Spanish control was shrinking. Spain had already lost large amounts of territory to the United States in North America earlier in the century. The influence of other European powers—including Britain, France, and Germany—were stronger around the world. The Spanish rule of Guam would soon come to an end.

Glass had little knowledge about the Spanish defenses on Guam. Information included with the orders warned of coastal guns and the possibility of one or two enemy warships in the area. The size of the Spanish garrison on the island was unknown. The Americans had little choice but to assume the island would be defended and prepared accordingly.

The small American flotilla arrived off Guam early on the morning of June 20, 1898. The weather was overcast with occasional rain squalls. With the transports staying further out to sea, Glass cautiously brought *Charleston* closer to the entrance of San Luis d' Apra Harbor on the western side of the island. He could see the deep-water harbor is formed by the Orote Peninsula on the south and Cabras Island to the north with jagged reefs near the coastline. The old Spanish Fort Santiago, positioned on a high bluff near the tip of the peninsula, stood as if a sentry guarding the island. The main city of Agaña was only a short distance to the northeast further up the coast.

Tensions aboard *Charleston* rose when an unidentified ship appeared ahead. The vessel was quickly determined to be a Japanese merchantman and of no threat. The warship's crew stood ready at battle stations, expecting a fight with the Spanish, as the vessel slowly moved into the harbor area.

Glass and his top officers could make out the silhouette of the fort as his ship moved along the northern coast of the Orote Peninsula. The cruiser passed Fort Santiago without firing, as *Charleston*'s guns could not be elevated high enough to hit the fort. Curiously, no cannons were fired from the fort.

The American warship continued further into the harbor approaching a second Spanish fortification—Fort Santa Cruz. A volley of cannon fire lashed out from *Charleston* on orders from her commanding officer. Again, there was no Spanish response. The American sailors had no way of knowing the island was virtually undefended. The old Fort Santa Cruz had been abandoned for years and was falling into ruins. The garrison of Spanish soldiers was small.[12]

A large group of curious residents were gathering on the shore at about the same time as *Charleston* was firing. The islanders were unaware a state of war existed between the United States and Spain. They believed the American warship was firing a salute to signal the start of an official state visit.[13]

Spanish representatives soon contacted Glass and were stunned to learn the two nations were at war. The Spanish governor, Juan Marina Vega, agreed to surrender after a short period of political negotiations and became a prisoner of the Americans.[14] Fifty-four Spanish soldiers and two officers were disarmed and taken aboard the transport *City of Sydney*.[15] Glass formally took control of Guam on behalf of the United States. The American flag was soon flying above the ruins of Fort Santa Cruz.

Little else was known about the Mariana Islands and the orders from Secretary Long only directed action against Guam. As a result, other islands in the chain—including Saipan and Tinian to the north—were left untouched. The American ships were soon back at sea for the remainder of the voyage to the Philippines.

The short expedition on Guam is often little more than a footnote in the history of the larger Spanish-American War. The conflict is frequently best remembered for headlines from Cuba and the Philippines. The bloodless takeover of Guam ended centuries of Spanish rule and ushered in a peaceful transfer of power on the island to the United States.

The Americans eventually returned to Guam. The territory was administered by the US Navy with a naval officer serving as governor. The islanders eventually became known as Guamanians.

The island remained mostly out of the public eye for almost forty-three years until the start of World War II in 1941. The local residents and American military personnel were suddenly thrust into a desperate situation when the global conflict reached the Pacific with the expansion of the Japanese empire. American control of the island abruptly—although temporarily—came to an end.

Chapter 1

ESCAPE

THE SHARP CRACKLE OF GUNFIRE suddenly interrupted the stillness of the early morning hours of December 10, 1941 on the island of Guam. The sound was enough to wake up forty-two-year-old Radioman First Class George Tweed from a sound sleep. War erupted between the United States and Japan only two days earlier. The island had been under attack by Japanese planes almost since the start of hostilities. The sounds Tweed was now hearing were different.

Tweed's small house, located on a side street in the main city of Agaña, was partially damaged by an errant Japanese bomb the day before. The damage, though, did not prevent the exhausted sailor from getting some deep sleep. "I was awakened about 2:00 a.m. by machine gun and rifle fire, but I'd been up so late and was so tired I was foggy and it didn't occur to me what it was," Tweed remembered. "I thought it was some of our men practicing. I swore at them a while and went back to sleep."[1]

The largely undefended American island was surrounded by Japanese territory. Thousands of miles separated Guam from any friendly military bases. About 3,800 miles to the east, across the International Date Line, Japanese carrier-based planes delivered a crippling surprise attack on American naval and air forces at Pearl Harbor, Hawaii to start the war. The staggering details of just how devastating the Pearl Harbor attack had been to American forces was not yet widely known.

The conflict raging in Europe for more than two years was now global—the United States was at war with the empire of Japan. Just about everyone on Guam—military personnel and local residents alike—knew a war with Japan would bring an immediate invasion and the forces on the island simply did not have the strength to repel an assault.

The gunfire heard by Tweed was not from men training—the Japanese invasion was underway. He previously gave a great amount of thought to what he would do when the war started and made his views known to some of the other navy men on the island. Becoming a prisoner of the Japanese was not something he wanted. Trying to flee into the jungle looked like a better option. "I didn't want to surrender," Tweed later recalled. "Anyway, I expected our navy would come back soon and retake Guam."[2]

Plaza de España, located in the central part of Agaña, was the seat of American government and not far from where Tweed slept. Many of the buildings prominently featured Spanish architecture dating from the long span of colonial rule. The plaza was surrounded by a variety of military and civilian buildings, including an administration building known as the Government House, the US Naval Hospital, the governor's mansion, and a jail. A large Catholic church and public school stood close by.

Located a few blocks away and up a hill was Radio Agaña. The three-hundred-foot antenna tower was a prominent feature of what was more informally known to some of the navy men as the Communications Office. The facility handled all radio traffic—both military and civilian—for the entire island.[3]

About two hours after the clamor of gunfire came the sound of a large explosion. "That brought me out of bed," Tweed explained. The sailor knew the Americans did not have any artillery on Guam—it had to be the Japanese. "I put on some clothes and went towards the Communications Office." The radio post was the island's link to the outside world. The sailor was certain it would have the most current information. He rushed out of his house wearing a khaki shirt and a pair of pants.

The destination quickly changed after Tweed encountered a frightened local resident who was a member of the island's guard force. Vincent Guevara served with the American sailors in the communications section.[4] He warned Japanese soldiers were close by and they had a machine gun position set up in front of the church.[5] Guevara knew of Tweed's plan to head into the jungle. He wanted to join him and urged the pair to get going fast.

The American sailor instead decided to head toward the Government House. "I was afraid that I might be accused of running out under fire or something if I just headed for the jungles," he recalled in an interview decades later. "So I wanted to get permission from somebody there to make me feel better about heading for the jungles."[6] Tweed rushed toward the main street of San Ramon. The murderous rattle of machine gunfire began almost as soon as he darted across the street.

Tweed made it safely to the backyard of the administration building only after some crafty maneuvering, including leaping over a fence and tumbling into a hedge. "And then I went up through the governor's garden and into the back door of the palace," he explained. The idyllic two-story Government House originally served as the governor's palace under Spanish colonial rule. The structure featured a cantilevered balcony and clay tile roof with administrative offices on the first floor.[7]

Radioman George Tweed is seen shortly after his rescue from Guam. The photo was taken on July 12, 1944, but the location is unidentified. (US Navy / National Archives)

Once inside, Tweed saw Captain George McMillin and Commander Donald Giles. Both naval officers seemed to be calm. McMillin was the highest American official on Guam and was serving the dual roles of leading both the civil government and the military contingent on the island. Giles was a close aide serving as vice-governor and executive officer of the small naval station.[8]

The top American leaders had few viable choices. They were facing a full Japanese invasion—likely with thousands of heavily armed troops. The enemy had complete control of the air and sea. The military contingent on Guam was small and lacked any type of heavy weapons. Giles asked Tweed if he had a gun. He did not. Guns were hard to come by for the Americans on Guam and there was little ammunition available.

"They told me the garrison would have to surrender because the Japs were bringing in artillery and the marines were almost out of ammunition," Tweed recalled of his conversation with Giles.[9] The commander gave him the choice of going on his own or surrendering with the rest of the garrison. Tweed wanted no part of surrendering. "I'll take the jungles," he replied. "When I saw what the situation was and learned at the Government House the garrison would have to surrender, I decided to go into the bushes, for I expected Americans to come back soon and take the place away from the Japanese."[10] The senior officers gave him no orders to the contrary. Giles simply wished him good luck.

Every single minute now counted in what may have been the most importance race to date in Tweed's life. The Japanese soldiers were on the move and getting closer. He rushed back to his house, again dodging enemy gunfire in the process.

Waiting back at home was Guevara, who patiently stayed behind, and Radioman First Class Al Tyson. The fellow sailor was a good friend and knew of Tweed's plans to flee. The two worked together in the Communications Office.

Staying in Agaña was not a viable option for someone not wanting to surrender. Tweed decided to use his old car for the getaway. He wasted no time in hurriedly grabbing a few possessions. "I got in my old 1926 Reo, packed some things and started up the road into the hills," he later said.[11] The fifteen-year-old vehicle was far from a modern mode of transportation. Tweed saw it as the only way for the threesome to get out of town fast.

The Japanese troops were on the verge of taking control of Agaña. To make it out of town, Tweed's car would first have to pass within range of the nearby enemy machine gun position. If he was able make it past the gun alive then he could get onto the main road leading out of town and the chances of getting away were good. He picked the right escape route—whether it was pure good luck may never be known. "They [the Japanese] proceeded into town from all directions on each of the roads except one," Tweed later recalled. "It happened that one bridge was destroyed, which blocked them from coming in that road."[12]

Tweed kept the car in low gear. He heard enough stories of people stripping the gears during a time of excitement and did not want to risk having it happen to him. The old Reo raced away with the driver keeping the gas pedal pressed to the floor. "When I got to the corner the Japs started shooting at my car, but they didn't hit it—not quite," he later explained. Bullets splattered all around the speeding vehicle. Maybe the gunner had bad aim or was not expecting to see a fast-moving car—or maybe it was Tweed's lucky day.

Once past the machine gun, the car sped up a hill leading out of town as the occupants kept their heads down. The light of a burning house in the distance silhouetted the car, making it a perfect target for an enemy sharpshooter. Apparently, none were close by in the immediate area. A sharp crack of an artillery gun sounded at about the same time. Tweed thought it was a Japanese cannon opening fire on the Government House at close range.[13] He was not going to wait to find out.

The car headed to the southeast as it hustled away from Agaña. The road led to a sparsely populated, and largely undeveloped, part of the island. "We got away safely," Tweed later recalled. "We went on out about eleven miles southeast of town on the other side of the island where we hid the car in the bushes and began looking for a place to hide where we could live."[14] Although the two sailors and their local companion made good on their escape from Agaña, their ordeal—and the nightmare of the remaining American military personnel on the Guam and the local residents—was just beginning.

GUAM

THE NAVY TRANSPORT USS *CHAUMONT* arrived in San Francisco, California on July 6, 1939 after sailing thousands of miles across the Pacific Ocean. The old vessel was a "regular" when it came to making the long trips to East Asia from the United States mainland, stopping at various ports and naval bases several times each year. The last year of the decade was a busy time for the ship with voyages to the Atlantic, Caribbean, through the Panama Canal, and Pacific already recorded in her logbook.

The *Chaumont* was again passing under the Golden Gate Bridge for another long voyage to Asia after only a fortnight stay in the area. Such trips typically began with visits to various American territories before arriving in China. She briefly stopped in Honolulu, Hawaii on July 27 to 29 before continuing west. Endless swells of blue water rolled against her hull as she plodded through the open ocean toward her next destination—the island of Guam.

Most Americans knew very little—if anything at all—about the small American territory in the Central Pacific. Guam is the largest and southernmost landmass in the Marianas chain of fifteen volcanic islands. The remainder of the chain was under the control of the empire of Japan in 1939. Only about 120 miles separates Guam from the populated islands of Saipan and Tinian to the north. The small islet of Rota was even closer—about fifty miles away. Most of the remaining Marianas were little more than volcanic rocks.

The area was considered by many to be the crossroads of the Pacific. The American territories of the Philippines and Hawaii are a long distance east and west, respectively. The Home Islands of Japan are almost directly north. New Guinea and Australia were to the south. Thousands of miles separated the assorted locations.

Various features of the island came into view as *Chaumont* slowly approached Guam on August 10, 1939. The white coral reefs and deep green jungle vegetation stood out in stark contrast to the surrounding blue ocean water. Ships typically sailed around the southern tip before arriving off the western part of the island. Those aboard could see the four-mile-long Orote Peninsula jutting outward to the west. Moving away from the main part of Guam, the peninsula becomes narrow—tapering down to only a half-mile wide—before widening to about one and three-quarter miles through the main part. The far western end comes to a point protruding out into the sea where sharp cliffs of up to 200 feet face the water on all three sides. Palm trees and various types of brush are scattered around the peninsula.

North of the Orote Peninsula lies Cabras Island. Shaped like a narrow finger and spanning a length of 500 yards, the island is part reef and part land. Taken together, the peninsula and island form Apra Harbor—the port of entry to Guam. Commonly known as San

Luis d'Apra during the time of Spanish rule, the deep-water harbor is perhaps the best in the Marianas.

The *Chaumont* moved through the calm, fluorescent blue and green water once inside Apra Harbor, giving sailors and passengers a good view of the surroundings. The small village of Sumay, on the Orote Peninsula, was home of the Pan American Airways seaplane station built in 1936.[1] The large Pan Am Clipper flying boats regularly traveled the San Francisco–Hong Kong route with intermediary stops in Hawaii, Midway, Wake, Guam, and Manila. In the opposite direction, the small Piti Navy Yard was nestled into the northeast corner of the harbor.

The unloading of cargo and passengers began at once, for the stop was to be brief. The transport was scheduled to continue her voyage west. Her next destination was Manila, Philippines.

Among the passengers disembarking from *Chaumont* was Radioman First Class George R. Tweed. The thirty-seven-year-old was a veteran sailor. He stood about five foot seven with light brown hair, blue eyes, and a fair to ruddy complexion. A weight of just under 140 pounds gave him a slender build. The sailor was married with a wife and young stepson back in California.

Tweed was an old navy hand. He first enlisted in the sea-going service on December 22, 1922 in Portland, Oregon, for a commitment of four years.[2] The new sailor rated as a radioman third class in November 1923 while serving aboard the World War I era destroyer *Paul Hamilton*. A lengthy list of ship and shore duties followed. One of the longer assignments took place when Tweed spent nearly three years aboard the aircraft carrier *Saratoga* in the early 1930s.

A later assignment sent Tweed aboard the battleship *Colorado* while she was operating in the Pacific. He was a radioman first class by the end of the decade. Tweed wanted his next duty to be on land. He sent a formal request through proper channels to the Navy's Bureau of Navigation. "It is requested my name be placed on the Bureau's eligibility list for duty at San Juan, Puerto Rico," Tweed wrote. "I have served at sea on board the *Colorado* since December 1938 and have served at sea for a period of eight years."[3]

Tweed's duty aboard *Colorado* concluded on June 28, 1939. He was at the end of a four-year enlistment period with a clean service record. He immediately wired the Bureau of Navigation from Long Beach, California with a Western Union telegram repeating his earlier request for duty in San Juan. "If this duty is available will proceed to port of embarkation on East Coast at own expense re-enlisting at Washington enroute," he wrote.[4]

There was no need for a radioman in Puerto Rico. Tweed was instead offered a similar position on Guam. He accepted and re-enlisted on July 11. It was Tweed's fifth re-enlistment. Orders directed him to *Chaumont* for the long voyage across the Pacific.

The sailors' new home encompassed about 225 square miles in a long and somewhat narrow rounded rectangle shape, giving Guam a land area slightly smaller than the city of Chicago. The island spans thirty-two miles from north to south with the distance across varying at different parts. It is widest at the north and south extremities where the cross distances measure about ten miles. An isthmus in the central part of the island narrows to four miles wide.

The location of Guam at the southern end of the Marianas puts it closer to the equator, making the island considerably more tropical than its neighbors to the north. The tropical vegetation is lush with forests, vines, high weeds, and underbrush, making travel on foot difficult in the many undeveloped areas. Man-made jungle trails provide travelable routes through the dense vegetation on some parts of the island.

The temperatures are mostly warm to hot and the humidity high. Northeast trade winds prevail during about half of the year, resulting in little rain. Monsoon winds from the southwest regularly blow from June to November, ushering in a rainy season with daily rains often occurring during the span of time.[5] Typhoons have occasionally struck the island with strong storms hitting in 1900 and 1918.[6]

Sharp ocean coral surrounds many parts of the island. The reefs are mostly narrow in width, although they can range up to 700 yards wide.[7] Deep sandy beaches, with limited coral obstructions, exist in several locations on the west coast.

The topography on Guam differs from north to south. For landscape purposes, the island can be divided into three areas—north, central, and south. The narrow central isthmus adjoins Agaña Bay on the western coast and Pago Bay on the east. A large portion of the central area is covered with palm trees. The coastal city of Agaña, located northeast of Apra Harbor, has long been the governmental capital and largest population center. Most other towns and villages are located on or near the coast. The more solidly constructed buildings in Agaña contrasted with those in some outlying villages. The structures in the small towns were often little more than grass-covered huts.[8]

The southern part of Guam is dominated by rugged hills favoring the west coast. Mount Lamlam, near the southwestern part of the island, stands 1,334 feet high with a series of other peaks in the area ranging from 800 to 1,100-foot heights.[9] The actual mountain tops feature partially barren volcanic rock with sparse vegetation.[10]

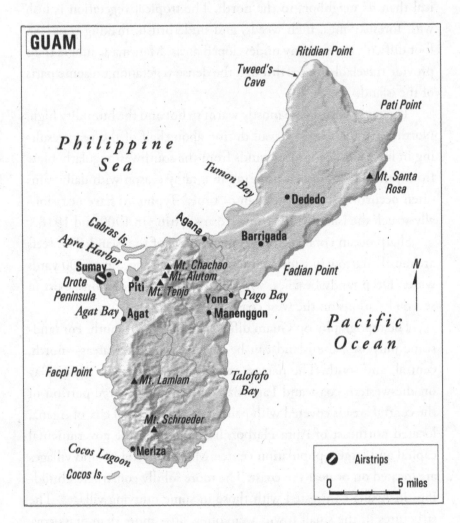

(Philip Schwartzberg - Meridian Mapping)

The northern portion of the island is mainly a 500-foot high limestone plateau. The rolling terrain includes various hills of less than 1,000 feet, including Mount Santa Rosa in the northeast. Large stretches of the northern coastline include limestone cliffs with heights ranging from one hundred to 500 feet. Dense tropical forests cover much of the northern region. Some limited open areas allowed for cattle ranching among local residents during the years before World War II.

Caves and ravines are found throughout the island's northern and southern areas. The three largest rivers—Talofofo, Ylig, and Pago—are in the central and southern regions and all flow toward the east coast.[11] A few swampy areas are located on the island.

The ability to move around Guam in 1939 included a mixture of paved roads, single-lane unpaved roads, and narrow jungle trails.[12] Although the road system was slowly developed during the time under American rule, traffic by foot, oxcart, bicycle, and jitney could be regularly seen at various parts of the island.[13] A main hard-surfaced road ran along the west coast from near the Orote Peninsula to Agaña and then extended further north, including a short branch to the northeast. A second main road stretched east-southeast from Agaña across the central part of the island to Pago Bay. Many of the unsurfaced roads became unpassable during the rainy season.

The sailor Tweed would later become intimately familiar with parts of the island's rough terrain. He was nothing more than a new arrival in the summer of 1939. The sailor certainly must have been eager to learn about his new home.

Chapter 3

AMERICAN TERRITORY

AFTER CAPTAIN GLASS IN *CHARLESTON* "captured" Guam for the Americans during a bloodless operation in June 1898, he made no further investigation of the remaining islands in the Marianas chain. The officer's orders were limited to seizing Guam, the seat of Spanish administration in the area, and the troops aboard his transports were urgently needed in the Philippines. Glass sailed away to Manila, with the small garrison of Spanish soldiers and top officials aboard his ships as prisoners.

The Treaty of Paris formerly ended the Spanish-American War on December 10, 1898.[1] Under the terms of the agreement, Spain relinquished Cuba, Puerto Rico, and Guam to the United States. Additionally, the Philippines was turned over to the Americans in exchange for $20 million.[2]

The historical record is not entirely clear whether American authorities assumed the capture of Guam meant the United States was to control the entire Marianas. The idea was wrong—if in fact it was the American assumption. The Spanish quickly sold the remaining Marianas, along with some other Pacific Island holdings (Caroline and Marshall Islands), to Germany for about $4 million.[3]

President William McKinley thought Guam could eventually become a showplace of American-style democracy in the Pacific, although the details of his thinking on the topic remain unclear.[4] He placed control of the island under the Department of the Navy by executive order on December 23, 1898.[5] A naval officer was to oversee the island as an appointed governor. The individual essentially held the combined powers of the executive, legislative, and judicial branches of the government under the United States system.[6]

The former Spanish colonies were added to a growing list of American possessions across the Pacific, including the Hawaiian Islands, Wake Island, American Samoa, and Midway Island. The value of Guam was clear from a strategic standpoint—the island was positioned directly on the almost 7,000-mile route between the United States and the Philippines. A small navy yard was built at the town of Piti inside Apra Harbor to serve as both a military base and port of entry.[7] A small contingent of marines and naval personnel were stationed on the island.

Navy Captain Richard Leary became the first American Governor of Guam on August 10, 1899.[8] He proclaimed all existing laws would remain in force until modified. Leary abolished the political powers of the Catholic clergy, essentially establishing the American doctrine of the separation of church and state.[9] A long list of American naval governors oversaw Guam in the following decades with their command generally benign—far different from the sometimes ruthless Spanish authority of the past.[10]

American ideals and practices gradually took hold on Guam. Some elements of the American Bill of Rights were incorporated into the local laws. A degree of civilian control was permitted with the establishment of a two-chamber congress, whose members only held advisory power to the governor.[11] The Guamanians were not official American citizens but were United States nationals. The two designations are very similar. The main difference is that nationals cannot vote in national elections.

Great advancements took place in health, public education, and economic matters during the time of American control. A bank and tax system were developed. The main economic activity was agriculture with crops ranging from corn, rice, and copra, to various types of fruit.[12] The local population rose at a steady rate during the early part of the twentieth century, from about 9,500 in 1900 to 21,199 in 1939.[13]

Guam was connected with the outside world at varying times by cable, radio, shipping, and airplanes. Shipping routes linked Guam with the Philippines, Hawaii, the United States, and China from the earliest days of American rule. A commercial cable station began operations in 1903 allowing communication by telegraph messages. The development of wireless radio later made the cable link obsolete. A navy-operated radio station kept in regular contact with Manila, Honolulu, and San Francisco.

The worldwide growth of aviation eventually brought commercial transportation to the island in the form of Pan American Airways. The seaplane service was a great addition for Guam with the first flying boat landing in late 1935.[14] The massive Boeing 314 Clipper later became a regular visitor to the island making four weekly stops.[15] The airline built a complete facility, with a hotel for overnight accommodations, repair facility, and office.

Tweed reported for duty at the Commandant's Office at the Guam Naval Station upon his arrival on August 10, 1939. He requested navy transportation for his family to join him shortly after he received his own orders to the island. Permission was approved in keeping with the standard navy policy for dependents. After Tweed's first wife Ida passed away in 1937, he married the former Mary Barger on December 15, 1938 in Yuma, Arizona.[16] Mary and step-son Ronald Tweed arrived in Guam aboard the transport *Henderson* in late December 1939.[17] The family eventually settled into a small rented house close to the hospital in Agaña.

The navy contingent on the island was small and numbered only a few hundred personnel. As a radioman first class, Tweed specialized in operating and maintaining all types of radio equipment. The isolated island was ideal for a sailor with his talents. He was assigned to join a small group of men working in the communications area.

Like many Pacific islands, Guam was close to a tropical paradise for sailors coming from the United States. The shores featured picturesque reefs, palm tree-studded beaches, and warm turquoise water teeming with assorted fish. The island was full of lush green vegetation and many types of fruits, including pineapples, bananas, and papayas. The morning sun rose beautifully in the eastern sky and slipped below the western horizon often surrounded by brilliant shades of red, pink, and crimson.

The duty on the island was far from strenuous for servicemen. Few military trainings or exercises, common at larger bases, took place on Guam. Options for rest and relaxation were plentiful for both officers and enlisted men alike. A Navy Officers Club was perched on top of a bluff near Agaña with a golf course nearby. The

Elks Lodge was popular with enlisted men, who were given honorary membership. Cheap drinks were served at the bar while the sounds of dance music flowed through the air.

The military facilities on Guam were not extensive—unlike the Philippines and Hawaii—making it easy for a newcomer like Tweed to quickly learn his way around. He quickly became acquainted with the personnel on the island. The military group included a small contingent of marines based on the Orote Peninsula near the town of Sumay.

The naval personnel mostly operated in Agaña and at the small navy yard. The modest station at Piti, comprising repair facilities and some warehouses, was never large enough to be a major operating base.[18] The base was home to a small group of ships affectionately known as the "Guam Navy."[19] The force included the small obsolete minesweeper *Penguin*, the old immobile oil ship *R.L. Barnes*, two small patrol craft, and cargo ship *Gold Star*. The latter served as Guam's station ship and much of her crew were Guamanians. She made regular voyages to the Philippines, Japan, and China to obtain supplies and shuttle passengers.[20]

In the days before World War II, the city of Agaña represented a colorful mix of native houses, structures of Spanish architecture, and newer modern innovations imported during the American era—electric lights, telephones, cars, soda fountains, and a movie theater.[21] The city's population of about 12,500 represented almost half of the people on the island.[22] The seat of American government and military headquarters was located at Plaza de España. The area included a large plaza, government administration building, communications center, and hospital. The stately Government House stood out prominently in front of the plaza with Spanish architecture and a beautiful garden about an acre in size. The American flag flew from a large pole nearby.

The white clapboard US Naval Hospital was not far from the Government House. The building was covered by a tin roof and featured a prominent red cross. The facility was staffed by a small contingent of doctors, five navy nurses, and an assortment of enlisted men. The hospital treated military personnel, their dependents, and local residents. Other buildings near the plaza included a jail, barracks, a large Catholic church, and a public school.

The 300-foot antenna tower of Radio Agaña was on top of a hill a few blocks from the plaza. The station was run by the navy and served as the hub for all—military and civilian—wireless traffic. A second communications center—Radio Libugon—was in a more isolated location a couple of miles southeast of Agaña. The station included four tall radio direction-finding antennas used to monitor Japanese radio traffic. The equipment was later upgraded to focus on naval communications, allowing radiomen to track the locations of individual Japanese ships. The Libugon radio intelligence work was a closely-held secret known to only a small number of navy men on the island.[23]

A daily newspaper was the main source of information for many Guamanians. The *Guam Eagle* was widely distributed throughout the island. It provided news from around the world and local stories. The publication was owned and operated by the navy.[24] Newsreels provided another source of information and were regularly flown in from the United States aboard the Pan Am Clippers.

Tweed's orders placed him with the sailors running Radio Agaña. He was involved in all daily activities needed to keep the station operating. Tweed likely split his time between both stations after settling into his duties.

The assignment was a perfect fit for Tweed. He had been tinkering with radios and communications equipment for almost his entire time in the navy. Outside of the service, he was a ham radio operator—essentially an amateur radio broadcaster. Ham radio operators obtained a license to operate their own private small-scale radio station.

"In 1931, while stationed in San Diego, I met a group of boys who were very much into radio," Tweed later explained. "In fact, they were so enthusiastic about it I asked them why." The group explained they were ham radio operators. Tweed was quickly sold on the idea. "I'd been in the navy for about nine years and in radio work all of that time, but never had given the ham game much thought," he continued. "This chance meeting with these fellows convinced me that the ham game must be fun." A fellow sailor helped Tweed get started. "It was a big day in 1932 when I got my license and went on the air as W6GJX in San Diego."[25] His ham radio operations continued while stationed on Guam.

World War II erupted in Europe by the time Tweed's family arrived. The conflict seemed far away for Tweed and the other servicemen on Guam. War worries, though, were soon to cast a long shadow over the Pacific.

Chapter 4

WAR PLANS

THE LONG DEBATE AMONG AMERICAN leaders about what to do with Guam from a military standpoint began shortly after the United States seized the island. The deliberations lingered for decades while the nation slowly drifted toward a war with Japan. Early supporters of fortifying the island included Admiral George Dewey and prominent naval strategist Alfred Thayer Mahan. Dewey was a naval hero of the Spanish-American War who defeated the Spanish Pacific Squadron in Manila Bay at the beginning of the conflict. "Guam occupies such a commanding strategic position in the Pacific, and one of such vital importance to our national interests in that ocean, that it is essential to hold it securely against any form of attack," the admiral wrote to the secretary of the navy in 1912.[1]

The strategist Mahan drew comparisons between Guam and the British fortress of Gibraltar in the Mediterranean. Both Dewey and Mahan passed away during World War I, silencing the voices of two strong advocates for Guam fortification. Interest in the topic continued to linger long after their deaths.

A range of proposals developed in December 1919 and again in the late 1930s provided options ranging from providing only enough military assets for a limited defense of the island, to creating a major operating base—essentially the fortress envisioned by Dewey and Mahan. None of the proposals were ever put in place.

Although American political leaders grappled with how to counter the growing power of Japan throughout the early twentieth century, the idea of building bases on Guam remained unappealing to the federal government. Many in congress looked to the vast Pacific Ocean as a form of protection for the nation and a reason not to become involved in foreign entanglements. "Japan, more than 7,000 miles from our shores, and with a navy only two-thirds as large as ours could make no successful attack on the Hawaiian Islands or continental United States," said Congressman John M. Robsion of Kentucky in 1939, summarizing the beliefs of many in congress.[2]

The roots of Imperial Japanese expansionism date back to the turn of the century when Japan gained influence over Korea, seized control of Formosa (present-day Taiwan), and defeated Imperial Russia in the 1904–1905 Russo-Japanese War.[3] The latter conflict included the spectacular Japanese naval victory in the Strait of Tsushima over the Russian Baltic Fleet. The Russian ships sailed halfway around the world from Europe to the Pacific, only to fall victim to a surprise Japanese attack.

The victors gained concessions and territory in China—an area long coveted by Japanese leaders as a source of valuable natural resources and agricultural space. The great victory announced Japan's arrival on the world stage as a major power, giving Imperial leaders the confidence that its fighting forces could defeat greater enemies.[4] Japan quickly rose to become the strongest power in East Asia and a possible future enemy of the United States.

The outbreak of World War I in 1914 found Japan aligned with European allies against Germany and other Central Powers. The move was in keeping with a decades-old treaty Japan signed with Britain to keep peace in Asia, although the Japanese clearly had the alternate motive of gaining territory. The British requested the Japanese Navy to search out and destroy German naval vessels operating in the Pacific.[5] The Japanese used the opportunity to seize control of Germany's Pacific territories, sometimes referred to as German Micronesia, including the Mariana, Caroline, and Marshall islands. The Japanese were given full custody of the islands after the war, which were often collectively referred to as "the Mandates."

The horrific killing on the European continent in World War I helped prompt the major world powers to begin disarmament negotiations in Washington, DC, during the early 1920s. The goal was to prevent an arms race among the victors by limiting the construction of large warships. The 1922 Washington Naval Treaty limited the construction of large warships for ten years among the signatories using the following ratio—United States (five ships), Britain (five), Japan (three), with lesser numbers for France and Italy. Although the allotment given to the Imperial Navy was sufficient to provide protection for Japanese home waters, the treaty increased animosity with the Western powers who were seen as not treating the Asian nation as an equal.[6] The treaty provisions were extended five years as part of the London Naval Conference in 1930. The Japanese later withdrew from further treaty negotiations.

The Japanese empire expanded in 1931 when troops invaded Manchuria in far northeastern China. American leaders deplored the aggression but took no action. China at the time was a nation split by civil war with different groups holding influence and power in various regions. A full-scale Japanese invasion of China began in 1937. Imperial land and air forces swept south to swiftly capture key cities with large population centers, including Nanking and Shanghai. The invaders unleashed horrific atrocities against civilians with aerial bombings, brutal torture, rape, and indiscriminate killings. The Chinese were eventually able to stop the Japanese advance.

The United States, Britain, and other countries long maintained a small military presence on the Yangtze River and in the city of Shanghai to protect Western interests. Relations between the United States and Japan were further strained when the small American river gunboat *Panay* was sunk by Japanese planes on the Yangtze River on December 12, 1937.[7] Japanese officials apologized for what they termed a case of mistaken identity.

The possibility of a conflict with Japan was something American military leaders had been planning for decades. The first version of what was termed War Plan Orange was completed by a select group of American Army and Navy planners in 1911.[8] The plan was part of a wider series of contingencies developed for conflicts with a range of potential enemies. Each possible adversary was identified by a color, with Japan assigned orange.

War Plan Orange assumed a Japanese attack on the Philippines with American and Filipino forces holding out until the United States Navy sailed across the Pacific for a decisive battle with the Imperial fleet. A key—and perhaps faulty—assumption was the Philippines would be able to hold out until the fleet arrived from bases on the west coast of the United States.

War Plan Orange was updated various times throughout the decades after World War I. American war planning shifted in 1939 based on developments in Europe and the Pacific. The "Rainbow" series of plans assumed United States and key allies would be fighting multiple enemies. The planning concluded with Rainbow 5 in 1941.

The scenario was based on the current situation of World War II in Europe with the United States and Britain, fighting several adversaries on a global scale. The plan focused on defeating Germany first due to the nation's strong military and large industrial capacity. More defensive operations were planned for the Pacific, although key portions of the older War Plan Orange remained.

The Japanese remained neutral when World War II broke out in Europe on September 1, 1939. Imperial leaders saw the conflict as an opportunity for expansion in the Pacific, especially after France surrendered to invading German forces in June 1940. The Japanese sought to create the Greater East Asia Co-Prosperity Sphere where nations in the region were to be freed from European colonial powers and put under Imperial rule.

Two events occurred in September 1940 to further strain relations in the Pacific. Japan formally joined Germany and Italy in the Tripartite Pact alliance on September 27, 1940 to form the Axis Powers.[9] The Japanese then moved military forces into the northern portion of French Indochina. In a counter move, an American embargo on the sale of scrap iron and aviation gasoline when into effect. The United States Pacific Fleet, traditionally based in California, moved west to a new home port in Pearl Harbor, Hawaii in 1940.

The continuation of Japanese expansion during the late summer of 1941 brought serious developments in the Pacific. All French Indochina, a colony comprising the current countries of Vietnam, Cambodia, and Laos, fell under Imperial control after weak local French authorities were powerless to resist. Japanese naval, air, and ground forces poured into the southern part of Indochina.[10] The expansion gave the Japanese bases to threaten British Malaya, Singapore, the Philippines, and the Dutch East Indies.

The American reaction was swift and struck right at the heart of the Japanese economy. President Franklin Roosevelt signed an executive order on July 26 freezing all Japanese assets in the United States and announced an embargo of all petroleum products to Japan.[11] He also recalled retired general Douglas MacArthur to active service and nationalized the Philippine Army. An immediate build-up of military forces in the Philippines was ordered with MacArthur in command.

The oil embargo quickly thrust Japanese leadership into an immediate crisis. There was little oil in the Home Islands, requiring Japan to import almost all vital resources with about 80 percent coming from the United States.[12] The lack of oil would have the catastrophic effect of paralyzing key industries in about a year and disabling the Imperial Navy.[13] The two nations began negotiations to forge a peaceful resolution to the situation. While the talks taking place in Washington stalemated, military leaders in Japan were secretly reviewing other options.

Imperial leaders decided on war. The key objective of the Japanese war strategy was to seize the oil- and resource-rich territories of Southeastern Asia, namely British Malaya and the Dutch East Indies, neutralizing United States Pacific bases, and capturing territory to create a strong defensive perimeter to protect the empire.[14] The operations were to be carried out simultaneously with a spectacular opening move.

Admiral Isoroku Yamamoto, commander in chief of the Combined Japanese Fleet, was the nation's leading naval planner. Although he opposed a conflict with the United Sates, having seen the nation's industrial might firsthand, a sense of duty compelled him to join the effort once the decision was made to go to war. Yamamoto saw the early destruction of the United States Pacific Fleet as an absolute necessity. He believed the only hope for a Japanese victory rested with a short war—an opening victory to lead the demoralized United States to the negotiations table where an agreement favorable to Japan could be secured.[15] He became the architect of a daring plan to attack the Pacific Fleet at Pearl Harbor with aircraft carrier-based planes. The operation was a closely guarded secret, known only to a select few at the highest level of Japanese leadership.

The diplomatic work continued throughout the second half of 1941 with the negotiations doing little more than buying time for both sides. The Japanese needed time to finalize war plans. The United States was focused on building up forces in the Philippines and ramping up the manufacture of war materials.[16] The countdown for conflict in the Pacific was underway.

Chapter 5

EVE OF WORLD WAR II

CONGRESS APPROVED MODEST MILITARY IMPROVEMENTS to Guam amid the increasing tensions in the Pacific. A manmade breakwater was constructed of limestone blocks to better enclose Apra Harbor.[1] The existing plan for a future airfield on the western end of the Orote Peninsula was put into motion. The 4,500-foot runway was cleared and staked out by late 1941, but no other work on the project was started.

Navy Captain George McMillin became the thirty-eighth American governor of Guam in April 1940.[2] His duty was to command all military and civil affairs on the island, although he was not to command troops in combat situations.[3] McMillin has been described as a thoughtful man who worked to improve relations between the navy and Guamanians.

The new leader set about restructuring the administrative government and encouraged local participation in the process. A series of departments were created to oversee the various depression-era government programs. McMillin eased an old restriction limiting outside businesses from setting up on the island, allowing for some economic expansion. New jobs were created in a soap factory and a business manufacturing purses made of shells for export. The economic activity was enough for McMillin to claim full employment by late 1941.[4]

Navy Commander Donald Giles was an early addition to McMillin's staff. He quickly assumed the positions of vice-governor and executive officer of the naval station. Giles was to play an important role as the island prepared for war.

The fear of a war with Japan was very real on Guam by the beginning of 1941. A presidential executive order signed in January prohibited foreign warships and commerce vessels from entering a three-mile Naval Defense Sea Area around the island, although exceptions could be made.[5] Japanese planes were spotted over the island in March. The potential enemy was clearly surveying the island and the reconnaissance flights continued into the summer. Japanese military radio traffic dramatically increased to where local residents could listen in on their home radios.[6]

The governor harbored no illusions about the prospect of war with Japan and the ability to defend the island. Security was always a top concern for McMillin. He was, after all, a military officer first and foremost. McMillin asked for troops from Hawaii and the Philippines to reinforce his garrison. The request was denied by officials in Washington.[7]

The military contingent on the island remained small. McMillin knew the resources to protect Guam were meager, making the island essentially indefensible. The war plan was to only offer token resistance and ensure all sensitive documents were destroyed before surrendering.

The strength of the Guam Navy remained largely unchanged from recent years—a few small vessels and cargo ship *Gold Star*. By then end of the year, there were a total of 271 navy personnel stationed on the island. The contingent was divided into various capacities, including an administration group, medical staff at the hospital, those assigned to the navy yard, and the sailors in the communications group manning the two radio stations.

The marine garrison numbered 153 soldiers under the command of Lieutenant Commander William McNulty. The force was essentially the size of a company and lacked any type of heavy weapons. The island had no artillery or shore defenses of any type. The soldiers were armed with outdated Springfield rifles, pistols, and a limited number of machine guns.

The third component of the security force was the Guam Insular Guard Force made up of Guamanians. The group was originally formed in 1901 as a type of local militia to guard the naval installations. The force was just short of 250 members by late 1941.[8] The guard members were armed, although there were not enough weapons for everyone. The Guam Insular Patrol, numbering eighty Guamanians, served as the island's police force.

The unstable situation soon required all American civilians to depart the island. Admiral Thomas Hart in the Philippines told McMillin he thought the diplomatic situation was worsening and he was sending home all dependents under his command.[9] The Guam governor decided to do the same. "The political situation in the Pacific was assumed to be tense during the Summer of 1941," McMillin later wrote. "After an effort extending over several months, arrangements were finally made to evacuate all dependents, including civilians, from Guam."[10]

The navy transport *Henderson*, accompanied by the heavy cruiser *Astoria*, arrived in Apra Harbor during the early afternoon of October

16, 1941.[11] The transport was making a return trip east after delivering troops and supplies to the Philippines. The *Henderson*'s mission was now to get civilians out of the Pacific. She was already partially loaded with civilians evacuating from the Philippines. Her stay in Guam was to last a little more than one day. A total of 104 American dependents of military personnel came aboard during the brief visit. The group was to be the last of the dependents to leave Guam.

There were undoubtedly many tearful goodbyes taking place in Apra Harbor as wives and family members prepared to return to the United States. Tweed's family expanded to four with the birth of son Robert in January. Like many sailors and marines, he was now having to say farewell as Mary and their two young sons climbed aboard *Henderson*. The two ships were sailing out of Apra Harbor by 4:00 p.m. on October 17. The vessels rounded the island and were soon pointed east for the long voyage to Hawaii.

Radio traffic and news reports kept the personnel on Guam apprised of the diplomatic negotiations taking place in Washington. Frequent news came in about the war in Europe, including Britain's struggle for survival and the German invasion of Russia. A growing sense of unease took hold on the island during the final months of the year.

The situation became bleaker in November when the news from Washington about the negotiations did not seem optimistic and Japanese planes continued flying over Guam. What had been occasional flights earlier in the year became daily occurrences. Giles remembered the planes flying with impunity over the island. "Looking back upon what transpired, I realize that these must have been reconnaissance flights collecting information on which to base attack plans," he later wrote. "They must have mapped and photographed the island down to the last inch."[12]

The War Department sent out an urgent warning message to commands around the world on November 27 as diplomatic negotiations in Washington faltered. The Navy Department sent a message with even stronger wording. "This dispatch is to be considered a war warning," the message ominously began. "Negotiations with Japan looking towards stabilization of conditions in the Pacific have ceased and an aggressive move by Japan is expected within the next few days."[13] The message included a brief mention of Guam. "Continental districts Guam, Samoa directed to take appropriate measures against sabotage."[14]

A secret observation post was set up on the northernmost tip of the island within a few days of the war warning. The station was manned by Insular Guard members who carefully watched nearby Rota Island for any naval movements.[15] Headlights on all vehicles were ordered blacked out, leaving just a small slit for emitting light.[16] The limited number of machine guns were deployed, including one placed on top of a hill near Agaña for anti-aircraft defense, and others in the city. McMillin ordered the process of destroying classified materials to begin on December 6.[17]

A small number of navy officers gathered in the officer's club during the early morning hours of November 30. The group huddled around the radio, with drinks in hand, to listen to the annual Army-Navy football game played in Philadelphia. The sailors struggled through less than stellar reception, although everything turned out good in the end with a navy victory. "This was to be the last event of our social calendar on Guam," Giles later recalled. "For some, it would be their last social event ever."[18]

Every serviceman on Guam was undoubtedly pondering the future as the calendar turned to December. "I felt war was imminent," Tweed later said of the time.[19] He had come to an important decision. "I realized that if we were taken prisoner that we'd be stuck in a prison camp for the duration of the war and I couldn't see that," he recalled years later. "So I thought that I would rather go out and hide in the jungle than to be taken prisoner."[20] He would soon be forced to put his plan into action.

The Pearl Harbor attack force began assembling on November 22, 1941 at Tankan Bay in the Kuril Islands north of Japan under the command of Admiral Chuichi Nagumo. The force included six large aircraft carriers, carrying hundreds of planes, and a small group of escorts. The preparations were carried out in extreme secret, even having false radio traffic created to make American intelligence think the carriers were further south in the Sea of Japan.[21] The plan was to attack Pearl Harbor at about 8:30 a.m. local time on Sunday, December 7, 1941.

The ships slipped out to sea in foggy weather on the morning of November 26 for the long voyage across the North Pacific. Nagumo was under orders to adhere to strict radio silence during the trip to Hawaii. The final decision to carry out the attack was made on December 1 with the coded message communicated to Nagumo, "Climb Mount Niitaka."[22] The Japanese force remained undetected once arriving at the launch position north of Hawaii. The first flight of 185 planes arrived over the island of Oahu at 7:55 a.m. on December 7. The Americans were taken by complete surprise as Japanese planes attacked airfields, ships, and naval facilities. The entire Pacific region was about to explode into conflict.

Chapter 6

WAR!

THE JAPANESE PLANS FOR THE invasion of Guam were already finalized by the time Admiral Chuichi Nagumo's ships put to sea. The November photo reconnaissance flights provided a good amount of information about the island. Japanese naval vessels began patrolling close to the island, but mostly at night to avoid detection. Once the Pearl Harbor attack was confirmed, Saipan-based naval planes were to begin bombing Guam to soften up the island ahead of the invasion scheduled for December 10.

The planes mounting the operation were from the 18th Naval Air Corps on Saipan.[1] The unit was equipped with Mitsubishi F1M2 "Pete" floatplanes. Manned by a crew of two, the slow biplanes were primarily used for reconnaissance and observation rather than attack missions. The lack of defenses on Guam, however, negated any possible disadvantages. The Pete was armed with three light machine guns—two forward firing and a swivel-mount rear facing gun—and could carry two 60-kilogram bombs (about 130 pounds).[2]

Patient Japanese air crews on Saipan were waiting for orders to start the attack as the first bombs were falling on Pearl Harbor. Only about one hundred miles separated the two islands, making for a short flight. The air units were notified to start the operation forty minutes after the Pearl Harbor attack.[3] A flight of nine Petes took off to begin the mission.

A sense of quiet covered Guam during the early morning hours of December 8, 1941. The island's position west of the International Date Line put the time one day ahead of Hawaii. The minesweeper *Penguin* was patrolling off Apra Harbor. The small warship's three-inch gun represented the most powerful weapon available to the Guam defenders. "This nightly patrol of the *Penguin* or a YP boat had been in effect for about six months," McMillin later wrote.[4]

Electrician Mate Second Class Edward Hale was a recent addition to *Penguin*'s crew, having arrived on Guam in early September.[5] He remembered the ship was in blackout conditions. "Below decks care had been exercised that no ports were open or that no lights were used that might leave strong reflections," he later wrote.[6]

The nightly patrol was uneventful and the ship headed for Apra Harbor. "At the break of dawn, the ship turned back through the narrow channel in the reef, moved up to one of the outer buoys and tied to it," Hale continued. "The motor launch took a few men immediately after breakfast and went to Piti Landing for provisions." The commanding officer, Lieutenant James Haviland, did not yet know of the Pearl Harbor attack.[7]

Managers were up early at the Pan Am station near Sumay. The Philippine Clipper was scheduled to arrive in Guam during the afternoon. The large flying boat was traveling westbound from California to the Orient and was just taking off from Wake Island, about 1,300 miles to the northeast. Passengers planned to stay overnight before the Clipper continued the next day to Manila.

A startling message reached Radio Agaña at about 5:45 a.m. from Admiral Hart in the Philippines and was rushed to McMillin by a messenger. "Japan started hostilities. Govern yourselves accordingly."[8] The news of the Pearl Harbor attack quickly spread around the island. The United States was at war.

Giles was in his quarters when he received an urgent phone call from McMillin about the start of the war. He quickly alerted Captain Bill Lineberry, head of the US Naval Hospital, before hastily dressing and rushing over to the Government House. He joined McMillin and a small group of officers. "Although we had known that war was imminent, we were stunned, both because the target of the Japanese attack had not been foreseen with any accuracy, and because of the manner in which the attack had occurred," Giles later recalled. "We were still fighting by gentlemanly standards and did not realize that war was no longer a gentleman's game."[9]

All the officers knew an attack on Guam was imminent. The men gathered around McMillin's desk as the governor outlined the next actions. The news was communicated to various military stations around the island. "Steps were taken immediately to evacuate the civil population from Agaña, and from the vicinity of possible military objectives, in accordance with a plan previously prepared," McMillin wrote. "All Japanese nationals were arrested at once and confined in jail."[10] Lights were blacked out across the entire island.

Many aspects of civilian life were suspended, including school, commercial businesses, and church services. Two urgent messages were sent to Wake Island to recall the clipper. The flight to Guam was cancelled. Many of the Pan Am employees and some civilian construction workers evacuated to Mount Almagosa, south of the Orote Peninsula.

Communication problems on Guam suddenly began at 7:30 a.m. Key phone lines were cut, most likely as an act of sabotage carried out by Japanese sympathizers. The local switchboard operators subsequently fled in fear for their lives.[11] Messengers took up the duty of hand-delivering communications.

Military units sprang into action across Guam. Parts of the marine contingent was located at various patrol stations around the island and were working with local administrators. "Because they lived in these villages, they knew the residents and were familiar with the local terrain," Giles explained. "These marines were our eyes and ears, serving as lookouts both prior to and during the forthcoming attack."

Most of the remaining marines were at the barracks near Sumay. They stayed in the area to use it as a base of operations against a possible Japanese landing in Apra Harbor and later took up defensive positions near the rifle range. The Insular Guard Force gathered at their barracks in Agaña. Weapons were distributed and the men were dispatched to Plaza de España to set up defensive positions around the Government House and other important buildings.

The various defensive preparations were still underway when the sudden roar of aircraft propellers revealed a flight of planes coming from the direction of Saipan. The spearhead of the Japanese attack arrived in short order—the nine Pete floatplanes. The planes were flying low at an altitude of about 1,500 feet. The attack began at 8:27 a.m.

Lieutenant Junior Grade Leona Jackson was part of the small contingent of navy nurses at the hospital. She was in her quarters when the chief nurse knocked on the door to pass along the news of the Pearl Harbor attack. "They'll probably be here next," her colleague warned. Jackson suddenly heard the distinctive sound of airplane propellers. "When they came over, I wondered for an instant, I think, if it was the Clipper returning but there hadn't been any Clipper in the day before and as the sound came nearer, I realized that it couldn't be a Clipper, it didn't sound like a PBY which had come sometimes to the island on their way to the Far East," Jackson later recalled.[12] She knew the enemy had arrived.

The station boat from the Piti Navy Yard just pulled alongside *Penguin* in Apra Harbor for a messenger to deliver a confidential envelop with the news of the war as the ship could not be contacted by radio. The general quarter's alarm was quickly sounded, sending men racing to their battle stations. The small vessel slipped her moorings and began slowly moving toward the harbor entrance.

Startled sailors suddenly heard the approaching planes. A trio of enemy planes sped toward the warship. To Hale, the aircraft looked like cruiser float planes. He knew they were Japanese after catching a brief glimpse of the red circles on the wings. "These were coming right at the *Penguin,*" he remembered.

The sailors opened fire with the three-inch gun and machine guns as the old ship made for the open sea. The fire seemed to cause the planes to move to a higher altitude, possibly reducing the accuracy of the initial bombing run.[13] At least one plane swooped lower to rake the ship with machine gun fire. The bullets gravely wounded Ensign Robert White who was manning the anti-aircraft gun. The officer fell into the arms of a fellow sailor and was able to speak a few words before taking his last breath. Many other sailors, including the skipper, were wounded in the attack.

Several near-miss bombs exploded close aboard during the final pass. Although not direct hits, the explosions ripped open parts of the hull, causing extensive damage. The ship began taking on water and listing. By 9:30 a.m., it was clear the *Penguin* was at the end of her fight. She was in open water about a mile and a half off Orote Point when Haviland gave the difficult order the scuttle the ship. Watertight doors were unlatched, and valves opened before the crew abandoned ship.

White's body was loaded onto a raft. The most seriously wounded men were given the limited remaining space. Many of the sailors had no choice but to swim. The wounded were transported by truck and car to the hospital with the help of marines once ashore. The sailors then witnessed the final minutes of their ship. Hale remembered "standing on the lava rocks of Orote Peninsula, we saw the Stars and Stripes, which still flew from her stern, sink beneath the quiet water."

The Japanese planes struck other parts of the island, including Apra Harbor and Agaña, while *Penguin* was fighting her last battle. The air attacks continued throughout the day before ending at about 5:00 p.m. Among the targets struck were the Piti Navy Yard, marine barracks, radio stations, and the Pam Am facility.

Jackson started her afternoon shift at the hospital and calmly went about her rounds even as the air attacks continued. "In about an hour, I should say, the casualties had come in," she remembered. The staff heard firsthand reports of the damage from *Penguin*'s wounded skipper and some injured marines. A stream of wounded people—both military and civilian—arrived at the hospital throughout the day.

Nightfall descending on Guam brought the eerie glow of fires burning from various targets hit during the air attacks. A native dugout came ashore near the end of the day close to Ritidian Point at the northern end of Guam and a group of occupants were seen to disappear into the jungle. A local patrol later apprehended the men, who were arrested and taken to the Government House for questioning.

The captured men were Chamorros from Saipan sent ahead by the Japanese to act as interpreters for the impending invasion. They told authorities the Japanese were set to land tomorrow morning just east of Agaña and that they were mistreated on Saipan. "I was inclined not to accept the story at the time since I thought it might be a trick to have the marines moved from Sumay to the beach during the night, in order that they might make a landing in the Apra Harbor area unopposed," McMillin later wrote. Time would prove the location of the landing was correct, but the timing was not.

The morning of December 9 brought the return of Japanese planes. A second day of bombing and strafing completed the destruction to most of the key facilities on the island. Warehouses, the machine shop, fuel dump, and other buildings at the Piti Navy Yard were heavily damaged or completely demolished. The Libugon radio station was damaged and abandoned. Many of the marine buildings at Sumay were destroyed. The nearby Pan Am facility was virtually wiped out. Although Radio Agaña escaped any direct bomb hits, near-miss explosions caused enough damage to knock the station out of commission.[14]

The remainder of the Guam Navy fared little better than *Penguin*, except for *Gold Star*. The station ship was visiting the Philippines and scheduled to return to Guam the day before the start of hostilities. Hart ordered her to stay due to the serious situation in the Pacific. The oil barge *Robert Barnes* was bombed and strafed, leaving her with a leaking hull. She was later captured by the Japanese while still afloat. Both small YP patrol boats were heavily damaged with one vessel completely destroyed by fire.

The damage reports trickled into McMillin's office throughout the two days and were difficult to confirm due to the limited communications around the island. It was clear to him the island was hit hard. Various reports included downed enemy aircraft. The gunners aboard *Penguin* thought their shells hit one of the attackers. However, there were no Japanese plane losses. All the men on Guam could do now was to wait for the invaders to arrive.

Chapter 7

FIRE FROM THE SKY

GEORGE TWEED ARRIVED AT HIS post in the Communications Office early on the morning of the first day of the war. Everyone in the office knew a Japanese attack was imminent. Perhaps even more unnerving was they also knew little could be done to stop the enemy. The Japanese planes arrived to find minimal resistance— no American airplanes, few anti-aircraft guns, and easy—almost defenseless—targets.

"We had no means of defense," Tweed recalled.[1] He knew the few machine guns were already divided up and given to various units. "One thirty-caliber machine gun was mounted on the hill above Agaña to repel air attacks," he said in recalling the ineffectiveness of the weapon. "The Japs soon learned that the gun was there and they flew higher as a result, although we did not bag any planes with that gun."[2] Though the gunner may have hit one or more planes—

or thought he did—the enemy suffered no plane losses during the bombing runs over Guam.

Many American servicemen rightly assumed the Japanese invaders would arrive with an overwhelming force of warships, strong air cover, and a large number of heavily armed soldiers. Tweed knew the defenders were at a great disadvantage and not just because of numbers. "We had very little ammunition there, so little that the Insular Force was unable to get any practice with machine guns prior to the war which resulted in very few of them having any knowledge of the operation of machine guns," he later said.

Tweed watched helplessly as the enemy aircraft arrived. He saw the planes fly "directly to Sumay, where they bombed the Standard Oil tanks and barracks of civilian workers for the construction company."[3] The radioman was given a special mission after the communication lines to the Libugon radio station were damaged early in the attack. "I was sent up that afternoon to a hill in a particular area with a portable radio to maintain communication with the communication office in town, as the telephone connection had been destroyed."

The sailor later wrote he was in an open field on a sloped hillside when his movements attracted the attention of at least one enemy plane who turned to make a strafing pass. Tweed watched in horror as the plane seemed to be coming straight at him. He dropped to the ground. His khaki uniform blending in with the dry grass may have saved him.

The actual Japanese target was likely a steel tower used as an airplane beacon about one hundred feet away on top of the hill. One or more bombs exploded on the ground, sending showers of deadly shrapnel cascading around the immediate area. Some of the red-hot particles landed on Tweed's clothes, burning small holes as he feverously tried to brush them away, and put a gash into his hand.[4] The planes eventually moved on to other targets. Tweed was still alive and the tower remained standing.

Some bad news awaited the radioman when he returned to town after the air attacks subsided. "On returning to Agaña at 2:30 p.m., I was told my house had been bombed," Tweed later said. "One bomb had dropped in town and it was on my house." He rushed to his residence to see the damage for himself.

The single bomb missed the intended target and slammed into the house. Tweed speculated the bomb was aimed at a nearby administrative building. Precision bombing was largely nonexistent in World War II, making collateral damage common.

He found the front door blasted wide open. It looked as though the bomb passed through the roof before exploding on the front porch. Although the concrete walls may have saved the structure from complete destruction, there was extensive damage throughout most of the rooms and the blast sent his personnel effects scattered around the immediate area.

There was little Tweed could do about his predicament. "I realized that I was terribly hungry and weak," he later wrote. "I found some cold meat and made some sandwiches before reporting to the Communications Office."[5] He arrived to find sledgehammers on the office table. The men were getting ready to smash the radio equipment when the Japanese invaded.

Tweed remembered the second day of the air attacks "was practically a repetition of the first" with Japanese planes attacking targets at will. "I stayed at the Communications Office until midnight and then went home to the wreckage of my house," he continued. "I dragged the bed out of the shattered bedroom and put it back where there was still some roof left."[6] The exhausted sailor was soon sound asleep. He would wake up to an uncertain future.

A small group of ships were sighted far out on the horizon shortly before the evening darkness shrouded the island. The sighting was an ominous sign of what was to come. Tweed remembered "the information was not widely spread."

The members of the Communications Office probably knew their section was to be a top target when the Japanese attacked. A small group of men from Radio Libugon were assigned on December 8 to set up portable radio equipment in the nearby mountains. The mission was accomplished by the morning on December 10 and the equipment was ready to operate except for the lack of one cable.[7] It is unclear if Tweed was involved in the operation.

A few short radio messages gave the outside world a brief glimpse of the events on Guam before the radio stations were later knocked offline for good. An initial message sent to Hawaii and the Philippines on December 8 simply said "Guam attacked." A later message provided more details. "Guam being attacked by air by two Japanese squadrons. Casualties four Chamorros on Pan American dock while securing radio station. Hotel destroyed. Gas tanks aflame. Office and machine shops machine-gunned."[8] Two subsequent messages received in the Philippines during the early afternoon simply reported Guam was under attack by six seaplanes.

The communications men were under orders to destroy all confidential materials and radio equipment to keep anything from falling into Japanese hands. Tweed later recalled all the equipment at Radio Libugon was broken up, piled up in the center of the station, and set on fire.[9] The Pacific Cable Station, Radio Libugon, and the Pan Am radio station were all abandoned. The Pan Am station was able to send off a quick "signing off" message.[10]

Radio Agaña later reported an ominous message. "One large ship believed to be a transport, two destroyers off Guam. Pending landing expected soon at several points."[11] The island was about to go dark to the outside world. In what may have been its final message, dispatched on the afternoon of December 9, Radio Agaña simply reported "All codes destroyed."

The main component of the Japanese Guam invasion force put to sea from Hahajima in the Bonin Islands at 9:00 a.m. on December 4 to begin the voyage directly to Guam. Four destroyers and a mine-layer accompanied nine transports loaded with almost 5,000 army soldiers.[12] The troops were members of a brigade-sized unit known as the South Seas Detachment under the command of Major General Tomitara Hori. The men were drawn from the 55th Division and included elements of the 144th Infantry Regiment. The group was assembled in Korea and sent briefly to Japan before arriving in the Bonin Islands during the last days of November.[13]

Additional support from the Imperial Navy included more warships and special amphibious soldiers. The heavy cruisers *Kako*, *Furutaka*, *Aoba*, and *Kinugasa* were under orders to provide bombardment support during the invasion if needed. A detachment of 370 Special Naval Landing Force troops (essentially Japanese marines) stationed on Saipan joined the armada en route.

The ships followed a course to the east of the Marianas and were not sighted by any Americans.[14] Rear Admiral Aritomo Goto commanded the ships from the heavy cruiser *Aoba*.[15] The forces devoted to the Guam operation were overwhelming for the lightly defended island. The Japanese estimate of military strength on Guam was reasonably accurate—about 300 men and 1,500 native soldiers.[16]

However, Japanese officers writing after the war recalled the concern of the Americans having coastal defense guns and artillery positioned at various points on the island.[17] The invaders were to quickly find the battle was going to be a one-sided fight.

Chapter 8

INVASION

THE JAPANESE INVASION FORCE ARRIVED in the Rota area on December 8, 1941. The ships loitered before receiving orders to begin the assault. The actual advance to Guam took place in smaller groups of ships with each moving to their designated landing area.

Army Second Lieutenant Yanagiba Yutaka was among the troops loaded in the transports waiting to take part in the invasion. The young officer had only been on active duty since October 1. "I was given a map of Guam Island said to have been drawn up from air photos," he later recalled of the voyage from Japan to Hahajima. "All place names were then turned to the Japanese language, and I was ordered to remember the geography."[1] He participated in additional training on land before force was again loaded into ships for the voyage to Guam.

Three Japanese transports used the cover of darkness as a cloak of protection to shield their approach to the Guam coast north of

Agaña.[2] The soldiers of the Special Naval Landing Force climbed into six small boats during the first hours of December 10. The craft glided through the water while slowly moving toward Dungcas Beach, about two miles northeast of Agaña.

Members of the Insular Patrol on beach patrol spotted ominous objects at sea around 3:00 a.m. The shapes quickly materialized into landing boats. Seaman Second Class Juan Perez fired off some shots in the direction of the leading boat before moving off the beach with the other members of the patrol. They then ran to Agaña to alert the American authorities—the invasion was under way.[3]

Word of the invasion reached Captain McMillin within an hour. He immediately ordered the implementation of the last elements of the war plan—destruction of any remaining important documents and materials deemed useful to the Japanese. The meager defense of Guam centered on Plaza de España in Agaña. Members of the Insular Guard Force, led by a small number of marines and sailors, set up defensive positions using overturned concrete benches, ditches, and sand bags. Most of their fire power resided in the three thirty-caliber machine guns. The weapons were set up in foxholes with sandbags providing some meager protection for the operators.

The soldiers of the Japanese Special Naval Landing Force met no resistance while coming ashore. They assembled at the beach before moving inland to a two-lane road heading southwest toward Agaña. The initial landing at Dungcas Beach was followed by the main invasion force. The South Seas Detachment came ashore in separate locations, including a battalion strength force at Tumon Bay (northeast of Dungcas Beach). A second group was scheduled to land at Merizo in the southern part of the island and advance north to the Orote Peninsula to secure the Apra Harbor area. The landing point was switched at the last minute after the Japanese realized there was no suitable road for the move north.[4] The delay meant the southern group would miss the short battle for Guam.

The Japanese troops moving toward Agaña showed no mercy to any civilians encountered along the way. A six-man guard patrol was bayonetted and shot not far from Dungcas Beach after meeting a large group of Japanese soldiers. Closer to Agaña, multiple groups of fleeing civilians were mercilessly attacked with gunfire, killing some and wounding others.[5] Two unlucky American sailors walking to see their girlfriends became the first prisoners taken on the island.[6]

Groups of Japanese soldiers approached Plaza de España from the north and northwest during predawn darkness with bayonets fixed to their rifles. Commander Giles strapped on his Colt .45 pistol and took up position with others, crouched behind a small stone wall. "The suspense was terrible until the enemy appeared along three streets, crouching in attack formation," he wrote. "Upon sighting these troops at the plaza, I ordered our forces to commence firing."[7] The morning silence abruptly ended with the rattle of machine guns and rifle fire. One of the machine guns momentarily stopped a group of Japanese soldiers moving toward the plaza near the church.

An officer attached to the administration group was near the Officer's Club on a bluff above Agaña and decided to join the fight. Lieutenant Graham Bright jumped into his car for the short drive to the plaza. Luck was not riding with the young officer. He drove directly into a cluster of Japanese soldiers, who riddled his car with bullets. Bright was dragged from the car and bayoneted to death.[8]

The Japanese advance into the plaza was twice stopped as the Americans and Guamanians put up a stiff resistance.[9] It was during the frantic battle for the plaza that George Tweed made his daring escape—initially from his home to the Government House, and subsequently to the countryside. The battle was short-lived for the out-gunned defenders.

Heavy rifle fire from Japanese soldiers promptly silenced the machine guns, allowing soldiers to pour into the plaza. The defenders began retreating to the west side of the plaza. The attackers quickly brought up machine guns and a small Pack Howitzer cannon. Machine gun bullets sprayed across the plaza. Many defenders ducked for cover as the sound of bullets echoed off buildings. Giles stayed in his position while bullets thumped into the wall behind him. The defense of the plaza was quickly becoming hopeless.

Enemy soldiers moved into position on the south side of the plaza to outflank the defenders. The Americans and Guamanians retreated into the Insular Guard Force barracks seeking shelter behind the concrete walls. After about twenty minutes of fighting, word reached the American authorities of additional Japanese landings.

After swimming ashore from their sinking ship, many of the unhurt *Penguin* sailors went to Agaña in search of clothes, shoes, and food. The men were assigned various duties, including nightly patrols, and ordered to stay in the armory. Edward Hale was thoroughly exhausted and hungry by the morning of the Japanese invasion. He spent the last two days on patrol and helping repair damaged communications cables connecting Agaña and points on the Orote Peninsula. The time included at least one brush with a Japanese plane.

The sound of gunfire from the direction of Dungcas Beach put everyone on alert during the predawn hours. Hale joined other sailors and guard members racing to set up the defense of the plaza. He remembered Chief Boatswain's Mate Robert Lane shouting directions on where to position the three machine guns.

The small minesweeper *Penguin* spent time in Chinese waters before her homeport was moved to Guam. The ship is shown off Shanghai, China in the late 1920s. (US Navy / Naval History and Heritage Command)

Suddenly, an unknown figure approached the plaza in the dark. Hale soon recognized him as shipmate Seaman First Class Thomas Haskins. The sailor was calm. He told them, "They are coming. Lots of them. They've got machine guns and bombs, and they're pulling carts of some type."[10] The latter was likely artillery cannons. Hale told him to see Lane for further instructions.

Time seemed to be moving slowly as Hale waited with a small group for the enemy to arrive. He only had twenty-two bullets for his .45 pistol. A hushed voice suddenly exclaimed the Japanese were moving near San Ramon Hill. "We jumped at the chance to do something," Hale explained. "Through the trees on the plaza, along the ledge, over the fence and along the road to San Ramon we ran."

The small groups scattered to hiding places in the brush part way up the hill. A large number of Japanese soldiers were seen moving in the distance. Hale quickly fired off some shots, emptying his pistol. All types of thoughts were racing though his mind as he reloaded the gun. Gunfire and screams were heard coming from the plaza. Two hand grenades exploded nearby, but the sailor was not hurt. The first rays of daylight were breaking across the sky when the shooting stopped. Hale suspected a surrender was about to take place.

McMillin was in his command post at the Government House while the fighting raged in the plaza. "The situation was simply hopeless, the resistance had been carried out to the limit," he wrote of the situation.[11] Giles earlier brought him the news of the additional Japanese landings. McMillin made the decision to surrender after briefly conferring with other officers. He communicated the decision to Giles, who was still outside in the plaza.

Giles began slowly moving toward his car, a Chevrolet parked near his position. "Carefully opening the door so as to not be targeted by the Japanese, I sounded three blasts on the horn, a signal recognized by anyone in the military as meaning secure," he wrote of the moment. The time was about 5:45 a.m. "This was not a pre-arranged signal to cease fire, but it seemed to be understood by both sides," McMillin explained.

The defenders stopped firing almost immediately and the Japanese continued for only a short time longer. Suddenly, a Japanese voice rang out, "Send over your captain." Giles and Lane slowly emerged and began walking toward the Japanese positions. Giles carefully turned the large head of his US Naval Academy ring inward so as not to attract unwanted attention from his soon-to-be captors.

The Japanese commander on-site did not speak English. Giles and Lane were placed under armed guard and marched to the landing site to meet with Commander Hiromu Hayashi. The Japanese naval officer also did not speak English. Since no interpreter was available, a strange conversation followed with both sides using sign language. It became clear the Japanese wanted to communicate with the top American official on the island.

The remaining defenders laid down their weapons back at the plaza. Men slowly rose from concealed positions with hands raised in the air. They were about to become some of the first prisoners of war in the Pacific.

Emissaries Giles and Lane began a march back to the plaza under the same heavy guard. They found McMillin already in Japanese custody. "I was captured in the reception room of my quarters about twenty minutes after the cease firing signal," McMillin wrote. "The leader of the squad of Japanese who entered my quarters required mine to remove my jacket and trousers before marching me into the plaza, where officers and men were being assembled, covered by machine guns."

The communication barrier still had to be overcome. When the Japanese commander learned there were Japanese citizens jailed nearby, he ordered their release and one became the interpreter. A formal letter of surrender was drawn up after some initial wrangling between McMillin and the enemy officer.

Chief Yeoman Luther Farris typed the short three-section letter, dictated by the Japanese, and the document was signed by McMillin.[12] "I, Captain George J. McMillin, United States Naval Station, Guam, by authority of my commission from the President of the United States, do as a result of superior military forces landed on Guam this date, as an act of war, surrender this post to you as the representative of the Imperial Japanese Government."[13] Two additional short passages noted the civil government was now the responsibility of the Japanese and both the civilian population and surrendered military forces would be treated humanely. Time revealed the latter two provisions were not followed by the Japanese captors. The news slowly spread around the island: all Americans were to surrender.

Chapter 9

SURRENDER

THE SURRENDER GAVE GUAM THE distinction of becoming the first American territory to fall into Japanese hands. Back in Agaña the hoisting of the rising sun flag made the surrender official, along with a proclamation issued by Major General Hori. "We proclaim herewith that our Japanese Army has occupied this island of Guam by order of the great Emperor of Japan. It is for the purpose of restoring liberty and rescuing the whole Asiatic people and creating the permanent peace in Asia. Thus our intention is to establish the New Order of the World."[1] The proclamation went on to warn of harsh treatment for any acts of defiance and spying, including the ominous threat of the intent to "execute said criminals by shooting."

When the fighting stopped, Japanese soldiers moved into the Communications Office, Piti Navy Yard, the US Naval Hospital, and other key points around the island. Second Lieutenant Yanagiba Yutaka was among the Japanese soldiers arriving in Sumay on the day of the invasion. His unit encountered no resistance. "The conquest of Guam was very easy, and it was like a journey overseas," he later said, marveling at how trouble-free the operation was carried out.[2] He marched to Agaña the next day and recorded his impressions in a diary. "Foreigners are luxurious," he wrote. "There are swimming pools, a golf course, and automatic record-changing phonographs."

Some members of the marine garrison at Sumay fled the area before the surrender. Those who remained solemnly gathered to await the arrival of the enemy, who were not long in coming. They lowered the American flag and buried it in the ground. The Japanese soldiers forced the marine prisoners to strip naked and sit on the golf course.

The short period of fighting and quick surrender prevented a high number of casualties during the invasion and battle in the plaza. The numbers were initially unclear. One source later recorded seventeen military defenders killed—thirteen American and four Insular Guard members—and thirty-five wounded. Thirty civilians were thought to have been killed. Japanese casualties have been reported as one killed and six wounded.[3]

Navy nurse Jackson was not a witness to the fighting on the plaza. Most of the small medical staff remained at the hospital. She remembered the firing stopped around dawn. "I think the most bitter moment in my life came at sunrise when standing in the library door I saw the Rising Sun on the flag pole where the day before the Stars and Stripes had proudly flown," she recalled.[4]

A group of Japanese soldiers appeared at the hospital in force around 8:30 a.m. They subsequently took over most of the facility and confined the American staff to a small area. Japanese authorities ordered the current patients to be moved to one side of the hospital to make space for wounded Japanese soldiers. The bodies of the American dead were initially put in a shed behind the hospital a couple of days after the invasion and buried together near a beach a short time later.[5] Most of the medical staff, including Jackson, remained separate from the rest of the American prisoners during the first weeks of the occupation.

Most of the prisoners were herded into the plaza shortly after the surrender order, where the men were forced to strip to their underwear. Communication difficulties added to the problems as Americans were not always able to understand Japanese orders. They quickly became familiar with the harsh treatment of their captors.

There was no shortage of brutal acts taking place as illustrated by the death of Marine Private John Kauffman. Although various accounts differ, Kauffman may have been slow to follow an order or possibly partook in some type of minor infraction. A Japanese soldier lunged forward to plunge his bayonet into the defenseless soldier's midsection. "He dropped to the ground and died," remembered Sergeant George Shane.[6] The lifeless body was dragged away by two Japanese soldiers and tossed onto a garbage pile. Some accounts have two other American soldiers brutally murdered after instinctively stepping forward to help their fallen comrade.[7]

Giles was among the officers mixed in with the prisoners. "With our dead and wounded shipmates lying nearby, we were held under heavy guard in the plaza for most of the day," he wrote. "There were no areas of shade, and the sun beat down incessantly, raising the temperature to an almost intolerable level. What an introduction to hell."[8]

Small groups of Japanese soldiers spread out looking for American stragglers as news of the surrender gradually made it around Guam. Captured soldiers and sailors were slowly moved to the main plaza. A group of sailors from the navy yard marched into Agaña under Japanese guard with their leader carrying a white flag. The marines from Sumay were eventually delivered via truck.

The arrival of daylight forced Edward Hale to make a decision. Hiding on a hill, he was weak and cold. The sailor thought seriously about going into the jungle and knew the locals would help him. However, he feared what would happen to those found to be aiding him and harbored doubts about how long he could hold out. He wondered what happened to his *Penguin* shipmates. Were they even still alive?

He saw some Japanese soldiers were nearby. They were calmly walking up the hill carrying weapons. Their dark green uniforms clearly stood out from the surroundings. Hale decided to surrender and began walking down the hill toward the plaza. "I could see the captured men sitting on the grass, surrounded by Japanese with bayonets and machine guns," he wrote of the moment. "At least they were alive."[9] A Japanese soldier suddenly ran up, yelling "Hands up!" The exhausted Hale complied, was searched, and soon joined the other prisoners gathered in the plaza.

As those on Guam were enduring their first days of Japanese rule, the details of what was happening on the island remained unknown to the outside world. A Navy Department Communique released on December 13, 1941 concluded the obvious. "The Navy Department announced that it is unable to communicate with Guam either by radio or cable. The capture of the island is probable.... According to the last reports from Guam, the island has been bombed repeatedly and Japanese troops had landed at several points on the island."[10] The military personnel were listed as missing in action.[11]

American authorities had no way of knowing most of the island's garrison was alive and prisoners of the Japanese in Agaña. The men spent the first couple of days confined to buildings near the plaza, including the Insular Guard Force's barracks, the small jail, and the Catholic church. The prisoners were fed two or three times a day—although the portions were smaller than what many considered normal—and no Americans were initially forced to do any manual labor.[12]

Sailor Robert Lane and some Japanese soldiers counted and recounted the Americans. The captors were almost certainly trying to determine how many Americans were missing. "Finally, a number was arrived at as being the official count," explained Giles.

The enemy was able to determine a small number of sailors were unaccounted for and considered missing. "Then came the bad news—not that we shouldn't have expected it. We were told that should anyone attempt to escape the rest of the prisoners would be shot."[13] Giles had few doubts the Japanese would carry out the threat given the brutality already witnessed in the plaza. He worried about one of the younger prisoners trying to make a run for it and the resulting dire consequences for the rest of the group.

The American captives knew little about what happened to the missing sailors. There was much speculation and rumors were circulating. "No one could account for a certain bit of portable radio equipment at that time, which led to the belief that a couple of missing radiomen may have escaped with it," Hale wrote.[14]

There was indeed some radio equipment missing from the main communication stations. A small group of sailors from the Libugon Station took emergency radio equipment up Mount Tenjo, southwest of Agaña and directly east of Apra Harbor. They hid in a cave during the attack. At one point, they were visited by Tweed, who was assigned to make sure the emergency equipment was working properly. Radioman Second Class Harold Joslin remembered Tweed leaving to get extra parts, only taking a walkie talkie with him. "We never saw him again, and we never got the radio on the air," he later said.[15]

The eight radio men were captured by Japanese soldiers shortly after the invasion.

The overall conditions for the prisoners began to deteriorate when the naval guards were replaced with regular army soldiers after only a couple of days of confinement. Food rations were severely reduced, and the incidents of abuse increased. Captives were required to stand at attention whenever a Japanese soldier entered the compound regardless of their rank. "The Japs stripped us of everything, even our GI clothes," remembered marine Don Manning. "They issued us the 'peanut suits'…with pants that ended around our knees and shirts that wouldn't even button."[16]

Strong punishments were handed out for any type of infraction. "Prisoners were punished severely for the slightest infraction or assumed infraction," Giles remembered. "Punishment was delivered on the spot, without any thought of due process. Normally it took the form of beatings, bamboo canes being the favorite delivery instruments, although in at least one instant a marine was struck with a wide belt having a large brass buckle."[17]

Most of the Americans were moved into the church and adjoining parish hall. As a place of worship, the church was not designed to be living quarters. The conditions were dreadfully overcrowded. Captives slept on pews, the floor, or any open space. There was only one indoor toilet and the water supply was minimal.

The reduced amount of food led to stomach ailments and diarrhea, making many of the prisoners weaker. "Most of us had no blankets and very few clothes," Hale remembered. "The early mornings were a bit cool, to say the least, but the real misery arose from the almost microscopic mosquitoes which came in skillions [sic) in the last evening to assail any part of the body. These insects were very difficult to see, and as individuals, the pests would scarcely be noticed."

One small contingent of captives were held at the hospital. The group included McMillin, Giles, and some of the administrative personnel. The conditions were only slightly better than the rest of the American confined to the church. One civilian, power plant manager Dominic Encerti, was allowed to leave regularly to repair equipment at the plant. "The Japanese were unable to keep anything going," Giles wrote.

Caption George J. McMillin (left) and three other officers return to Washington, DC on September 7, 1945 after being freed from a Japanese prisoner of war camp. The naval officer was serving as the American governor and military commander of Guam at the time of the Japanese invasion. (US Navy / National Archives)

The prisoners were allowed to bury their dead. A total of fourteen Americans—four marines, nine sailors, and one civilian—were laid to rest in a cemetery near the location of the initial Japanese landing. Full military honors were provided.[18]

The change of leadership on Guam was not complete without some type of parade by the invaders. The American prisoners were made to stand at attention in Plaza de España about a week after the invasion. They watched a parade of about 2,000 Japanese troops, complete with vehicles and horses. General Hori proudly straddled a white horse. He gave a long lecture about the new order Japan was creating in the world and extolled the prisoners to be obedient.

Some of the prisoners helped unload a Japanese supply ship at Piti close to Christmas. Many volunteered for the assignment to get out of the crowded conditions. The recently arrived ship to Apra Harbor was full of rice and other foodstuffs for the soldiers. The hard labor closed out a very difficult month.

OCCUPATION

THE JAPANESE WASTED NO TIME in taking complete control of Guam while the American prisoners were held in Agaña. The invaders soon gave Guam a new name—Omiya Jima, the Great Shrine Island.[1] The city of Agaña was renamed Akashi—the Red City. The renamed island was now part of the Japanese empire.

The dawning of a new year—1942—held great uncertainty for the captives. "We had little idea what the Japanese would do with the captured Americans," the sailor, Edward Hale, wrote. "Surely the stories we had read in American magazines offered no encouragement."[2]

Commander Giles summed up the issues facing the captives. "While held on Guam we experienced three primary problems: inadequate food, mental and physical abuse by our captors, and uncertainty as to our future," he recalled.[3] The prisoners' situation was about to get much worse.

Word spread quickly among the captives in early January that they could soon be moved. A few stragglers in hiding surrendered and joined the group. The prisoners made the march to the Piti Navy Yard on January 6 with some nurses and wounded men riding in vehicles. Rumors abounded as to where they could be going—a new camp on the island, a prisoner exchange, or some other destination—no one really knew.

The journey included walking past some Guamanians along the route, possibly as a humiliation for the beaten-down and worn-out Americans. "The unforgettable picture that will never fade from my memory on that miserable march was the expressions on the faces of the hapless Chamorros," Hale later wrote. "I could see hope itself turned into a torturing memory on the faces as we pass along the street." It seemed as if the islanders somehow thought the mere presence of Americans on Guam would help keep the Japanese from mistreating the civilians.

Nurse Leona Jackson was among the Americans about to depart the island. "We knew that something was going on because the night before, the doctors and the hospital corpsmen who had been assigned for the maintenance of the hospital were taken over to the church with the rest of the prisoners, so we realized that we were ready for a move," she later recalled.[4] She loaded up a suitcase and headed by truck for the harbor.

The Americans could see a variety of ships in Apra Harbor, including some old rusty transports. The situation gradually became clear for the prisoners—they were about to leave Guam. The departure day was set for January 10, with the ship *Argentina Maru* providing the transportation.

Marine Captain Charles Todd served as an aid to Captain McMillin. "Who can forget that day?" he said, years later. The men were counted again and then herded aboard decrepit lighters for the short trip to what looked to be the nicest ship in the harbor. The *Argentina Maru* was a luxury ocean liner built in 1939. She spent most of her time as a civilian vessel traveling between Japan and South America before requisition by the Imperial Japanese Navy in 1941.[5] The Guam prisoners, and those transported from Wake Island to Japan, were the only captives sent aboard ocean liners. Less fortunate captives, from the Philippines and elsewhere, made the voyage in old decrepit freighters.[6]

A total of 483 Americans were put aboard the transport.[7] Manning remembered a higher total. "There were about 650 of us packed in the hold of that ship, half construction men and half marines," he said.[8]

Marine Private Garth Dunn had no illusions about having any first-class accommodations. "True to my prediction, we descended lower and lower into the bowls of the ship. Finally, we couldn't go any lower," he recalled. "The hold was dark, dank, and warm. The heat settled over the crowded men like an oppressive blanket."[9] Giles recalled, "We were taken past the luxurious first-class cabins and herded down into the hold—four decks down, deep in the bowels of the ship."

The nurses and a couple of civilians went into stewards' cabins while the rest of the prisoners went below into the cargo hold. Jackson shared a cabin. She considered the compartment to be luxurious accommodations compared to those below deck. The transport departed after sundown on January 10. She traveled without escort through waters possibly prowling with American submarines.

Marine Marvin Roslansky was among those crammed aboard the ship. "It was just a hold," he later said of the accommodations. "Your bunks were there and the latrines were just off the side. There was really nothing."[10] The bunks were stacked six high, making for impossibly crowded conditions. The meager diet was heavy on rice. "We went up in different groups for air once in a while," Roslansky continued. "They let us up for that. But it was strong supervision."

A rumor the ship was going somewhere in the South Pacific circulated among the prisoners shortly after departure. The idea was quickly dispelled when the weather started turning colder on the second day at sea—the ship was clearly heading north. The *Argentine Maru* arrived at the Port of Tadotsu in southern Japan on January 14.[11]

Gone was the idyllic island surroundings of Guam and the tropical climate. The men were now in winter conditions. The prisoners were taken to Zentsuji, a coastal city facing the inland waterway on Shikoku Island. The Americans were about to start a brutal stretch of time at a prisoner camp and were destined to spend the rest of the war in Japan.

A preview of the cruel treatment the civilians were to endure under Japanese rule on Guam took place on the morning of January 6. A small group of Agaña residents was summoned to watch the execution of two Guamanians in a cemetery. Alfred Flores tried to smuggle a message to an American construction company worker. Won Pat was a caught by Japanese authorities taking supplies from a warehouse. Both men were sentenced to death for their actions. News of the killings quickly spread among the local population—they understood in the clearest terms that even the smallest infractions would result in the harshest punishments under Japanese rule.[12]

The army assault troops were redeployed once the island was secured. The Imperial Navy assumed control of Guam in March 1942, about three months after the invasion, with Commander Hayashi Horace initially installed as the military leader. The commander was a naval officer among the invasion troops. He set up his headquarters in the Government House in Agaña. He dispatched a contingent of soldiers to the former marine facilities in Sumay.[13]

Only a small garrison of about 300 men—members of the 54th Naval Guard Unit—remained to occupy the island.[14]

Most of the naval troops stayed to themselves and did not have a lot of direct interaction with the civilians. Sailors often dressed in their white uniforms to stroll around Agaña during weekend liberty time. Over one hundred "comfort girls" were brought to the island, mainly from Korea, to satisfy the sexual wishes of the military men.[15] The enforcement of laws and rules gradually fell to the police force.

Life under Japanese rule changed quickly for the Guamanians as the new occupiers sought to impose "Japanization" on their new subjects. The civilian government was placed under the control of Minseibu, or the civilian affairs department of the Japanese Army, in January 1942. The Minseibu offices were set up at the St. Vincent de Paul building, adjacent to the Catholic church in Agaña. Many of the officials came from Saipan, including five or six Chamorro interpreters.[16]

The Minseibu controlled daily administrative affairs on the island. The strong influence of the military never seemed far during the occupation. Lieutenant Commander Homura, an elderly officer, served as the head of the Minseibu and governor of the island.[17] The officer gave regular propaganda talks at the church, with often required attendance for civilians, creating ill feelings among the Guamanians.

All Guamanians were now the subjects of the Japanese emperor. The practice of bowing was established as a show of respect to the Japanese. The time-honored tradition in Japan was completely foreign to Guamanians, and commonly viewed as a way to humiliate the civilians. Failure to bow often resulted in a swift kick, slap, or beating—the punishment was up to the discretion of the soldier involved.[18]

Japanese replaced English as the official language. Schools reopened with new subjects, including Japanese thought, culture, and the reasons for the conflict—the Greater East Asia Co-Prosperity Sphere.[19] The American dollar was outlawed, and the Japanese yen became the new currency. Guamanians could exchange their dollars at a very unfavorable rate. The Japanese authorities allowed two Catholic priests, Father Jesus Baza Duenas and Father Oscar Calvo, to stay on the island. The pair, along with a Baptist minister, were to care for the islander's spiritual needs.

The police sought to keep order, root out any American sympathizers, and hunt down the missing American personnel. They regularly searched for hidden weapons and radios. Beatings and torture became the preferred methods of gathering information.

"They seemed to believe that if they beat you long enough and hard enough, you would tell them what they wanted to hear. If you didn't, they would at least know that you knew nothing. In either case, they received information," wrote Ben Blaz, a teenager during the war.[20] His father worked as a government official under the Americans and was taken in for "questioning." He was freed only after undergoing a terrible beating.

As with all lands in the Japanese sphere, the administration sought to exploit any natural resources for the benefit of the empire. On Guam it included manganese. Small quantities of the trace mineral were found in the southern part of the island and mining efforts began early in the occupation.

Agriculture became an important initiative for the Japanese. Almost all arable land in some communities was turned into rice or vegetable fields to be maintained by local workers.[21] Some of the product was to be turned over to the Japanese through the enforcement of mandatory food quotas. Individual Japanese soldiers often visited farms to help themselves to produce, eggs, chickens, and anything else they wanted. Food rationing for civilians was initiated.

The occupiers used the local population for construction projects. Laborers were recruited to work on the Orote airfield and later airstrips. The lack of adequate heavy equipment resulted in much of the work having to be done manually. They received a handful of rice—or no compensation at all—for their strenuous efforts. Some islanders escaped into the jungle to avoid the forced labor.

Many Guamanians believed the Americans would eventually return. Until then, they had to co-exist with the Japanese as best as possible. The situation for the civilians was to become worse as the war progressed.

Chapter 11

ON THE RUN

THE GROUP OF THREE MEN who slipped out of Agaña just ahead
of the Japanese invaders was lucky to have escaped. George Tweed,
fellow sailor Al Tyson, and Vincent Guevara, a member of the Insular
Guard Force, were out in the country by the time Captain McMillin
was signing the surrender order. Tweed believed his departure approximately coincided with the time of the surrender. "It was just about at
this time that I left town," he later said.[1]

Tweed's old car was the means of their daring escape. Guevara
decided it was best if he went to stay with his family instead of being
with American servicemen on the run—a wise choice under the circumstances. He parted ways with the sailors, leaving them in Ordot
just south of Agaña.[2] The two sailors continued into the rural area.
"We got in my car and proceeded about eleven miles from town
where we left the car in the brushes and proceeded to find a hiding
place," Tweed explained. The two sailors were on their own, trapped

on an island now rapidly falling under the control of the Japanese, and in need of a secure place away from the enemy. The pair were in the vicinity of Yono, a small village almost straight south of Agaña and close to the eastern coast.

The fast-paced action of the escape may have now seemed like a blur to Tweed. "I had prepared some boxes of food and supplies for a tentative flight, but I delayed leaving until the last possible moment," he later explained of his departure. "Finally, I decided that if I was going, I'd better leave—fast!" He remembered the sound of gunfire as they sped away in the car. "Then a machine gun started firing at the car as we drove by, but I had no lights on and they missed us and the tires, luckily."[3]

Once carless, the sailors were immediately confronted with having to move through thick and prickly underbrush. The vegetation was dominated by an aggressively growing plant covered with small thorns, recognized by various local names in tropical areas around the world. The plant was commonly known as lemonchina in Guam. The invasive plant grew wildly, forming a thick underbrush at the ground level under the forest canopy.

The Americans could never have survived for any length of time without the help of local residents. "I knew the Chamorro people pretty well before I went into the jungles," Tweed related years later. "I know that they are generous to a fault. They'd give you their shirt off their back if they felt that you needed it."[4]

The sailors were content to wait for the Americans to return. Both expected the American Pacific Fleet to arrive soon. Tweed expected to be rescued in about two or three months. He later settled on June 1942 as the time he believed the Americans would return.[5] The sailors had no way of knowing the extent of the damage to the fleet at Pearl Harbor or of how badly the war was going for the Americans in the opening weeks of the conflict. No fleet was sailing across the

Pacific to liberate Guam and no Americans were returning to the island anytime soon.

The Yono region where Tweed and Tyson were hiding was largely an agricultural area. The sailors were initially helped by an area farmer named Francisco Ogo.[6] The older gentleman lived in a small house with his wife and some extended family members. A young girl who spoke some English acted as an interpreter for the adults. The family generously provided food and water. Tweed and Tyson were fearful the Japanese might find them in the house. They set up a small camp in the nearby jungle brush.

The two sailors were not the only ones hiding from the Japanese. Four other Americans—all navy men—successfully eluded the enemy. Two were also from the Communications Office in Agaña—Yeoman First Class Adolphe Yablonsky and Chief Aerographer's Mate Luther Jones. Tweed knew both sailors well. The other pair eluding capture were two men from the sunken *Penguin*—Chief Machinist's Mate Michael Krump and Machinist's Mate First Class Clarence Johnston. The latter was a relative newcomer to Guam, having reported for duty aboard the ship in May 1941. Krump arrived on station in April 1940, giving him a little more familiarity with the island.[7]

The four other sailors were hiding near Manenggon, about three miles from Tweed and Tyson.[8] Although the distance was not great, the two groups were separated by thick jungle, swamps, and the Ylig River. The sailors were brought together by another Yona area farmer named Manuel Aguon. Tweed and Tyson were introduced to the husky Guamanian by another local resident. Aguon gave them a warm welcome. He led the pair through the dark of night on a trek to meet up with the other Americans. Tweed and Tyson could only speculate as to the identities of the others—they really did not know who they were going to see.

The small group hiked up a hill on a rough trail. Tweed was able to make out the faint outline of a small shelter and sniff the smell of smoke once on level ground. Two figures, on guard duty nearby, slowly became clear in the darkness. Aguon confirmed his identity to one of the Guamanian guards before the American fugitives were put in contact with each other.

The small group gathered in the jungle hideout. The motley crew was bedraggled in appearance and donning long hair and beards. Their clothes were in tatters, but they were happy to see each other. Their survival was heavily dependent on several local Guamanians who brought them food, water, and supplies.

Jones explained his small group was hoping to leave town in another sailor's car. Chief Machinist's Mate Malvern Smoot was one of four men who attempted a daring escape from the Government House during the battle on the plaza. A small group of sailors were planning to reach Smoot's car to pick up the other sailors and leave town.

The men divided into pairs after racing out the back entrance. Smoot was running with civilian employee John Kluegel. They immediately came under fire by Japanese soldiers. Smoot was able to return fire with his pistol before both Americans were gunned down. Although they were probably already dead, a Japanese soldier bayoneted Kluegel and an officer used his sword to decapitate Smoot.[9] The other two fleeing Americans were wounded during the attempted escape. Both survived to become prisoners.

Jones and the others set out on foot after Smoot never showed up with his car. They were able to slip out of the area along the same road used by Tweed. Only after comparing notes did the sailors realize their paths had crossed during the escape. Jones and the others jumped into the brush after hearing the speeding car approaching, thinking it was a truck full of Japanese soldiers. They suddenly realized it was Tweed's car. The men yelled out as soon as the car sped past. It was too late for their voices to be heard.[10]

The four men narrowly escaped a group of Japanese soldiers near an abandoned chicken ranch in the hills. They spent days wandering through the thick forest, trying their best to keep out of sight. The sailors were eventually found by Aguon and were set up with a place to hide. The hideout was near a cliff with a commanding view of a nearby valley and river.

The sailors were careful not to let their guard down as they enjoyed each other's company.

They took turns keeping a careful lookout. Yablonsky was standing watch when he suddenly spotted a large group of Japanese soldiers crossing the river. He rushed back to tell the others.

The men scattered into hiding places in accordance with a premade plan to make a last stand. They were to stay hidden, until the Japanese reached the top of the hill and were surrounded, before springing up in a surprise attack. The odds were against their survival. The sailors could only muster three pistols among them for weapons while facing heavily armed enemy soldiers. Johnston gave one of the guns to Tweed. Hours of tense waiting followed with each man hiding still in their appointed position. The sailors returned to the shelter of their hideout only after receiving the all-clear from Yablonsky—the Japanese patrol was going back down the hill.

The Japanese were indeed looking for Tweed and the other escapees. The occupiers initially knew little about the missing American sailors. Tweed had an idea why the enemy wanted to find him so badly. "The Japs learned from the start the fact that I was in the bushes because they tried to repair some of the transmitters, radio transmitters and generators that we had smashed before they came in," he explained. "They got the idea of finding the American radio material man to help them. They found out who he was, which was me."

The knowledge that Tweed was a radio repairman was information the Japanese could have easily found either from rosters in the Communications Office or through the interrogation of prisoners. "They went over to the church where the American prisoners were confined and asked them to send me out," Tweed continued. "Of course, he received the answer that Tweed was not there, so they knew almost immediately that I was in the bushes, and because they were afraid that I would build a radio transmitter in the bushes and communicate with the Americans, therefore, they were more anxious to find me than the other fellows."

The sailors were forced to go on the run in the days following the initial scare when enemy search parties returned. They quickly packed up their belongings and were careful not to leave any traces of their presence before heading out through the thick jungle. The group narrowly escape detection on at least one other occasion. Help from the local residents often allowed them to stay one step ahead of the Japanese, although the one step was sometimes pretty close.

The reunion of the six sailors was short-lived. Staying together in a larger group was a dangerous undertaking. The men could not move about the island without leaving traces of their location and route. An additional complication occurred when Aguon was arrested by Japanese authorities after a search party found a small piece of khaki clothing, apparently left by Jones, at his ranch. He was taken to the jail in Agaña and beaten mercilessly while the Japanese pressed him for information on the whereabouts of the Americans. Aguon never revealed anything about the fugitives.

The sailors decided to break into pairs for greater agility and safety. Tweed simply remembered "the Japs came up and we were forced to disband and separate again."[11] He opted to stay with Tyson.

Chapter 12

DISASTER IN THE PACIFIC

THE PACIFIC ERUPTED IN AN inferno of war while George Tweed and Al Tyson were making their escape from the Japanese invaders on Guam. Imperial Japanese forces unleashed a series of carefully planned attacks against American, British, and Dutch possessions in the immediate aftermath of the Pearl Harbor surprise. The two closest American possessions to Guam—Wake Island and the Philippines—were hit hard in the opening days of the conflict.

The isolated Wake Island, some 2,000 miles west of Pearl Harbor, been described as one of the loneliest atolls in the Pacific in the opening days of the war due to the long distance from potential help.[1] However, unlike Guam, Wake was not defenseless. The three small atolls, collectively known as Wake Island, were defended by a garrison of 378 marines under the command of Major James Devereux. The soldiers were equipped with five-inch coastal defense guns, a variety of anti-aircraft guns, and machine guns for beach defense.[2]

The land was barely above sea level and there was little in the way of trees or vegetation. A marine squadron of twelve Grumman Wildcat fighters arrived on December 4 to begin operations from the newly constructed 5,000-foot runway.

After a preliminary bombing from land-based planes flying from the Marshall Islands, an undersized Japanese invasion force arrived off Wake in the early hours of December 11. The Japanese woefully underestimated the size of the defending garrison. Their latest intelligence reports indicated the air attacks knocked out at least half of the coastal guns and destroyed all the airplanes.[3] The reports were far from accurate.

The determined marine defenders repulsed the first Japanese attempt to invade the island. Coastal guns hit the destroyer *Hayate*, causing a tremendous explosion toward the stern of the ship. She broke in two before rapidly sinking. Only one sailor survived.[4] A second destroyer sank after bombs from a Wildcat fighter ignited a rack of depth charges on the warship's stern.

Several other Japanese ships sustained damage before the invasion force turned away.

The expulsion of the Japanese attack offered a brief glimpse of good news from the otherwise bleak Pacific front. A relief mission to bring more troops and planes to the beleaguered island floundered as leadership of the Pacific Fleet changed in the aftermath of the Pearl Harbor disaster and the navy lacked clear intelligence on the whereabouts of key elements of the Japanese fleet.[5] The enemy returned with a more powerful force to take control of the island on December 23. A last radio message from the American garrison reported, "The enemy is on the island. The issue is in doubt."[6] The overwhelmed defenders put up a fierce fight before surrendering.

The largest Japanese operation mounted against American territory in December 1941 took place about 1,500 miles west of

Guam in the Philippines. The rushed buildup of military forces in the American territory, under the direction of General MacArthur in Manila, had been underway for months before the war started. The general oversaw an air force of 277 planes, including 35 of the new B-17 Flying Fortress bombers, and about 100 frontline fighters.[7]

The buildup of the Filipino army was taking place with the help of American advisors and army units, although the process was far from complete. Many ground units were understrength and lacked adequate weapons, equipment, and training. More reinforcements were scheduled to arrive from the United States late in the year and in early 1942. Even with the buildup incomplete, the Philippine garrison represented the second largest concentration of American Army forces in the Pacific outside of Hawaii.[8]

The tenuous supply line connecting the United States to the Philippines was extremely long—stretching thousands of miles across the Pacific—making the territory isolated like Guam. Strong Japanese forces were positioned to the north in Formosa (Taiwan). American war plans called for defending the area around Manila Bay to deny the enemy use of the harbor. Imperial war plans called for the Philippines to be occupied as part of the larger operation of seizing British Malaya and the Dutch East Indies. The attack on all three began simultaneously after the Pearl Harbor strike.

The Japanese were able to catch many of the American planes on the ground during a devastating air attack on key air bases on the main Philippine island of Luzon—hours after the news arrived of the Pearl Harbor attack. The dreadful blow to MacArthur's air force saw half of the B-17 bombers and more than a third of the fighters demolished in a short period.[9] The enemy quickly won uncontested control of the skies.

An amphibious invasion followed with about 35,000 Japanese soldiers, accompanied by thousands of additional support personnel, coming ashore in a six-day span in northern Luzon and advancing south toward Manila.[10] The capital city was later abandoned without a fight. The last days of 1941 found American and Filipino ground forces in Luzon retreating toward the Bataan Peninsula. The mountainous finger of land on the west side of Manila Bay was an ideal place to hold out until help arrived or to serve as the location for a last stand. More than 80,000 soldiers and 26,000 civilians were soon crammed into the peninsula.[11] MacArthur commanded the operations from the nearby fortified island of Corregidor off the southern tip of Bataan.

The American and Filipino forces were short on supplies and food. No reinforcements were available from the United States. MacArthur was later evacuated to Australia on direct orders from President Roosevelt. The beleaguered Bataan garrison held out under unrelenting Japanese attacks until surrendering on April 9, 1942.

The defenders on Corregidor held out for less than a month before surrendering on May 6, 1942. The Corregidor capitulation included all American remaining servicemen in the territory. The battle of the Philippines was over.

The loss of Wake Island and the Philippines were bitter blows to the United States. In the weeks following the attack on Pearl Harbor, Japanese amphibious and air forces swept south and west, seizing the Gilbert Islands and attacking British Malaya along with various islands in the Dutch East Indies.

The leaders of Thailand fell into alignment with Japan after a brief invasion. Imperial ground forces attacking from mainland China forced the surrender of the British Crown Colony of Hong Kong on Christmas Day. The bleak news from the Pacific front continued into 1942. A hastily assembled command of American, British, Dutch, and Australian forces, informally known as ABDA, was organized to stop the enemy advance in the Dutch East Indies.

Japanese forces raced down the Malaya Peninsula toward Singapore after landings at the start of the war. The island fortress was the lynch pin of all British operations in the Far East. British Prime Minister Winston Churchill told American officials only a month earlier that Singapore could hold out for six months under siege.[12] The island surrendered on February 15, 1942 after just two weeks. Churchill lamented the loss of Singapore as "the greatest disaster and capitulation in British history."[13]

The important islands of the Dutch East Indies—including oil-rich Borneo and Sumatra—fell one by one to Japanese forces carefully advancing under the constant umbrella of air cover. The decisive defeat of ABDA naval forces in the Battle of Java Sea during the last days of February paved the way for all the Dutch East Indies to fall under Japanese control by the middle of March. The Imperial threat now loomed large over Australia.

The American road to victory was to be long and difficult. By the middle of 1942, the Japanese empire controlled a vast swath of territory spanning thousands of miles from Burma in the west to the Marshall Islands in the east, Manchuria in the north, and all the way south to just north of Australia. Guam was a small island far from any American-controlled territory. Tweed and the others on the island likely knew nothing about the disaster befalling the Allies in the Pacific. One thing was certain: the United States Navy was not returning to Guam anytime soon.

Chapter 13

LOCAL HELP

FUGITIVES GEORGE TWEED AND AL Tyson hid in the jungle near Yona for the first couple of months after escaping Agaña just ahead of the Japanese invaders. The pair eluded search parties while frequently moving around and living in rough conditions. Tweed later credited his outdoor instincts to his upbringing in a rural area in southern Oregon. He spent a lot of time outdoors, including frequent trips hunting in the woods with a rifle. The experience taught him a sense of direction and some basic survival skills.[1]

The men received help from many local Guamanians. Manuel Aguon, a rancher, was among the first to offer aid by allowing the Americans to stay on his farm. He later underwent brutal treatment by Japanese authorities after having been arrested and accused of aiding the American fugitives. Aguon had indeed helped the American sailors, although he kept the precious information to himself. He gave his captors no useful information, suffering greatly because of his loyalty to the Americans.

His brother Vincent met with Tweed and Tyson to share the news of Aguon's arrest. He also brought some terrifying information. "They'll kill you," Vincent warned them of the Japanese. Life on the run was starting to wear on the sailors. Any ideas of possibly voluntarily giving themselves up likely changed given the unwelcome news from Vincent.

The American prisoners were already sent off the island by ship. Vincent explained the Japanese no longer wanted any additional captives. He communicated in writing with a Japanese officer who learned English at a university almost ten years before the war. The soldier no longer remembered how to speak English, although he was still able to read and write the language. "Any Americans captured in the brush will be killed," he emphasized to Vincent in written form.[2] Turning themselves in did not seem a viable option anymore for the runaway sailors.

The two Americans eventually decided to part ways. "About two months after we had been in the bushes, we had been chased by searching parties and so forth, Tyson had decided that he wanted to go to a ranch of a friend of his," Tweed explained. The ranch was thought to be about eleven miles away. "I told him that I thought it was too far to go, that he couldn't get that far along the road, it was too dangerous. However, he insisted on going and I told him if he went, he would have to go alone."[3]

Tyson ventured out on his own after the pair divided up their meager supplies. "So, he left me and started for his friend's ranch." The lone sailor, however, did not get very far. "He got about three miles down the road when he became tired and sleepy and crawled into the bushes and went to sleep. The next morning when he woke up, he appealed to the nearest native ranch for assistance."

Fortunately, those he approached were not sympathetic to the Japanese. "They agreed to help him, they took him, put him in a hiding place, gave him food and water and he continued to stay there," Tweed later said. "About a month after he left me, I went down to visit him to find out if he was making out all right because I felt sort of responsible for him. He had no bush experience and could not go anyplace alone or do anything on his own without someone showing him where to go or what to do."

Tweed felt bad about letting him go on his own. "However, when I went down to see him, the man who was helping him said that if the Japs did come on out after him, he would go to the bushes with Tyson, would guide him, show him where to go and help him," Tweed continued. "So, I felt that he was in good hands and at the time Tyson seemed to resent the fact that I had come down to visit him, so I didn't see him after that."

Now alone, Tweed was again on the move and worried about his ability to survive. At one point, he went to the ranch of Juan Cruz. Around the same time, he received a pistol from Agaña businessman Joaquin Limtiaco.[4] "When I left Agaña I didn't have a weapon of any sort, but after being in the bushes about two, two and a half months a native brought me a .45 pistol with plenty of ammunition and I also got ahold of a machete," Tweed recalled. "The pistol came in very handy at times."

Tweed spent most of 1942 moving about in the rural central part of Guam, including stays near Yona, Tamuning, Barrigada, and Manenggon.[5] The region included dense jungle forest and some agricultural areas with ranches. His survival was largely based on assistance from others.

One of Tweed's stops was a cave on the property of Manuel Cruz near Yona. The family provided food and worked to keep his location a secret. Cruz became frustrated at things the sailor sometimes did to jeopardize his cover, according to son Manny Cruz. He recalled his father once scolding Tweed after spotting smoke spiraling upwards from his cave and other confrontations, including the sailor picking oranges in broad daylight.[6] Tweed soon found other helpers.

Among the many locals helping Tweed were two pairs of brothers—Juan and Joaquin Flores and Felix and Jose Torres—along with Limtiaco and Jesus Reyes. Some of the men constructed Tweed a small shelter. They brought him an assortment of food, including canned goods, for about three months of meals.

Some of the helpers were later arrested by the Japanese, who accused them of aiding Tweed. According to Felix Torres, the area residents who suffered the most were Limtiaco and the Flores brothers. "They were brutalized in such a way that their hands and feet would be tied together and then hung from a beam, and the Japanese would swing their bodies against the walls."[7] Torres suffered beatings to his face. They did not give away any information about the sailor, even while undergoing the ruthless interrogations.

The Japanese sometimes employed the assistance of an individual known as the "lash man."

The chunky native from Saipan was able to hit harder than the Japanese police due to his strong arms.[8] It did not take long for the lash man to become well-known to the Guamanian civilians.

Limtiaco took Tweed to Reyes after the Flores brothers were arrested. Reyes in turn arranged for the sailor to temporarily stay with another local named Wen Santos.[9] A woman named Agueda Johnston played a crucial role in helping Tweed during his early time on the run. She was about as pro-American as any Guamanian, and for good reason. The Guam native was married to American William Johnston.

Johnston has been described as an adventuresome young man from Tennessee. He joined the marines and was given orders for duty on Guam. He later became a successful teacher on the island. Johnston fell in love and eventually married one of his students—Agueda Iglesias. The couple started a family and enjoyed a comfortable life on the island up until the start of the war. Agueda became a teacher at the local school in Agaña. Johnston left the marines to become a civilian employee working for the navy under the Bureau of Yards and Docks.[10] He also became a successful businessman. Johnston was still working for the navy when Guam fell to the Japanese. He was sent away with the other American prisoners and later perished in a Japanese prison camp.

Agueda was left behind to care for the family alone while still working as an educator. She soon took on the additional roles—at great personal risk—as morale-booster and patriot. Her involvement in helping Tweed included providing food, clothes, and reading materials. The books were often smuggled to Tweed through others.

The Japanese authorities came to suspect her involvement in aiding the fugitive. She underwent a series of severe interrogations. Like so many other Guamanians, she, too, suffered great hardship while protecting the American sailor. On one occasion, she was stripped of her clothes and lashed twenty-five times. The whippings cut into her flesh and left her lying in a pool of blood.[11] Still, Agueda refused to give her tormentors any information. She was eventually set free.

Throughout the occupation, Agueda communicated progress of the war to help boost the spirits of the Guamanians. The information often came from secret radios, kept hidden from the occupiers. The news was sometimes clandestinely spread through writings on the inside of soap wrappers made by her family—often passed to people right in front of oblivious Japanese guards.[12] Her efforts greatly helped the local population suffer through the long occupation.

Before long, too many Guamanians knew of Tweed's whereabouts and it was only a matter of time before Japanese officials found out. Additionally, the sailor's own actions put him at risk of being captured. "When I was in Yona, there were so many people, they'd bring so many visitors there to see me that I felt that it didn't matter so much if I did go out roaming around at night because everybody knew where I was anyway," Tweed later rationalized.[13]

Only decades after the war did Tweed publicly admit he went out to a party one night. He referenced receiving a phone call from a woman on Guam asking him of reports he was often showing himself in public and going "out at night running around the whole island at night attending parties." Tweed spoke of his response in an interview. "So I told her, I says there was only one time that I ever went to a party and I says the only reason I did then was because everybody knew where I was anyway," Tweed said. "The party was given by Agueda Johnston...and that's the only time. I says yah, I used to go out a night and roam around and go here and there."

The situation for Tweed was unsustainable. The Japanese were diligently looking for him. Local residents suffered at the hands of their occupiers to keep the sailor's whereabouts a secret, but he often acted carelessly. His days of living life in hiding were bound to come to an end—unless something changed.

Chapter 14

KING AND NIMITZ

IN THE AFTERMATH OF THE attack on Pearl Harbor, during what many historians consider as some of the darkest days in the history of the United Sates Navy, two new leaders emerged to carry the seagoing service forward into war. Both Admiral Ernest J. King and Admiral Chester W. Nimitz already had long naval careers spanning decades before each rose to prominent command positions. The pair were to play an important role in the Pacific War as a whole, and specifically in the operations ultimately leading to the retaking of Guam.

King assumed the role of commander in chief of the United States fleet in December 1941 and became chief of naval operations three months later.[1] He held supreme command over all naval forces worldwide and was the highest-ranking uniformed navy officer. The admiral was responsible directly to the president.[2]

King was born in Lorain, Ohio on November 23, 1878. His time at the Naval Academy included sea duty on the warship *San Francisco* during the Spanish-American War. He graduated in 1901 and subsequently spent time aboard a variety of large warships, small naval vessels, and an assortment of land stations. King spent many years involved in the growing field of naval aviation, including duty at the Bureau of Aeronautics and serving as commander of the Naval Air Station in Hampton Roads, Virginia. His time as captain of the aircraft carrier *Lexington* provided practical and valuable experience in aviation. King was promoted to rear admiral in 1933 and became chief of the Bureau of Aeronautics.[3]

A navy reorganization in early 1941 created three separate fleet commands—Atlantic, Pacific, and Asiatic. King was promoted to lead the Atlantic Fleet. The move came at a time of escalating tensions with Germany. The conflict waging on the European continent was also taking place in the Atlantic Ocean where German submarines were attempting to interdict the flow of war materials to Britain. The circumstances led to a sort of undeclared naval war with American warships taking an increasing role in patrols and convoy escort duty.

King was heavily involved in war planning after the United States formally entered the conflict in December 1941. He helped develop and shape strategy as a member of the American Joint Chiefs of Staff and with the Combined Chiefs of Staff. The latter was a union of the top American and British military officers whose recommendations went directly to President Roosevelt and Prime Minister Churchill. King was always guided by a basic principle, "We must do all that we can with what we have."[4] He was known for having a confounding mix of iron will, high intelligence, and a comprehensive knowledge of naval subjects, along with plenty of arrogance and aloofness.[5] The admiral has frequently been described as callous and abrasive to both subordinates and equals.[6]

Nimitz was born in Fredericksburg, Texas on February 24, 1885. His family was not wealthy and it was clear early on there was no money for him to attend college. He hoped for an appointment to the United States Military Academy (army) as a high school student, only to be disappointed when no spaces were available. Undaunted, the young man instead secured an appointment to the Naval Academy and left high school early to join the Naval Academy Class of 1905. He proved to be an excellent student and graduated seventh in a class of 114.[7]

A long list of duty stations on sea and land followed throughout the early decades of the twentieth century. The officer spent nearly twenty years in submarines and played an important role in building the submarine base at Pearl Harbor in the 1920s.[8] He studied at the Naval War College, held various staff positions, and spent time as the executive officer of the battleship *South Carolina*. Nimitz became the commanding officer of the heavy cruiser *Augusta* in the early 1930s while the warship was serving as the flagship of the Asiatic Fleet based in the Philippines.

Flag rank was achieved with a promotion to rear admiral in 1938 while stationed in Washington, DC.[9] The admiral was assigned a four-year term as the chief of the Bureau of Navigation in 1939. His situation suddenly changed—like so many other naval officers—with the attack on Pearl Harbor.

Nimitz was home listening to the radio on the fateful Sunday morning, like millions of other everyday Americans, when the first news of the surprise Japanese attack was broadcast across the air waves. He rushed to his office in downtown Washington. Other admirals, officers, and civilians arrived in haste as the news became widespread.

The admiral was summoned to the office of Frank Knox a little more than a week later. The Secretary of the Navy just returned from a personal inspection of Pearl Harbor. He decided

Admiral Husband Kimmel was to be relieved of duty as the commander in chief of the Pacific Fleet in the aftermath of the disaster.

The once powerful fleet commander soon slipped into retirement—seen as a villain by some for unpreparedness and as an unjustified scapegoat by others.

The secretary spoke to Nimitz about the sense of gloom hanging over Pearl Harbor. Knox wanted a new leader, one capable of changing the mood in the Pacific. He wanted someone who would be ready to undertake offensive operations. "How soon can you get ready to travel?" Knox suddenly asked. "You're going to take command of the Pacific Fleet."[10] Nimitz was quickly on his way to the Pacific. He was appointed as the new leader of the Pacific Fleet on December 17, 1941, just ten days after the start of hostilities.[11]

Top American naval commanders of the Marianas Campaign meet aboard the heavy cruiser *Indianapolis* on July 18, 1944. Pictured from left to right are Admiral Chester W. Nimitz, commander in chief of the Pacific Fleet, Chief Naval Operations Admiral Ernest J. King, and Commander of the Fifth Fleet Admiral Raymond A. Spruance. (US Navy / National Archives)

Nimitz maintained a trim figure. His face featured penetrating blue eyes and featured a head of whitening hair. He espoused a calm and humble demeanor and was known to be friendly and pleasant. The admiral had little interest in publicity.[12] Under the humble shell was an officer filled with brilliant intelligence, fighting toughness, discipline, and audacity. Nimitz was someone who liked to lead by example.[13]

The new leader arrived at Pearl Harbor on Christmas Day with only his flag secretary. He found fear, low morale, and the gloomy atmosphere Knox had described. His fleet sustained serious damage with most of the battleships stationed at Pearl Harbor having been either sunk or heavily damaged. However, his submarine force was largely intact and a small group of codebreakers were frantically working to unravel the main Japanese Naval Code JN-25.

Nimitz called together the staff he inherited from Kimmel. "There will be no changes," he told them. "I have complete confidence in you men. We've taken a terrific wallop but I have no doubts as to the ultimate outcome."[14] The process of getting the Pacific Fleet back into fighting shape would not be easy. Nimitz and his staff began work immediately.

As the top naval leader, King was immediately confronted with a global situation unparalleled in military history. The United States was forced to fight a two-ocean war. The Pacific Theater often dominated the headlines and public attention in the immediate aftermath of Pearl Harbor. Often away from the headlines, a serious situation faced the Americans in the Atlantic at the same time. The Germans launched a submarine offensive against the United States with merchant ships coming under attack all along the eastern seaboard, sometimes in plain sight of American cities and civilian onlookers.

King proved to be adept at dealing with both crises simultaneously. He was instrumental in gaining resources for offensive operations against Japan, despite an overall strategy directing most military assets to the European side of the war—the previously agreed-to Allied strategy of "Germany First." King and Nimitz, along with a large supporting cast, were to play a critical role in forging and implementing a strategy for the war in the Pacific—a strategy that ultimately led to American operations in the Marianas and the liberation of Guam.

Chapter 15

TURNING THE TIDE

THE GOAL OF THE NUMEROUS Japanese military operations taking place around the Pacific in the first months of the war was the completion of the planned defensive perimeter. Japanese leaders anticipated the United States would be ready for a peace settlement after suffering a series of devastating defeats. The American leaders, though, showed no interest in a negotiated peace. The attack on Pearl Harbor instead served as a rallying point and the public wanted retribution.

Admiral Nimitz used the meager naval resources under his command to strike back, albeit on a small scale. American submarines began unrestricted undersea warfare against the Japanese merchant fleet. Carrier-based planes raided Japanese-held islands during a series of rapid operations in February and early March 1942. The targets included Wake Island, Marcus Island (an isolated coral atoll between Wake and Japan), and the large base Rabaul in the Solomon Islands.

The attacks were small operations, causing little damage, but had important ramifications. The strikes gave American pilots combat experience and provided a morale boost—good news at an otherwise bleak time while causing mild embarrassment among Japanese commanders who boasted the United States would be in no position to strike back for many months.[1]

New bases were established in Australia where the United States began to assemble an army under the command of General MacArthur. The continent could be used as a staging area for a counter attack against the Japanese empire. Steps were taken to safeguard the United States to Australia supply line that perilously stretched across the South Pacific.

The Combined Chiefs of Staff gave operational control of the Pacific front to the United States. American planners subsequently divided the theater into two broad command areas in early 1942. MacArthur was made Supreme Allied Commander of the Southwest Pacific Area. His region included Australia, the Philippines, most of the Dutch East Indies, and New Guinea. Nimitz commanded the vast Pacific Ocean Area. His region included most of the Pacific not under MacArthur's control and was later subdivided into three smaller regions (north, central, and south) with Nimitz assuming direct command over the central and northern areas.[2] The Solomon Islands was divided between both command areas.

The two leaders were given the same mission—contain Japanese expansion, defend the North American continent, keep open the vital line link between the United States and Australia, and prepare for counter-offensive operations. The American Joint Chiefs of Staff still decided all high-level decisions on strategy. MacArthur and Nimitz were then responsible for the field implementation.

Imperial Japanese leaders suffered an unexpected blow on April 18, 1942, when American Army Air Force B-25 bombers under

Lieutenant Commander James Doolittle bombed targets around Tokyo. The normally land-based planes took off from the aircraft carrier *Hornet* in the audacious operation. The actual damage was slight. The strike was front-page news in the United States and served as a great morale booster. The attack was a psychological blow to the Japanese. Imperial naval leaders were overwhelmed with shame for allowing American naval forces to come so close to Japan.[3] The Doolittle raid had far-reaching effects, including the redeployment of fighters from the frontlines to homeland defense.[4] More importantly, the Japanese were convinced to accelerate plans to extend the defensive perimeter—east to Midway Island and south in an attempt to cut the American supply line to Australia.

The tide of war was to eventually turn in favor of the Americans in the Pacific after the Japanese advance was halted in two critical naval battles. Imperial forces were ready to push closer to Australia by the end of April 1942 by seizing control of the southern portion of the Solomon Islands and Port Moresby in the southeastern corner of New Guinea. Japanese leaders were certain MacArthur was planning to use Australia as a base for a future counterattack and controlling Port Moresby—only 300 miles from the northern tip of the continent—provided air bases to threaten Australia and keep the American general in check.[5] The moves were also preliminary steps for later plans to advance on New Caledonia, Fiji, and Samoa—important locations in the Australian–United States supply line.

A naval battle ensued in the Coral Sea after American intelligence discovered the Port Moresby plan. The encounter began on May 4 and was mostly fought by carrier-based planes. The Battle of Coral Sea became the first naval battle in history where the opposing ships never sighted each other.[6] The outcome was a tactical victory for the Japanese whose planes sank the aircraft carrier *Lexington*, destroyer *Sims*, and a tanker, and damaged the aircraft carrier *Yorktown*.

American planes hit two aircraft carriers in return, sinking the small carrier *Shoho* and damaging the large carrier *Shokaku.*

The Japanese carrier air groups were severely battered, resulting in the postponement of the Port Moresby invasion.[7] The Battle of the Coral Sea is considered an American strategic victory for stopping the Japanese advance southward.[8] The battle put two large Japanese aircraft carriers temporarily out of service, preventing their participation in an even larger Midway operation then in the final stages of planning.[9]

The setback at Coral Sea did not prevent the Japanese from moving forward with plans to extend the defensive perimeter east with an attack on Midway Island. Situated only 1,135 miles to the northwest, Midway was widely viewed as a "sentry" guarding the approaches to the Hawaiian Islands.[10] Admiral Yamamoto greatly appreciated the vast American resources and knew time was running out for Japan to score a complete victory over the Pacific Fleet.[11] He believed Midway could be occupied quickly, with little American interference, prompting a counterattack from the remnants of the American fleet thought to be in Pearl Harbor. He would be waiting with a superior naval force to win a pivotal battle.[12] An attack on the Aleutian Islands of Alaska was set up to be a diversion to the main operation.

The bulk of the Japanese fleet moved east toward Midway. Arrayed in seven task forces, the massive armada of ships included four heavy aircraft carriers, two light carriers, seven battleships, fourteen cruisers, forty-three destroyers, along with an assortment of submarines and support ships.[13] The four large carriers—all veterans of the Pearl Harbor attack—were together in a task force known as the First Mobile Force under operational control of Admiral Nagumo.

Nimitz could counter the large number of attackers with only meager resources—three large aircrafts carriers, a handful of cruisers and destroyers, and some land-based planes on Midway. The carriers included the damaged *Yorktown*. She was quickly repaired after returning from the Coral Sea to make ready for the battle.

Although outnumbered in ships and planes, the American possessed the key advantage of having ships equipped with radar. The new equipment allowed for an early warning of approaching planes, giving the American time to prepare for an air attack. The Japanese ships did not have radar and had to rely on human lookouts.

American code breakers were able to discern that a large enemy naval operation involving the Combined Japanese Fleet moving eastward was in the offing, although the exact target was initially unclear. Intelligence officers at Pearl Harbor gave enough clues to convince Nimitz the objective was Midway.[14] He deployed his carriers in two task forces to an area believed to be a perfect location to wait in ambush—all three were on station about 350 miles northeast of Midway on June 2 under the overall tactical command of Rear Admiral Frank Jack Fletcher aboard *Yorktown*.[15] The other two carriers—*Enterprise* and *Hornet*—were in a separate task force commanded by Rear Admiral Raymond A. Spruance. The presence of an American warship stationed at the French Frigate Shoals, a small group of coral islets between Hawaii and Midway, prevented the Japanese from refueling long range seaplanes by submarine to reconnoiter Pearl Harbor.[16]

The actual battle occurred in several stages, including a pre-invasion attack on Midway by Japanese carrier planes and American land-based aircraft unsuccessfully striking the enemy fleet. The key day of the battle was June 4 when American carrier planes carried out a surprise attack on the main force of Japanese carriers, disabling three—*Akagi*, *Kaga*, and *Soryu*. A counterstrike by planes from the remaining operational Japanese large carrier *Hiryu* badly damaged *Yorktown*, causing her to be abandoned. She later sank after sustaining additional damage from a Japanese submarine.[17] A subsequent American air attack scored direct hits on *Hiryu*. All four Japanese carriers were lost.

The loss of the four carriers compelled Yamamoto to abandon the Midway invasion plans and the Japanese fleet began a long retirement to the west. The Battle of Midway is widely considered the decisive turning point of the Pacific War. In addition to the sinking of the four carriers, the Japanese lost a large number of irreplaceable veteran pilots. With their expansion plans halted, the Japanese settled on a strategy of aggressively defending the large amount of territory under their control.[18]

The Midway victory set the stage for limited offensive operations by the United States to take place in the South Pacific. The plan approved by the Joint Chiefs was for a step-by-step advance toward the large Japanese naval and air base at Rabaul through the Solomon Islands and along the northern coast of New Guinea. Leadership was to be divided owning to the area straddling the border between the Pacific and Southwest Pacific Command areas.[19] The Solomon Islands' part of the operation was under Nimitz.

Soldiers of the 1st Marine Division landed on Guadalcanal and the nearby island of Tulagi in the south part of the Solomons on August 7, 1942. The operation was done with meager resources at a time when most military assets were directed toward Europe under the Germany First strategy. A series of sharp land-and-sea battles took place over the next six months before the Americans emerged victorious in early 1943.

The New Guinea portion of the advance was fought by American and Australian forces under MacArthur's command. The operation began with the defense of Port Moresby. A second Japanese amphibious invasion of the strategic coastal city was never attempted. Imperial Army troops instead tried to capture the city with a ground attack from the north by traveling overland through the rugged and mountainous Kokoda Trail. The Port Moresby garrison was reinforced with battle-hardened Australian troops, veterans of the fight against the Germans and Italians in North Africa.[20]

The operation was a disaster for the Japanese, who faced a host of tropical diseases and near starvation during the difficult overland journey on the Kokoda Trail. The attackers were stopped short of Port Moresby and ordered to retreat north in late September.[21] The defeat prompted an Allied counterattack setting off a long and slow advance along the northern New Guinea coast.

The Allied offensive operations started in 1942 were of limited scope in the South Pacific. Although successful in the Solomon Islands and New Guinea, the moves amounted to little more than pinpricks on the edge of the vast Japanese defensive perimeter. The American leaders faced a series of critical strategic decisions in 1943.

Chapter 16

RADIO AND NEWSPAPER

THE RESIDENTS OF GUAM ENJOYED a daily newspaper, the *Guam Eagle*, in the years leading up to the start of the war. Like many of the basic necessities on the island, the publication was owned and operated by the navy. The newspaper provided news from around the world intermixed with local stories. The start of publishing approximately coincided with the beginning of the island's first commercial radio station, K6LF.[1]

The *Guam Eagle* abruptly disappeared in the aftermath of the Japanese invasion. The newspaper—or at least a new version of it—was temporarily resurrected for about four months in 1942 by George Tweed while he was hiding from the Japanese. The key to the rudimentary operation was a radio and for that, the sailor needed help from the locals along with his own ingenuity.

Tweed was used to tinkering with radio equipment outside of the communication section because his ham radio hobby followed him from California to Guam. "Of course, I took my gear along," he said of his amateur radio equipment. He restarted broadcasting his ham station in 1940. For about a year, he was able to connect with ham stations on other Pacific islands and some in the United States.

The broadcasting continued until the navy put a stop to it. "On June 10, 1941, when censorship was started on the island, the navy officially closed down all amateur activity on Guam," he later explained.[2] "We were ordered to suspend operation, pack and crate all our transmitting equipment. It was taken to the Communications Office where it was sealed and stored for delivery to the rightful owner at some future time." He was permitted to keep his radio receiver, allowing him to keep listening even if he could not broadcast.

Japanese authorities banned the use of all radios shortly after taking control of the island. Any radios still in the hands of civilians were ordered to be turned in to their headquarters in Agaña by a designated date. Violators were threatened with severe punishment if any radios were found after the deadline.[3] Although most radios were likely turned over to the occupiers, a small number remained hidden and Tweed wanted to get his hands on one.

"The natives kept asking me what I wanted, so I told them I wanted a radio receiver," he later recalled. "They promised to get me one." The islanders more than kept their promise, bringing him not only a radio, but also some tools—including a screwdriver, a pair of pliers, a soldering iron, and a supply of batteries. "These batteries came from wrecked cars on the island," Tweed continued. "I had a stock of six storage batteries, so I could listen plenty."

Initially, each battery had to be taken away to be charged after running out of power. The situation changed after the Guamanians brought Tweed a small portable gas-powered generator. The gas supply mostly came from the numerous abandoned cars scattered around the island. Wire and lightbulbs later arrived, allowing Tweed to make a rudimentary light system. "But I could only run one thing at a time; it was a choice between the iron, the lights or the radio receiver."

Jesus Quitugua was among those instrumental in getting the sailor what he needed. The civilian formerly worked at the Communications Office and knew Tweed from his previous work. The smuggled radio needed some work to get it back into operating condition—not an easy task with no spare parts—but Tweed was up to the task. Tweed recognized the radio as having belonged to another navy man and recalled previously repairing it.

At some point, Tweed received a second radio of the same make and model as the first one. "Only, the trouble was, it was inoperative because it had been stored carelessly and the dampness had got to it," he explained. "I stripped parts from it to fix up the first receiver."[4]

The fugitive sailor never did get a working transmitter—a radio allowing him to send out messages—although it was not due to lack of trying. "Yes, I did try," he later recalled. "I gathered parts to make a simple transmitter of about 30 watts output. I had the usual collection of junk from old sets and I worked on it for a time." A Guamanian offered to take the parts into town where it would be easier to work on. Tweed never saw the individual or the transmitter parts again. The Japanese were rumored to be killing anyone found with radio equipment and perhaps the individual suffered a horrible fate. "I did not get my transmitter back and never got enough parts to build another."

The radio gave Tweed a link to the outside world shortly after beginning to work. Wires were hung from some coconut trees for an antenna. "I listened most for the news as I was starved for news of the progress of the war," he remembered. He was eventually able to pick up KGEI in California.

The station began operation in 1939 and was owned by the General Electric Company. A powerful transmitter, located in a nondescript two-story building in Redwood City, California near San Francisco, beamed the signal out into the Pacific. The station was the only one on which news from the mainland United States could be heard in the Pacific at the time—even as far away as the Philippines.[5] Tweed was readily familiar with the station, having regularly listened to it before the war. Announcers often began their programs with "This is the United States of America."[6]

Tweed later wrote of listening about good news and bad, including the April 18, 1942 American bombing of Tokyo led by Lieutenant Commander Doolittle and the fall of Corregidor—the last American holdout in the Philippines.[7] He initially passed along bits and pieces of news to his contacts. Then came the newspaper.

"Since word-of-mouth news is apt to be distorted, I got the idea of writing out the news," Tweed explained. "I wrote the news in pencil for some time." He switched to typing after an old typewriter was delivered and the new *Guam Eagle* came into existence.

The newspaper—and the radio—became instant hits among the islanders who were eager to learn about how the war was going. He received a plentiful supply of food in return for spreading the news. "During that time, I made five copies of the news which I distributed to trusted friends."[8]

Former Insular Guard member Ben Pangelinan was among the locals helping to distribute Tweed's newspaper. He was showing the newspaper to others in Joaquin Limtiaco's Agaña home when the residence was suddenly raided by Japanese soldiers. Pangelinan avoided arrest by quickly flushing the newspaper down the toilet.[9]

Both sources of news soon became a problem. Each night, just as the antennas were strung up, a large group of Guamanians came to listen—often numbering as much as forty to fifty people.[10] The large gatherings could not be kept secret for long and were sure to raise suspicions among the Japanese authorities once they caught wind of the gatherings. When the occupiers found out, they would either be on the trail to finding Tweed, torturing more local residents, or both.

"However, this didn't last because people were eager to tell about the news, so at the end of about four months I was forced to abandon the radio and bury it," Tweed explained. "The last day I listened to the radio, I listened to KGEI at San Francisco, and it was announced on that day that the Americans had made their first landing in the Solomon Islands and were consolidating their position before any further expansion. That was the last day I listened to the radio." The news would have placed the time as early August 1942. The popular newspaper abruptly ended with the discontinuation of the radio.

Tweed later added some additional details about the episode. "The Japs thought that I had a radio on the air, a transmitter," he said. "They heard radio signals and blamed me at first, which spurred their hunt for me, but failing in this they accused three natives of operating the radio from a small gasoline electric plant, but after separating the natives and ordering them to various portions of the island to keep them separated, the radio continued."

The authorities were determined to find the source of the radio signals. "By using direction finders and continuing their efforts they finally located the man who was operating the radio. It was a small walkee-talkee [sic] set which the Japanese officers used to communicate with their planes. It was being operated by a Japanese officer." Tweed believed the officer was killed for his actions.[11] Hidden radios continued to be intermittently operated by Guamanians on the island during the occupation.

The Japanese efforts to find Tweed increased throughout 1942. A price was put on the heads of the American fugitives, Tweed in particular. Distributed handbills prominently featured his photo. Tweed was warned of this by Jesus Quitugua.[12] The torturing of Guamanians and dispatching of search parties continued.

The Japanese patrols were often accompanied by Guamanians, with the local residents frequently used as forced participants. A common arrangement was for the islanders to form a long line and walk forward, combing through the thick brush while soldiers marched right behind them. The Guamanians often made enough noise so that any nearby Americans would have advanced notice to avoid detection.[13] The Japanese soldiers seemed oblivious to the tactics.

Even though the Guamanians were facing a worsening situation in assisting the Americans on the run, they continued to provide help. A young storekeeper named Tommy Tanaka did his part in helping Tweed. Tanaka knew he was taking a big risk—including torture and death—but he wanted to be loyal to the United States. "We were under American flag at that time, even though my name is Japanese," he later said.[14]

Tweed was soon again on the move. He knew from previous conversations that he could trust Tanaka to provide aid and keep his location a secret. However, he needed help in getting to Tanaka's house. Tweed asked to be taken to meet with a local priest named Father Oscar Calvo.

All missionaries were removed from heavily Catholic Guam by the Japanese in early 1942. Only two Catholic priests remained on the island—Father Calvo and Father Jesus Duenas. Father Calvo was ordained a priest on April 5, 1941 after previously attending a seminary in the Philippines and serving as a diocesan seminarian on Guam.[15]

Father Calvo worked tirelessly in the early days of the occupation, initially moving out church items from the Agaña Cathedral after the building was taken over by the Japanese. He regularly conducted burials and often administered last rites after someone returned from being "questioned" by the Japanese authorities. He tried to meet the spiritual needs of the local population as best he could under the difficult circumstances, frequently reminding civilians "One day the Americans will come."[16] Father Calvo ultimately stayed at his father's ranch in Maite and focused on the northern half of the island, while Father Duenas worked in the south.

Tweed and Father Calvo eventually met one night. "He welcomed me...is there anything he could do to help me and all of that sort of thing and I told him yah," Tweed later recalled. "There's a man had told me that I can come to his place and he would be glad to help me, but I says that I don't know how to get there." Father Calvo arranged for a meeting between Tweed and Tanaka.

The fugitive sailor stayed at Tanaka's house for a time and the family cared for him. They washed his clothes, gave him food, and provided the weary sailor a place to sleep—on an actual mattress. However, Tweed's stay did not last long. Rumors of another Guamanian knowing of his new location prompted yet another move. He later attributed the leak to one of the priests, helping to create a controversy after the war about the sailor's interactions with the two clergymen.[17]

Tanaka was later taken by the authorities to the Agaña jail. The Japanese suspected his involvement in helping the American sailors. "Without any preliminaries, I was tied to a beam and then the Japanese, including the Chief of Police Shimada, took turns hitting me from all sides," Tanaka he said of the dreadful episode. "I felt so helpless that I began thinking that either I kill them...if I ever get the chance...or I kill myself."[18] He endured the beatings and incredibly did not give away any information.

Tweed was again on the run to a new hiding place. Moving in a hurry was now becoming a common happening. He was then immediately faced with some horrifying news—enough to likely have sent a bolt of terror through him. An islander told him some other fugitive Americans had been captured and killed.

DOWN TO ONE

AN UNKNOWN NUMBER OF GUAMANIANS helped George Tweed escape capture by the Japanese during the years of occupation. Some of their efforts have been well-documented, while others have slipped away to become lost to history. Whether their role was large or small, everyone who provided assistance helped keep the sailor one step ahead of the enemy authorities. One individual whose role was not well-understood until after the war was Adolfo Sgambelluri.

Sgambelluri was the son of an Italian-American navy musician who settled on Guam after marrying a local woman. His complexion made him easy to be mistaken as an American. He became a Guam police officer in 1935 and later did intelligence work for the navy.[1]

He held a sterling record as a policeman and later assumed the duties of a detective. "Roberto and Sgambelluri were the detectives who investigated all the incidents involving the local people, and I don't recall their leaving any case uncleared. They were feared, but highly respected," said Marine Captain Charles Todd of Sgambelluri and another detective. "In many instances, they assisted in other cases involving naval personnel and their dependents."[2] Todd served as the island's chief of police before the war.

The Japanese authorities may have also seen the same abilities in Sgambelluri as those described by Todd. He did not depart the island with the other American prisoners and instead became a police officer for the occupation forces, a position certainly not endearing to much of the island's civilian population. Sgambelluri likely had no choice in the matter. His role included acting as a translator and liaison between the military occupiers and residents.

The police officer's regular contact with Japanese officials gave him access to inside information. Sgambelluri remained loyal to the Americans and decided to act as a double agent—at great risk to his own safety. He clandestinely passed information to Guamanians about searches and investigations whenever possible, especially when it came to the American fugitives and hidden radios. Sgambelluri often gave the secret information to a very select group of individuals, including Joaquin Limtiaco and Agueda Johnston.[3]

According to Sgambelluri, Japanese authorities tabbed Limtiaco to help them find Tweed and the other Americans in hiding.[4] The officer often met with Limtiaco ahead of his questioning sessions to discuss what information he was to pass along. The routine helped keep the Americans just ahead of the Japanese searchers. Limtiaco was reported to have been brutally beaten a total of eight times. He knew the location of the Americans on every occasion, but told nothing.[5]

The other five American sailors in hiding were not nearly as lucky as Tweed. They successfully eluded the Japanese for the first half of

1942 before their time ran out. Sgambelluri was abruptly summoned to police headquarters on September 11, 1942. He was instructed to wear dark clothes and sensed something big was in the works.

The policeman was ordered to join a group of Japanese soldiers and two local guides—Francisco Aguon and Felix Aguero—in a truck. Sgambelluri remembered a Japanese officer with the last name of Kimura in charge of the operation. The group departed sometime after midnight. They were driven to an area about nine and a half miles north of Agaña in the general vicinity of Togcha and Manenggon. Someone told him during the ride that they were going to bring in a group of Americans. His role was to act as an interpreter.

The group set out on foot and quickly disappeared into the dark jungle on a trail. The trek lasted more than an hour. Sgambelluri was given a list of questions to ask the fugitives by a Saipanese investigator during a brief stop. "Although I was hoping we would never find the Americans, I agreed to do as ordered," he later recalled.[6] The force later divided into two smaller groups.

The two guides led the soldiers directly to the locations of the Americans. It was believed Aguon betrayed the sailors, possibly after undergoing brutal torture and having threats leveled against his family.[7] Sgambelluri heard a single pistol shot just before 5:00 a.m. The Americans were sleeping and taken by surprise. The three sailors were Luther Jones, Michael Krump, and Adolphe Yablonsky.

"Jones was the first one I saw coming out from amongst some trees in the savanna," Sgambelluri later said. "Then Yablonsky and Krump as they stated their names. They were all made to stand up with their hands behind them tied." The police officer went about asking his list of questions as ordered, including if they had a radio, who had been helping them, and if they knew the location of the other Americans. The sailors gave no useful information. A search of their belongings found some canned food, a knife, and some pistols.

All three Americans were then mercilessly beaten. The information Tweed had received of the Japanese not keeping any prisoners unfortunately proved to be true for the captured sailors. They were made to dig their own graves as the Japanese soldiers stood around them in a circle. "I thought the Japanese treated their prisoners better than this," Krump was reported to have said.[8] The question generated a laugh from Kimura after going through an interpreter.

Krump was beheaded by Kimura's sword. Jones and Yablonsky were ruthlessly bayonetted. The two guides, Aguon and Aguero, were forced to cover the graves with dirt, even as moaning came from below the soil. There were now only three American sailors on the run and the Japanese were diligently looking for them all. Patrols of up to twenty soldiers were dispatched on an almost daily basis to conduct searches through the jungle. The local population continued to be terrorized in the ongoing effort to get information.

Al Tyson joined up with *Penguin* sailor Clarence Johnston sometime after leaving Tweed. The pair successfully escaped detection of the Japanese authorities in the area north of Agaña before arriving at the ranch of Frank Perez. The rancher constructed a makeshift jungle shelter, made of bamboo and other materials, about half a mile from his house and not far from a cliff overlooking the ocean in the general vicinity of Tumon.

The sailors visited the Perez ranch twice daily—every morning and evening. They received prepared meals that were always taken back to the shelter for consumption. Only a small circle of people knew of the hidden location. Father Duenas was a regular visitor, seeing the men at least once a month, often arriving on horseback.[9]

The stay lasted about six months. The situation suddenly changed when Japanese authorities became suspicious of Perez operating a contraband radio. It was clear Tyson and Johnston needed to move to a safer location in a hurry. Perez personally took them to the ranch of Tommy Torres about ten miles north near Machanao. A group of soldiers visited the Perez ranch not long after the sailors' departure.

The life on the run for the two fugitives ended abruptly during the early morning hours of October 22, 1942 when a group of about fifty Japanese soldiers arrived at the Perez ranch. The islander was threatened with death before he reluctantly led them to the area where the Americans were hiding. He took the soldiers through a narrow jungle trail before arriving at a row of abandoned chicken shelters—nothing more than poles propping up tin roofs.

The Americans were unaware of the approaching searchers. The Japanese clearly knew the Americans were hiding somewhere on the Perez ranch, although who gave away the information was never fully established. Tweed later wrote of Juan Perez (Frank's cousin) as the culprit.[10]

"They sneaked up on them at night, also, and Tyson was sitting by the fire while Johnston laying asleep," Tweed explained. "They waited about two hours for Tyson to go to sleep also, but after that length of time they decided they'd better get it over with before it started getting daylight."[11] Morning light could give the fugitives a better opportunity to slip away into the jungle.

The Japanese quietly surrounded the shelter where the Americans were hiding. "So they formed a sort of semi-circle around the place and simultaneously yelled 'hands up' and one shot was fired in the air," Tweed continued. "Tyson became frightened ran out the other side of the camp and hid behind a bush, Johnston awakened from his slumber grabbed his gun and started shooting at the Japs." The soldiers took cover and waited for Johnston to run out of bullets before opening fire in unison. The sailor never had a chance. "Three bullets penetrated Johnston's chest, one grazed the side of his cheek and another one hit him in the forehead, which dropped him."

The Japanese quickly moved into the camp area. "They went in and saw that Johnston was dead, saw that Tyson had left his gun behind and that he was unarmed, so they proceeded to search for him," Tweed continued. "Tyson had no flashlight, but the Japs did. He waited until they were very close, he knew that he had little chance for escape under the circumstances, so he stepped out from behind a bush with his hands up in an effort to surrender."

The soldiers immediately opened fire, hitting him in the head at close range. Tyson most likely died instantly. The number of fugitive American sailors was suddenly down to one.

Chapter 18

ARTERO

WHILE HIDING OUT AND CONSTANTLY on the run, George Tweed quickly became a symbol of the United States—both for the local population and the occupiers of Guam. He represented hope for the Guamanians—optimism the Americans would eventually return to liberate the island. Some islanders believed the return of the United forces was dependent on Tweed's survival. For the Japanese, Tweed exemplified a threat and a stumbling point in their efforts to surpass all American influences on the island.[1]

The news of the other American sailors killed at the hands of Japanese searchers traveled fast though the island's grapevine and certainly must not have taken very long to reach Tweed. He was now the last holdout and knew the Japanese were making every effort to find him. "They then, after catching these [five] men, they concentrated their efforts on me," he later said. "They detailed a fifty-man searching party as a permanent detail to search for me."[2] The search continued for two years. "During that time, they came very near me several times, but were never quite able to make contact."

The year 1942 was entering the final months and Tweed was certain he needed a more secure hiding place. The month of October was typically rainy on Guam—enough to make survival in the outdoors even more challenging than what the sailor thus far encountered. The Japanese increased their reward for Tweed from 50 to 1,000 yen. The Japanese money was now the legal currency on Guam. Authorities distributed leaflets, covered with his picture, around various parts of the island.[3]

Maybe the Japanese would just stumble upon Tweed's hideout or perhaps a local resident might give out a key bit of information while undergoing torture. In either case, the searchers were getting closer, and it was likely only a matter of time before the sailor's luck ran out. "At times they were only a few jumps behind me," Tweed recalled of the Japanese search parties. "On one occasion, they came out, surrounded the place where I was hiding and closed in, arriving at my hiding place about three o'clock in the morning, but when they got there it was empty since I had left there after dark the night before, just a few hours before they came out."

Perhaps the sailor's narrowest escape came during the timeframe when he was hiding in a cave near Fadian Point in late 1942. The small promontory was in a rugged area on the eastern coast of the island. Tweed returned to his cave one day to find a papaya with a message carved on it. Although the letters were crude and appeared to have been done in a hurry, it seemed to be some type of warning. The message likely came from one of his local helpers. The meaning was not clear—stay in the cave or go?

Tweed then became worried the next day when his contact, who typically visited promptly every morning, did not show up. "The next time they tried to get me I left more or less on a hunch," he explained. "I thought it was time to leave, so I packed up and started getting out of there. The more time that went by the more eager or anxious I became." He packed what he could carry and moved any excess supplies out of sight into some tall grass.

"Finally I left the place, climbed over a cliff, had gone less than one hundred feet along a dim trail through the bushes when I heard someone coming," Tweed continued. "I got off the trail about fifty feet, squatted down behind the bush and watched the trail." He held his breath as a Japanese soldier walked past on the trail where he had just been moments ago. Tweed was able to see the distinctive round cap and khaki shorts. The man was carrying a rifle.

A second soldier appeared right behind the first and then another and another. Beads of sweat rolled down the sailor's neck as he carefully counted the number of passing soldiers. "I sat there and watched fifty Japs with rifles go past heading right for the cave that I had just left," he later said of the tense moment.

Tweed knew he had to get out of there—and fast. He was stiff from his day's hiding in the cave and needed to lug along his sixty-pound bag of supplies. He started down the coarse trail heading inland, initially struggling with cramps and sore muscles.[4] No matter the circumstances, he was still alive and again on the move—one small step ahead of the Japanese.

Among the many Japanese occupiers looking for Tweed was a petty officer in the 54th Naval Guard Unit named Hirose Hisashi. Although not part of the initial invasion force, he arrived later to participate in the occupation. He heard about a naval man hiding out on Guam, from an American prisoner in Japan, before he even arrived on the island. Hisashi's recollections after the war offered some insights into the Japanese perspective of the effort to find Tweed.

The soldier recalled the high concern about Tweed having an operational radio. "The military took a serious view about his owning of a communication instrument," Hisashi later said. "If he had not owned such an instrument, the military would not have investigated him to such an extent. The Communication Squadron studied how to trace back this American soldier's communication but couldn't track his transmission place."[5]

The search process involved getting information from Guamanian leaders of villages and the police force. The former likely came from threats, intimidation, and torture. The information was often unreliable. "It was speculated that Tweed was hiding in Yona, Talofofo, or Pago because there were edible trees in those places," Hisashi continued. "We thought he couldn't hide in Yigo or Merizo because there was no food." The soldier remembered searching near one of Tweed's hideouts at Fadian Point—possibly the narrow escape Tweed spoke about. "When there was information, we stretched curtains on hills around these areas for a stakeout."

Hisashi remembered the searches were many times exhausting endeavors. He appreciated the bravery of those involved. "I could well understand the scary emotions of the US soldiers who hid for as long as two and a half years," he later said. "I admired their emotional strength to live off the land. I think the Chamorros hid them with sincerity."

An exhausted Tweed eventually arrived at the house of friend Joaquin Flores. He walked about ten miles, with painfully blistered feet, after his narrow escape from the Japanese patrol. Flores smuggled the sailor to Juan Pangelinan in the northwestern part of the island.

Pangelinan was a former US Navy man in his fifties. He served aboard the American steamer *Pensacola* during World War I and later retired as a chief machinist's mate. Tweed later described him as a loyal and patriotic American citizen.[6]

The retired navy man hid Tweed for about a week. Suddenly, Pangelinan came to believe the Japanese were heading for his property. He appeared to be very nervous and terrified, more about his family's safety than his own. Tweed later identified the time as early October 1942 and gloomily noted, "The past ten months I had lived in eleven different places, not counting one-night stands in rain-soaked cornfields, bushes, and cow pastures."[7]

Tweed was again on the move and traveling north. Pangelinan definitely did not want to abandon him. Rather, he arranged for the fellow sailor to meet someone who was to become one Tweed's most important helpers. His name was Antonio Artero. The dizzying sequence of events took place just before Al Tyson and Clarence Johnston met their end.

"On the 21st of October 1942, I finally met Antonio Artero. He was one of the few people who could keep a secret," Tweed explained. "The other people, while they were very willing to help the Americans, they were proud of the fact and they would tell all their friends and relatives about it, but Artero he [didn't] do this, realizing the danger of the situation and kept it to himself."[8]

Artero was a member of one of the island's most prominent families. His father was Don Pascual Artero y Saez, a Spanish soldier during the fading days of the empire, who settled on Guam around the turn of the century. He became patriarch of a growing family, a successful businessman, and one of the island's largest landowners with holdings that included hundreds of acres. Pascual established two large ranches on the northern part of Guam, in the regions of Dededo and Yigo, with ample pasture lands for cattle.[9]

The ranches provided meat for the island through a meat market store in Agaña. He also operated a saw mill producing lumber and various wood products. The businesses allowed the family to build wealth during the decades leading up to the war. Differing sources make it unclear if the patriarch knew of the true extent of his son's involvement with Tweed.[10]

The torturing and brutalization of those suspected of helping Tweed were well-known among the local population. Artero was fully aware any association with the fugitive sailor was extremely dangerous for his whole family.[11] He became so frightened that he was having trouble eating and sleeping.

The two talked about the situation shortly after his arrival. "I asked him if he wanted me to leave the ranch," Tweed recalled of the conversation. "I told him I wouldn't stay there if he wanted me to go." The reply was a firm no. "I don't want you to go," Artero said. "If you leave here, they'll catch and kill you."[12]

Tweed reminded him the risks were much larger. "Well, if I stay here and get caught here, they won't only kill you, but they'll kill your wife and children," he said. Although Artero was scared, he was unwilling to abandon the sailor. "Yes, I know that, we must be very careful, that's all," Artero concluded.

The American was truly grateful. "So I told him that if I lived to get back to the States that he wouldn't be doing that for nothing, that I would pay him back for what he was doing," Tweed said. Artero would have nothing of it. "No, I don't want any pay from you," he told the sailor according to Tweed. "I won't take any money from you. I'm not doing this for pay." He told Tweed he was "doing this just to save your life." Artero needed to make some quick decisions about how to hide Tweed—the decisions could mean life and death for himself, his family, and the sailor.

Chapter 19

THE CAVE

LIFE ON THE RUN EVENTUALLY started to wear on George Tweed. "After the first year I began to lose hope," he said.[1] "I felt I would sooner or later be caught," he continued. "But I was determined to do my utmost to postpone that day as long as possible."[2]

Teacher Agueda Johnston urged Tweed to continue his holdout and not to surrender regardless of the circumstances.[3] She generously provided food, clothing, and reading materials for the sailor. Her situation became tenuous when the Japanese began to suspect her involvement in helping the fugitive. She was taken into custody and interrogated about his hiding place. Agueda was beaten and whipped before she was eventually freed. She revealed no useful information to her captors.

Tweed was now in the northwestern part of the island—far from his initial area of hiding further south. Retired navy man Juan Pangelinan arranged for him to meet Antonio Artero. The devoted

Catholic wanted to help the American sailor. He was also very con-cerned about his own safety and that of his family. The Japanese hunt for Tweed was common knowledge among the Guamanians. Those even suspected of aiding the sailor were facing drastic conse-quences. Artero wrestled with his conscience and consulted with his wife Josefa before deciding it was his Christian duty to help Tweed.[4]

Artero decided the best course of action was to hide Tweed in an isolated area on his family's property—a well-hidden cave on the face of a high cliff. The location was about four miles from the northern tip of the island near a place known as Pugua Point. The cave faced west, overlooking the Pacific Ocean with a spectacular view.

Getting there was not an easy undertaking. Artero knew the area well—very few others did. The trek first required hiking on a narrow deer trail running near a cliff. Next came a climb up a steep limestone cliff once off the rough trail. Two large rocks, each over thirty feet high, were perched on top of the cliff. Although commonly referred to as a cave, the space was actually a gap between the two rocks. The hiding place was a narrow crevice measuring about six feet wide and thirty feet long. The nearby cliff featured a sharp drop of about 300 feet. The place seemed like a perfect location for someone not want-ing to be found.

Tweed was not at his hideout for very long when Artero brought him the news about Tyson and Johnston. He explained the details of their killing at the hands of Japanese soldiers. A sick feeling overcame Tweed. He was now the last American left and more determined than ever to hold out until the island was liberated—whenever that might be.[5] The key was to keep his location a secret from others on the island. The more Guamanians who knew his location, the greater the risk of the information reaching the Japanese.

The narrow confines of George Tweed's cave hideout are examined by American military personnel. The undated photo was taken after the American liberation of Guam. (US Navy / National Archives)

It was clear Artero was now the key person in Tweed's survival and would continue to be so as long as the sailor remained on the island. Neither Tweed nor Artero had any way of knowing the time was to span almost two years. "During this time he came to my hiding place, which was about a mile and a half or two miles from his ranch house and would bring me food every week," Tweed explained.[6]

The small cave now became the sailor's home—there was no more living on the run. He worked to make it livable with Artero's help. "Now there was nothing to keep rain from coming in there because it was all open," Tweed said years later. "As I say it was just a crevasse and it was open at the top."

The solution was to build a small roof. "Antonio brought me a couple of sheets of metal roofing. Oh, that guy would bring me anything that was available…that he felt that I needed."[7] A tilted portion of the roof allowed water to drain into an old drum. A cloth cover stained out bugs and debris to give Tweed a plentiful supply of water.

Tweed next worked to fashion furniture out of some rough sawed wood boards, also provided by Artero, and bamboo sticks. He initially worked with only a machete and pocket knife although Artero later brought him a hand saw to use. The sailor crafted a crude table, a basic chair with a high back, and a small cupboard to store his few cooking utensils. A homemade light fixture was crafted from a sardine can. With the use of a crude wick and coconut oil for fuel, it provided light when needed.[8]

Tweed tried to shave about once a week using the sparse collection of razors he collected in his travels. He later recalled the blades "almost pulled my face off" as he did not have any shaving soap. Although he had some bouts of illness during his time in hiding, the sailor for the most part stayed healthy. "I guess the mountain air agreed with me," he said, also adding, "there wasn't much of my catching any contagious diseases"[9]

The American's pistol offered more than just a sense of protection—it came in handy, although not for shooting at the Japanese. Wild deer were prominent in that area of the island. "I shot two deer with the pistol, the first one solely for the meat, but the second one I wanted the deer for the hide more than the meat," he explained. "I was running short on shoes."[10] He skinned the second deer and arranged to have the hide taken into town to be tanned.

"I had an old pair of shoes there that had been made in the Philippines that had rubber soles," he continued. "The uppers were of canvas, but in the bushes and the rough jagged rocks that I was forced to travel over, the canvas uppers didn't last very long, even though the rubber soles were still good." Tweed fashioned a new pair of shoes using the deer hide and old rubber soles. "Of course, the deer meat also came in very handy." He likewise fashioned some homemade shoes for Artero's family.

The sailor initially only had a 1941 calendar in his possession. He worked feverously during his time in isolation to create new calendars, even carefully crossing out days. Tweed paid good attention to the phases of the moon. "It was pretty important for me to know when the moon would be full and when the nights would be dark," he recalled.[11] The added months extended far into 1943 as the sailor carefully kept track of time the best he could.

On a clear day, Tweed could see far down the western coast of Guam, making out Agaña, the Orote Peninsula, and points around the harbor area. However, he was not able to make out individual ships. He looked out into the blue Pacific Ocean and dreamed of the day American ships were to appear on the horizon.

Tweed eventually fell into a general routine to pass the time. He occasionally walked on the trail at night. He obtained a small number of smuggled magazines and books—all brought in by Artero. The reading materials, along with playing cards, helped break the isolation. The diet for the hiding sailor varied based on what Artero provided. Food included eggs and rice. Fresh fruit, such as bananas and papaya, also became regular fare.

Tweed became as self-sufficient as possible in many areas. He harnessed the power of reflected sunlight, using a small half-cylinder made of glass to start fires when needed. A small fire was typically used for cooking. The sailor became adept at drying coconut meat and then squeezing out the oil. "Coconut oil makes good cooking fuel," he later explained.[12]

Thoughts of the Japanese were never far no matter how routine life became for Tweed. He later wrote about having vivid and terrifying dreams involving his capture or killing by the enemy. Tweed knew the other Americans in hiding were taken by surprise and thought of the grim possibility of waking up to find soldiers standing over him.

The nightmare scenario prompted him to develop a rudimentary warning system using a windup alarm clock attached to a long cord fashioned from tree bark. The clock was placed on the trail leading up to his cave. The system at least gave Tweed some assurance he might have just enough advanced warning to escape if the Japanese were to sneak up on him.

The sailor's very survival rested upon the ability to keep knowledge of his location to as few people as possible. Artero tried to keep the secret by telling only a few immediate family members. He did not tell any friends.[13] The family went to great lengths to keep any amount of information from slipping out. At one time a maid became suspicious of some extra clothes in the wash, prompting Artero's wife Josefa to tell her the clothes belonged to her brother.[14]

"When the Japs had lost my trail and couldn't pick it up again, they tried to threaten me out of the bushes," Tweed recalled.[15] "First, they announced that as soon as they found the man who was helping me they would kill him. That brought no results, so they enlarged the threat to include his wife and his children." The threats were enough to strike fear in the local population. "There was no doubt in anyone's mind that they would carry out their threat. This brought no results, so then they enlarged the threat to include the man, his wife, and his children, the commissioner of the district that I was in, and one hundred people selected at random from that district," Tweed continued. "This made a number of commissioners and a number of the people very nervous because they didn't know what district I was in and they might be the victims of the Japs if I was hiding in that district."

The occupiers turned to help from religious clergy when all else failed. Two Japanese Catholic priests were sent to Guam—Monsignor Dominic Fukahori and Father Petro Komatsu. The clergymen were on the island to presumably help with religious matters and assist in relations between the local population and Japanese authorities.[16] Father Komatsu wrote an open letter to Tweed in late 1943.

The letter urged Tweed "to give yourself up and thus relieve the suffering and anguish of the Chamorros."[17] In exchange, Father Komatsu pledged he would not be killed. Rather, Tweed would be sent to Japan to be with the rest of the American prisoners. Copies of the letter were distributed around the island. Tweed did not accept the proposition and the trail for the Japanese searchers remained cold.

The arrival of Christmas Day 1943 brought a special surprise for the American. Artero lumbered up the trail, one day earlier than his normal weekly food delivery, with two large baskets slung over his shoulders. He delivered a smorgasbord of food for the holiday, including roasted chicken and a custard pie, along with the normal weekly food delivery. He also brought a few wrapped gifts—a razor and smoking set.[18] The calendar soon turned to 1944.

Chapter 20

PACIFIC DRIVE

AFTER GIVING UP HIS RADIO in early 1942 and living a life of isolation in his cave, George Tweed was cut off from news about the Pacific War. He had no way of knowing American forces were on the offensive against Japan and slowly moving closer to Guam. New and more powerful warships were now joining the fleet as the United States was building a powerful navy—a fleet so formidable it likely could have never been envisioned by the secluded sailor on Guam.

The year 1943 marked a time of strategic decisions for American leaders on how to proceed in the Pacific. The American victories at Coral Sea, Midway, and Guadalcanal were merely pinpricks on the fringes of the Japanese empire. The enemy still controlled a vast amount of territory behind a strong defensive perimeter, designed to shield the Home Islands from direct attack.

Most of the strategy decisions for the Pacific front fell to the American Joint Chiefs of Staff.

Navy boss Admiral King was the leading advocate for more resources and action against Japan at a planning conference in early 1943. He wanted to "keep moving" in the Pacific before the Japanese had sufficient time to consolidate their territorial gains.[1] Many other leaders were more interested in the European theater.

The admiral spoke with conviction of his desire to attack in the Central Pacific through the Marshall and Marianas Island groups, with the discussions sometimes becoming heated. King believed a front close to Japan offered a good chance of drawing the main Japanese fleet into a decisive battle where it could be destroyed by superior American naval forces.[2] Leaders agreed in early 1943 for an uneasy compromise with a statement for "maintaining pressure on Japan, retaining the initiative, and attaining a position of readiness for a full scale offensive against Japan" once Germany was defeated.[3] The agreement authorized planning for various operations in the Pacific, including King's Central Pacific offensive.

The theater-level decisions to implement the strategy involved a mix of complex planning issues, inter-service rivalries, political concerns, and strong personalities. The process pitted two strong characters—General MacArthur and Admiral King—against each other. MacArthur was overseeing operations in the South Pacific. He was known to be a constant seeker of publicity and resented the navy's— and King's—strategic leadership in the Pacific.[4]

MacArthur advocated for a continued advance through the Solomon Islands and along the northern coast of New Guinea to the Philippines. He argued the advance could be made under the constant umbrella of air cover from land bases. Freeing the Philippines was politically popular—the nation was an American territory—and MacArthur had publicly promised to return with a liberating army.

King would have nothing of it. "The idea of rolling up the Japanese along the New Guinea coast…and up through the Philippines to

Luzon, as our major strategic concept, to the exclusion of clearing our Central Pacific line of communication to the Philippines, is to me absurd," he adamantly declared.[5]

The admiral's Central Pacific strategy was a more direct route to the Japanese Home Islands Naval leaders liked the familiar route due to the Orange pre-war planning, the flexibility offered by the plan, and plenty of open waters for the deployment of the growing battle fleet.[6] However, the operations involved long movements and advances without the shielding cover of land-based aircraft.

President Roosevelt refused to press the issue, ultimately leading to a compromise where both advances were approved to move forward simultaneously.[7] The dual strategy eventually proved profoundly successful and was proficient in keeping the enemy off-balance. The Japanese leaders were constantly having to divide resources during the next two years to fight the approaching enemy on two different fronts. The Central Pacific offensive was to begin with the seizure of the Gilbert Islands in November 1943, followed by an attack on the Marshall Islands in early 1944. The Caroline Islands and the Marianas were to be invaded in July and October, respectively.

The situation facing the leaders of the Combined Japanese Fleet in 1943 were considerably less desirable than the American position. The Japanese incurred serious losses in ships, planes, and experienced pilots during the 1942 naval battles. Shipyards in Japan were producing only a fraction of the vessels their American counterparts were churning out. The enemy suffered a tremendous blow when Admiral Yamamoto was killed in the Solomon Islands when his plane was shot down by American fighters on April 18, 1943 after intelligence officials decoded his travel schedule.[8] Yamamoto's successor was Admiral Mineichi Koga.

The Imperial Navy was still a very powerful force, especially in battleships and cruisers. Koga reorganized the Combined Fleet into task forces built around aircraft carriers. The shrinking carrier force would have to heavily rely on naval land-based aircraft going forward to halt the American counterattack.

Assuming a more defensive posture, the Japanese sought a decisive naval battle with the American fleet to turn the tide of the war. Koga developed a series of plans, known as Operation Z, to be fought when the Americans penetrated the Philippine Sea from various possible points of entry, including through the Marianas.[9] The implementation of the battle plan was to fall to yet another Japanese admiral after the death of Koga in a noncombat plane crash.

Turning the Central Pacific drive into action fell to Admiral Nimitz and his staff at Pearl Harbor. Two key subordinates were selected as onsite commanders—Vice Admiral Raymond Spruance as the overall commander and Vice Admiral Richmond Kelly Turner (commonly known as Kelly Turner) was the commander of the amphibious forces.

The Nimitz team initially focused on planning the Gilberts and Marshalls operations. Both island chains were far from Pearl Harbor—the Gilberts were about 2,400 miles away—and possessed the similar characteristics of low-lying tropical coral atolls of various sizes and shapes. The invasions were to be the first island "assaults" with troops landing directly against well-prepared and dug-in defenders.

The Gilberts operation was the first opportunity for Nimitz to deploy the full power of his growing fleet. Spruance led a force of 200 vessels and 27,600 assault troops.[10] The primary target was tiny Betio Island. The largest islet of the Tarawa Atoll—about 300 acres arrayed in a long and narrow shape—was crammed with 2,600 Japanese soldiers and about 2,000 additional construction troops. An extensive network of defenses included British artillery guns from Singapore, fourteen tanks dug into the sand, and over one hundred fortifications—pill boxes, machine gun positions, and bunkers—with overlapping fields of fire focused on the beaches.[11]

American planners were counting on a robust pre-invasion bombardment from the sea and air to knock out many of the defenders. The early morning hours of November 20, 1943 was greeted with the thunderous roar of gunfire from three battleships and supporting ships. A total of 3,000 tons of shells rained down on the island. Waves of carrier planes followed before the assault troops of the 2nd Marine Division moved toward the island.

The pre-invasion bombardment proved to be ineffective against many of the defenses. The assaulting marines met a firestorm of resistance. Inaccurate estimations of the tidal conditions caused even greater problems. A coral reef, extending hundreds of yards offshore, blocked the approach for many of the landing craft, forcing marines to wade ashore under heavy fire.

An American general ashore radioed Turner a grim message about eight hours after the landing began—"Issue in doubt."[12] By evening, the men ashore were pinned down in a narrow beachhead nestled among the dead and dying. The marines eventually pushed forward and prevailed in heavy fighting. The island was secured after a brutal and bloody battle lasting seventy-six hours.

Nearby Makin Island was lightly defended and secured with light casualties. Just over 1,000 Americans were killed and about 2,100 were wounded in the combined operations.[13] Almost the entire Japanese garrison on Betio was wiped out.[14] The Japanese fleet did not seriously challenge the operation.

The Tarawa invasion was sensationalized by the American press as an unnecessary tragedy. Reports of heavy casualties sustained in just a few days of fighting, coupled with pictures of dead marines on the beach, shocked the nation.[15] Nimitz and his staff immediately set about studying the battle to make improvements for future operations.

The Gilberts quickly became a forward operating base for the next move in the Central Pacific offensive—the Marshall Islands. The chain comprised many small islands and atolls spread out over a wide area. About 750 miles separated the northwestern and southeastern corners of the islands.

The final plan incorporated a heavier pre-invasion bombardment than Tarawa, better coordination between the amphibious and support forces, and the concept of island-hoping—assaulting some islands, while bypassing others. The tactic was already used in the South Pacific to allow for a faster advance into Japanese territory with fewer American casualties.

The three main targets were the strategically important islands of Majuro, Kwajalein, and Eniwetok. Kwajalein was one of the world's largest atolls with more than ninety individual islands surrounding a large lagoon. The atoll served as the hub of Japanese military activities in the Marshalls and the center for logistics among the entire outer defensive perimeter.[16]

The amphibious landings began on January 31, 1944 with army soldiers coming ashore on Majuro in the southeastern portion of the Marshalls. The undefended island was secured in one day and quickly turned into an advance base. Subsequent landings took place on areas of the Kwajalein Atoll complex and Eniwetok Atoll. The objectives in the Marshall Islands were secured with relative ease and the Americans suffered a fraction of casualties compared to the Tarawa battle.

The heavily defended islands of Woetje, Maloelap, Mili, and Jaluit were bypassed by the Americans. The airfields on these islands were neutralized by bombing. Unable to be resupplied, the trapped garrisons literally spent the rest of the war starving. The Japanese fleet again offered no challenge to the American invasions. The Marshalls invasion was a symbolic defeat for the Japanese—the first loss of pre-war territory.

The Gilberts and Marshalls operations allowed for the development of a logistical system for sustaining a large naval force far from a major base, such as Pearl Harbor. The newly acquired territory became advance bases for throngs for warships, planes, and men. The coordination of the fast carriers and amphibious forces proved to be a model successfully used throughout the remainder of the war.

The speedy capture of the Marshalls enabled American planners to reconsider the timeline for the invasion of the Marianas. The islands provided a more direct route to Japan than the Carolines, although the decision came after a new dimension was added to the strategic debate—the B-29 Superfortress. The new and advanced long-range bomber was expected to be ready in sufficient numbers by the middle of 1944 to be deployed against Japan.

Army Air Force leader General Henry "Hap" Arnold needed a base within 1,500 miles of the Japanese Home Islands. The Marianas were a perfect fit. The Joint Chiefs recommended naval forces go directly to the Marianas after seizing the Marshalls with the hope the islands "might be in our hands by July 1944."[17] The Marianas quickly became the centerpiece of the Central Pacific offensive.

Chapter 21

OPERATION FORAGER

THE MARIANAS WERE BEHIND THE frontlines for the Japanese during the early years of the war. The islands largely served as a supply and staging area for forces fighting in other areas and the number of troops stationed on there was low.[1] The situation changed in early 1944 when it became clear the Marianas would likely be the target of an American invasion at some point during the year.

Faced with advances on two fronts, the Japanese focused on holding their Absolute National Defensive Zone—a line running through the Marianas, Palaus, and the western end of New Guinea. The Imperial leaders understood the critical importance of the Marianas in the defensive shield. Preparations taking place behind the defensive line included the construction of additional airfields, assembling troops for deployment, and massing the fleet for a possible decisive battle with the American Pacific Fleet.[2]

Admiral Soemu Toyoda became the new top naval leader after the untimely death of Admiral Koga. He updated Koga's Z plan to become Operation A-Go. The objective of the plan was the same—to fight a decisive battle in the Philippine Sea.

While the navy planned for their sea battle, the army deployed troops to defend key island holdings. The Japanese 31st Army was established in March 1944, under the command of Lieutenant General Hideyoshi Obata, to defend the Marianas and Truk.[3] Much of the army's land fighting thus far during the war had been on mainland China and islands in the South Pacific. Army units in China were drawn upon for filling the ranks of the new force to be deployed to the Marianas.

American submarines were waging unrestricted warfare against Japanese sea commerce since the early days of the war, sinking merchant ships and slowing the supply of raw materials back to Japan from all corners of the empire. A bevy of submarines prowled the waters around the Marianas throughout early 1944, aiming to disrupt the flow of reinforcements and supplies to Saipan and Guam. A significant number of Japanese army units arrived in the Marianas without their weapons and essential equipment due to the submarine attacks. The result was the formation of various ad hoc odd units composed of mix and match survivors.

The last major reinforcement convoy making transit to the Marianas lost five of seven ships to American submarine torpedoes in early June. By the middle of the month, Japanese defenders numbered 31,629 military personnel on Saipan, and about 18,500 on Guam. Much smaller garrisons were stationed on Tinian and Rota.[4]

The American Joint Chiefs of Staff formally approved the next phase of the Central Pacific offensive in a sweeping March 12, 1944, directive outlining future operations in various Pacific areas. The military leaders ordered the southern islands of the Marianas to be occupied with a target date of June 15.[5] The occupation of the Marianas represented the ultimate end goal of the Central Pacific offensive. Admirals King in Washington and Nimitz in the Pacific both knew what was at stake—a forward operating base for an eventual attack on Japan, airbases for the new B-29 bomber to strike the Home Islands, and the possibility of luring the dormant Japanese fleet into a decisive battle.[6]

The directive gave Nimitz the ability to begin detailed tactical planning for what was to be the largest American undertaking in the Pacific to date. The three islands of Saipan, Tinian, and Guam were identified as the main targets. Saipan was given top priority due to the better quality of its existing airfields. Planners fixed a June 15 target date for the Saipan landing and the invasion of Guam was tentatively set for June 18.[7]

Nimitz again turned to Admiral Spruance, his trusted subordinate, to lead what was soon christened Operation Forager. Spruance's long naval career began with graduation from the US Naval Academy in 1906. He received additional education in electrical engineering within a few years. An extensive series of land and sea duty followed, including commanding five destroyers and the battleship *Mississippi*. Shore positions entailed time at the Naval War College, posts in intelligence and engineering, and commandant of the Tenth Naval District based in Puerto Rico.[8] Spruance was promoted to rear admiral and assumed command of a cruiser division in September 1941. His ships escorted Vice Admiral William Halsey's aircraft carriers during raids on Japanese-held islands during the early months of the war.

The rise of Spruance to prominence began with the Battle of Midway. Halsey, one of the top aircraft carrier commanders, was confined to the hospital on the eve of the battle after developing a serious skin condition. Doctors would not release him despite the admiral's strong opposition to the confinement. Following Halsey's recommendation, Nimitz selected Spruance as his last-minute replacement.[9] Although second in command during the engagement, Spruance's remarkable leadership of two carriers during the battle contributed to delivering the first decisive defeat to the Japanese in over 300 years.[10]

Spruance has been described as a quiet individual and someone who liked to keep a low profile—essentially staying out of the spotlight. Aside from the shy exterior, the admiral was meticulous and calculated, carefully planning his every move.[11] He became the chief of staff for Nimitz shortly after the Midway victory. He then became the commander of the Central Pacific Force on August 5, 1943.[12] The growing battle force included most of the critical elements of the Pacific Fleet, including a growing number of new aircraft carriers.

Nimitz initially procrastinated in giving Spruance the sea command, although it had nothing to do with his qualifications. The admiral was not sure he could part with Spruance on his staff.[13] The year together at Pearl Harbor was time well spent for both admirals. Nimitz and Spruance made a good team. "The better I got to know him the more I admired his intelligence, his open-mindedness, and his approachability for any who had new or different ideas, and above all, his utter fearlessness and his courage in pushing the war," Spruance later recalled about Nimitz.[14]

The Unites States Navy maintained one large group of ships as the main battle fleet in the Pacific and occasionally changed the name of the force in a somewhat unique situation in the annals of war. The designation changed based on who was the commander. The ships became the Fifth Fleet when under the command of Spruance during the Central Pacific offensive.

The same vessels were the Third Fleet when led by Halsey supporting the drive to the Philippines. Spruance and Halsey alternated command of the big fleet during major operations as the United

States attacked the Japanese empire on two fronts. As one admiral commanded the fleet, the other and his staff were behind the frontlines planning the next operation.

The vast array of naval forces under Spruance's command for Operation Forager included 535 ships of all types. The force was primarily divided into three large groups: Fast Carrier Force, Joint Expeditionary Force, and Forward Area Central Pacific.[15] The latter force was the designation for land-based air units supporting the operation. The fast carrier force, designated Task Force 58, was under the command Vice Admiral Marc Mitscher. Essentially, in the main battle fleet, the formation included fifteen aircraft carriers (carrying almost nine hundred aircraft), seven new battleships, twenty-one cruisers of various types, and sixty-nine destroyers.[16] The force was divided into four smaller task groups of three or four carriers and escorts. The task force made far-reaching air attacks into Japanese territory throughout the early months of 1944. The seven fast battleships occasionally operated as a separate task group, as dictated by the tactical situation, under the command of Vice Admiral Willis Lee.

The Joint Expeditionary Force, designated as Task Force 51, under the command of Admiral Turner, was the actual invasion force. Turner was by then considered a leading expert on amphibious warfare, having led multiple large-scale invasions beginning with Guadalcanal. The force was divided into two smaller groups. The Northern Attack Force, embarking two full divisions of soldiers for Saipan and Tinian, was under Turner's direct control. The Southern Attack Force for Guam, led by Rear Admiral Richard Conolly, included one-and-a-half divisions of soldiers. The 105,859 assault troops assigned to the operation, including 66,779 for the Northern

Attack Force and 39,080 for Guam, was a mix of army and marine units.[17] Tactical command of all ground forces ashore rested with Marine Lieutenant General Holland M. Smith.

The logistical challenges facing the planners of the operation were substantial both at sea and on land. The closest forward operating base was Eniwetok in the Marshall Islands—just over 1,000 miles away. A series of temporary floating bases, including fuel barges, repair shops, floating drydocks, and tugboats, were positioned to support the large number of the ships. The actual invasion forces were coming from great distances—Hawaii (3,500 miles) and Guadalcanal (2,400 miles)—which meant soldiers were to be crammed aboard transports for a long period of time.

A variety of challenges also confronted those planning the land portion of the operation. The landscape of the three target islands combined some of the hazards previously encountered in island invasions—coral reefs to impede the approach of landing craft, rugged jungle terrain, and plenty of caves for hidden guns and concealed strongpoints.[18] The islands of Saipan and Guam were large enough for the enemy to conduct an in-depth defense with room for the defenders to maneuver and counterattack, unlike the smaller coral atolls in the Gilberts and Marshalls where the key battles were fought on or near the beachhead. Saipan was home to a sizable population of Japanese residents—a new threat not previously encountered by American soldiers in the Pacific.

Few up-to-date maps existed for the islands, particularly with Saipan and Tinian, and little detailed information was known about the enemy defenses. Long-range American bombers, modified with cameras, began regular reconnaissance flights to give the planners some photographic resources. Submarines assisted in the planning by reconnoitering the target islands and scouting beaches.

The first American air raid was delivered on Saipan by planes from Mitscher's carriers on the morning of February 23, 1944. The aircraft sank two freighters and some small craft and damaged dock facilities while striking targets all around the island. Japanese records indicate 168 plane losses because of the attack.[19] Aerial strikes, delivered by carrier and land-based aircraft from the Marshalls, continued to occur at various intervals until the invasion.

The initial plan called for the marines to carry out the assault on all three islands with army units held in reserve. The ground forces participating in Operation Forager included the 2nd Marine Division, 3rd Marine Division, 4th Marine Division, and 1st Provisional Marine Brigade. The army's 77th Infantry Division and 27th Infantry Division served as reserves. The 77th was to be a distant reserve stationed in Hawaii, while the 27th was to be a floating reserve available on site in the Marianas for use on any island as needed. The forces assembled and trained while leaders worked out the final details of the tactical plans.

The first American aerial bombing of Guam took place on June 11–12 when the island was struck by carrier-based planes. The bombing began to steadily increase as American forces came closer to converging on the Marianas. Carrier planes made regular appearances over the island. The American planes were a welcome sight for Guamanians and the lone American sailor in hiding—George Tweed.

Chapter 22

AMERICAN PLANES

TIME IS OFTEN VIEWED AS a precious commodity with people frequently trying to use it judiciously. For someone like George Tweed, isolated while hiding in a cave on Guam, he had an abundance of the asset and plenty of time to think. For starters, he took the examination for chief radioman shorty before the start of the war. The promotion would put him at the top rating for his specialty. He had no idea if he passed the exam.

Tweed still possessed his checkbook from the Bank of Guam showing a balance of $221.81.[1] He should still be getting paid—unless he was declared dead. How much has he accumulated in back-pay? Would he even survive the war to collect it?

The sailor often wondered about his family and how they were doing back in the United States. His mother still lived in Oregon. His wife and kids—Mary and the two children left Guam with the other dependents shortly before the start of the war—resided in

California. "Suppose my wife's name isn't Mrs. Tweed any longer?" he later recalled thinking. "I really couldn't blame her if she remarried."[2]

The Japanese attack on Guam was part of an avalanche of bad news reported to the shocked American public in the weeks after the attack on Pearl Harbor. The news was particularly unnerving for those with relatives on the island or elsewhere in the Pacific. Initially, there was no information available for family members about the fate of the servicemen stationed on Guam.

Tweed's mother was Mrs. Roscoe Bennett. She requested information in a handwritten letter addressed to the Navy Department in Washington, DC, dated December 27, 1941. "Is there any way possible that you could get any information concerning my son," Bennett wrote. She added, "I am sixty-three years old and my health isn't very good."[3] The Navy Department responded less than two weeks later explaining communications with the island has been cut off. The official noted, "At present, the Department can furnish you no definite information, and furthermore cannot now predict when positive information will be available."[4]

Both Bennett and Mary Tweed received nearly identical letters from the Navy Department in the coming months. The documents confirmed George Tweed was on the island at the start of hostilities. "As his name does not appear on any causality list thus far received it is probable that he is a prisoner of war."[5] The department pledged to pass along any additional information as soon as such became available.

By early May, the sailor's status was changed to missing. The information was communicated to Tweed's relatives by letter. "You are informed that according to information received through the International Red Cross your son...is reported missing following action in the performance of his duty when the Japanese attacked the island of Guam," read a letter to Tweed's mother from the Navy

Department.[6] Information on the location and status of Tweed then fell silent.

By early 1944, Tweed had become accustomed to his life of mostly isolation in his cave hideout near the northwest corner of Guam. He largely lost contact with the outside world and had no reliable knowledge of who was winning the war. His dream of a great fleet of American ships arriving off the horizon never yet materialized.

The Japanese propaganda machine continued to boast of great victories even after the tide of war turned against Imperial forces and the Americans started winning crucial battles. Like all information on the island, the news filtered in small bits and pieces through the local population and was eventually related to Tweed by Antonio Artero. He could only hope the Americans were winning the war and getting closer to Guam.

The sailor began to hear of changes to the Japanese garrison early in the year. He previously heard most of the Japanese invasion troops left sometime after the American prisoners departed. "Three hundred Jap navy men were put ashore to operate the civilian government," he later recalled of the occupation group. "About six months later this number was cut in half, 150 of the navy men being taken to the island of Rota a short distance to the north of Guam, as the Japs said, to fortify Rota. This condition continued with only 150 Japs in Guam until March 1944."[7]

Tweed pegged March as the month when a large number of regular Japanese soldiers began arriving on the island. If the information he was hearing about the enemy garrison was correct, then it could only mean the Americans were getting closer. "The Japs made the statement that the Americans had said that they would return to

Guam on the 1st of April, so they made hurried preparations for defense of the island," Tweed said later. "When April the first arrived and nothing happened, the Japs became angry and shouted that the Americans were liars, that they said they were coming on the first of April, but they didn't come. This was apparently someone's April Fool's joke."

The grapevine had some Japanese troops subsequently leaving the island. "However, the following month more troops began being poured in there," Tweed continued. "Ship loads [sic] of concrete and supplies, guns, fortifications, anti-aircraft guns were brought there. Concrete gun mounts were constructed, also pits for anti-aircraft guns." The occupiers were clearly expecting an invasion to begin sometime in the very near future.

The arrival of new troops, coupled with the frantic buildup of defenses on the island, may have reduced the Japanese effort to find Tweed. "Finally, the Japanese officially pronounced me dead in April, 1944," he later explained. "There had been only navy men on Guam until March, then army men came. The navy was afraid the army might find me, so officially pronounced me dead to save face."[8]

Tweed longed for the days of having a radio to get reports from KGEI in San Francisco. He decided to venture out from his cave, against Artero's advice, to visit a friend named Ramon Rojos near the village of Barrigada. Tweed wrote of having left Rojos a radio and some possessions before escaping when the Japanese took over. The trek required walking a good distance on a jungle trail. The risks were great—the sailor could get lost and be unable to find his way back to the cave, discovered by a Guamanian who would pass the information to the authorities, or even be found by a Japanese patrol. He decided it was worth the risk and ventured out, carrying his pistol for protection, with the hopes of returning before Artero's next food delivery.

At some point in the journey, Tweed left the trail under the cover of darkness and began walking on a road near Dededo. Tweed likely did not know there was a Japanese guard post in the area. He continued to walk down the road and then suddenly was upon it. The post was a house with a Japanese sentry inside. Tweed knew the only course of action was to keep walking in the hope of not being noticed—any type of abrupt movement or turning around was sure to attract attention.

Suddenly, there was movement in the building. The clumping of heavy shoes on a wooden floor penetrated the silence of the night as the sentry opened the door. A brilliant stream of light protruded out from the open door intersecting the road just ahead of Tweed's path. He now had no choice but to stop. Tweed slowly came to a halt and clutched his pistol ready to fire if needed. He already made up his mind to shoot the Japanese soldier if he came out into the road.

The Japanese guard stood in the doorway looking out into the inky black darkness. "I stood perfectly still, my finger on the trigger," Tweed wrote of the moment. "After about a minute, he turned and went back into the house, closing the door."[9] The tense moment passed, allowing Tweed to continue walking on the road while putting his pistol away. He later thought of what an absurd idea it had been to shoot the sentry—either he could have been caught on the spot or many Guamanians could be killed as the Japanese searched for the person responsible. The repercussions to the local population would have definitely been severe.

Tweed arrived safely at Rojos's house only to find the radio was gone. It had been removed and Tweed's possessions burned. The Japanese authorities took Rojos in for questioning and torture after suspecting his involvement in helping the American.[10] Tweed's journey back to his makeshift home was successful, although he initially struggled in finding his way back to the cave and became exhausted along the way.

The date of June 11, 1944 was a monumental day in Tweed's long ordeal on Guam. The watershed day was the first time the sailor saw American planes over the island. "They were a long time coming but they're here at last," he later said of the joyful moment.[11] "I knew it would not be long," he continued, thinking of the American fleet's arrival.

The air activity over the island quickly became a regular event. The view from his cave hideout gave Tweed a grandstand seat for the American bombardment of Guam. He could occasionally see clouds of smoke rising from the port area after an air attack and relished the idea of sunken Japanese ships in the harbor. "At the beginning our planes came from the southeast and then they started coming from the north," he said. "I figured the fleet was operating up there, and, another thing, I saw Japanese planes heavily loaded with bombs flying northward." He rightly concluded an American attack on Saipan was underway. "Then I was pretty certain."[12]

Tweed heard stories of what happened to the American pilots who were shot down. He recalled the report of one pilot who was forced down by anti-aircraft fire. "After he landed the Japs were afraid to approach the plane so they went to a native ranch and detailed a native to go talk to the pilot since they knew that he could speak English," he explained. "There were also some native girls there who went with the native and approached the plane."

The Guamanians were happy to see an American. They approached the plane, shook hands with the pilot, and talked with him for some time. The pilot told them "on his way down he had decided to fight until he was killed, but since the people were so friendly, he felt that he had friends on the island and would surrender."

Japanese soldiers soon approached the plane and an officer saw the pilot's shoes. "He took the shoes off the American feet, wore them himself and forced the American to go barefoot," Tweed continued. "Then he picked up a club and began beating the pilot. After beating him for some time he was taken to town where he was held for four days under torture for information." Tweed heard the pilot was later executed.

Tweed made careful observations and gathered whatever information he could about the Japanese defenses. He later explained the operation of an anti-aircraft gun emplacement. "They would dig a pit about fifteen feet square and cover the pit over with one inch of steel," he later said. "The anti-aircraft gun would be mounted near the edge, one edge of the pit." About thirty men were assigned to the gun. "One man would remain up inside and operate the anti-aircraft gun. If this man was killed, one more Jap would go up and take over his duty of firing the gun. In this manner it was impossible for more than one Jap to be killed at a time unless a direct bomb hit was scored on the cover of the pit."

One thing was for certain—the Americans were close. The invasion of Guam could be only weeks—or even possibly days—away. Tweed knew he needed to survive long enough to see liberation.

Chapter 23

SAIPAN

MUCH OF THE WORLD'S ATTENTION on June 6, 1944 was focused on Europe where Allied forces were beginning the long-awaited invasion of France with an amphibious landing at Normandy. At the same time, on the other side of the world in the Pacific, the vast armada of ships involved in Operation Forager were preparing for the invasion of the Marianas. The Marianas operation numbered only 22,500 less troops than the those deployed during the initial phase of the Normandy operation.[1] Although both were large-scale amphibious operations, the two invasions were very different in terms of distance. The invaders at Normandy only needed to cross the English Channel before hurling into the heavily defended coast of France. The Marianas operation required the entire assault force—everything, including ships, men, supplies, and equipment—to travel thousands of miles.

The ships of the Northern Attack Force and other supporting units came from Hawaii—3,500 miles from the target. The force included Admiral Spruance making the voyage in his flagship heavy cruiser *Indianapolis*. The Southern Attack Force sailed north from Guadalcanal—2,400 miles away. The carriers of Task Force 58 were at Majuro in the Central Pacific.

The great rendezvous among the groups took place in the Marshall Islands. Coral atolls and lagoons were soon overflowing with ships of all types. The flagship *Indianapolis* sailed from one lagoon to another, allowing Admiral Spruance to marvel at the base development since the recent American invasion. "The progress in four months in clearing away the wreckage and in building up from nothing again is phenomenal," he wrote in astonishment.[2]

The admiral held meetings with his senior commanders for a final review of the operation plans. American land-based air from the Marshalls and elsewhere were to suppress Japanese airpower in the Caroline Islands. The carriers of Task Force 58 would eliminate enemy air strength in the Marianas, Volcano, and Bonin Islands along with providing protection from any naval incursions by the Japanese.

The immense fleet set sail for the more than 1,000-mile voyage to the objective. An American fighter pilot flying above the mass of the ships marveled at the mighty fleet. "I looked down on this power and wondered what kind of fools these Japanese were. They had made one of the greatest miscalculations of all time, and boy, were they going to pay the price."[3] The landing on Saipan was scheduled for June 15 with the invasion of the much-smaller adjacent island of Tinian to take place concurrently. The invasion of Guam was planned for June 18.

Admiral Mitscher's carriers were sailing about two hundred miles west of the Marianas on June 11 when two hundred planes took off for an afternoon attack on Saipan, Tinian, and Guam. Enemy fighters and bombers were thought to be plentiful on the airfields of the target islands. The American planes swopped to attack, appearing to catch the Japanese by surprise. An estimated fifty Japanese planes were destroyed in the air and on the ground.

During the night hours, Mitscher dispatched small teams of planes to circle the enemy airfields and occasionally make strafing attacks. The tactic was designed to keep the Japanese awake through the night and leave them exhausted the next day.[4] The enemy plane losses increased during the following days as American strikes continued to erode Japanese air strength in the region.

The naval bombardment on Saipan began one day later when seven fast battleships, diverted from carrier escort duty, pummeled the island with 2,432 sixteen-inch shells and 12,544 rounds of five-inch.[5] The gunners and spotters, however, were not used to shore bombardments and the barrage had little effect on the defenses. The shelling duty was taken over the next day by a group of older battleships and smaller warships—the regular bombardment unit. Their barrage was more effective, although not enough to neutralize the defenses.

Saipan is the second largest island in the Marianas with an area of eighty-five square miles.[6] The dominant features are Mount Tapochau, rising to a height of over 1,500 feet near the center of the island and the indentation of Magicienne Bay in the southeast. The town Garapan on the west coast served as the Japanese administrative capital for the Marianas. The Aslito airfield on the southern part of Saipan was considered by the Japanese to be the most important airbase between Japan and Truk.[7]

American intelligence officials used aerial photographs and radio intercepts to estimate the Japanese garrison on Saipan at about 15,000 to 17,000 troops.[8] The actual number was almost 30,000 with strong fortifications and heavy artillery. The command of the defenses fell to Lieutenant General Yoshitsugu Saito of the Japanese 43rd Division.

The overall area commander was Lieutenant General Hideyoshi Obata. He was away on an inspection tour of other islands when the Saipan invasion began. His attempted return only made it as far as Guam. The American attack prevented his moving to Saipan. Also on Saipan was Admiral Nagumo. The Pearl Harbor victor was reduced to commanding a token naval force in the Marianas after the disastrous Battle of Midway and other setbacks.

The amphibious landing on Saipan took place as scheduled on the early morning of June 15 with elements of the 2nd and 4th Marine Divisions coming ashore at beaches on the southwest coast of the island. A diversionary move toward a beach further north failed to fool the Japanese.[9] The marines quickly learned from the withering enemy fire that the pre-invasion bombardment failed to knock out the defenses. Well-concealed machine guns, mortars, and artillery poured heavy fire on the invaders from protected positions.

The marines initially focused on holding narrow beachheads to allow more troops and equipment to come ashore. American artillery batteries engaged in furious counterbattery duels with enemy positions as soon as the big guns came ashore.[10] There were 20,000 Americans on Saipan by sunset.[11] Japanese counterattacks and greater than expected resistance slowed the advance but failed to halt the invasion. The beachhead area was secured the next day, allowing American forces to advance into the southern portion of the island. The floating reserve—the Army's 27th Infantry Division—was landed due to the heavy fighting.

Concurrent to the landing operations were a series of ominous reports of Japanese ship movements. A concerned Spruance kept abreast of the developments. Although the possibility of a large naval battle had been discussed by Nimitz and Spruance, both admirals thought the Japanese would likely not attack the Marianas.[12] "I was of the opinion that the Japanese fleet was waiting for a time when they could count on strong shore-based air to help them," Spruance later explained. "Outlying groups of islands, such as the Marianas, could not be counted on for this, as we had demonstrated our ability to smother them with our superior carrier air strength."[13]

American submarines previously noted the presence of a large number of enemy surface ships in Tawi-Tawi, in the southwest part of the Philippines near Borneo. The movement of ships into the Philippine Sea was reported on June 15 by the submarines *Flying Fish* and *Seahorse*. Spruance was now aware of at least two large groups of Japanese ships heading east toward the Marianas. Confronted with the possibility of a major sea battle, with the fate of the Marianas operation potentially hanging in the balance, he postponed the landings on Tinian and Guam.

American land forces took control of a large portion of southern Saipan, including Aslito Airfield, while a sea battle was playing out in the waters to the west (the details of the naval battle will be covered in the next chapter). General Saito ordered a defense to the last bullet when it was clear no reinforcements were coming. By the end of June, American forces were taking heavy casualties while slowly advancing into the northern portion of the island. About another week was needed to root out the remaining defenders.

Saito and Nagumo both died by suicide in the closing days of the battle. Most of the remaining Japanese servicemen perished in a terrifying suicidal charge on American positions. Saipan was declared secured on July 9 after more than three weeks of fighting.[14] A final tragedy played out on the rocky northern tip of Saipan near Marpi Point when Japanese civilians, convinced the invaders were barbarians and cajoled by the few remaining servicemen, committed mass suicide by jumping off the cliffs into the ocean below.

The human cost of the Saipan victory was staggering. A total of 3,119 Americans were killed and an additional 10,992 were wounded or missing, bringing total casualties of the invasion to 14,111.[15] The Japanese lost almost their entire garrison of 30,000 men and an untold number of civilians.[16]

The adjacent island of Tinian was secured after about a week of fighting in late July. The garrison of about 9,000 Japanese troops was defeated by the first day of August, although mopping up operations continued well into 1945.[17] The main focus of Operation Forager now turned to Guam.

Chapter 24

TURKEY SHOOT

THE PHILIPPINE SEA IS THE vast expanse of the western Pacific between the Philippines and the Mariana Islands. The east-west span of more than 1,500 miles contains a few islands. Both American and Japanese pre-war planners envisioned the possibility of a decisive naval battle—one capable of deciding the outcome of a war—taking place in the Philippine Sea. It was the topic of strategic planning, war games, and annual naval exercises.[1] In June 1944, the area became the scene of the largest naval battle since Midway.

The Combined Japanese Fleet largely avoided major battles in the aftermath of the Midway defeat. The American invasion of the Marianas, however, was too close to the Home Islands for Japanese naval leaders to ignore. The Imperial Navy was under new leadership. The top command now rested with Admiral Soemu Toyoda. He assumed the reins after the untimely deaths of admirals Yamamoto and Koga.

Toyoda inherited the Operation A-Go strategy of committing the fleet to a decisive battle, although not specifically based on the invasion of the Marianas. Japanese leaders originally expected the next American attack to take place about 1,000 miles away at Palau Islands.[2] Toyoda put his plan in motion for the defense of the Marianas once the American forces were sighted and it was clear the operation was not merely a raid. He issued the following simple order to exhort his sailors to victory: "The fate of the Empire rests on this one battle. Every man is expected to do his utmost."[3]

The Japanese Navy was reorganized into the First Mobile Force on March 1, 1944. The arrangement was similar to a US Navy task force with the larger fleet divided into smaller task groups.[4] The Mobile Fleet was a powerful force under the command of Vice Admiral Jisaburo Ozawa, although it was smaller than the number of ships available to Admiral Spruance. Ozawa could muster nine aircraft carriers (with four hundred thirty planes), five battleships, thirteen cruisers, and twenty-eight destroyers.[5] The American Task Force 58 counted fifteen aircraft carriers.

Toyoda and Ozawa were faced with a host of disadvantages beyond the number of ships. Severe fuel shortages, largely a result of proficient American submarine actions, limited the radius of Japanese naval operations and kept the fleet close to oil sources in Borneo. The fleet needed to travel a great distance to reach the Marianas from Tawi-Tawi, taking away the element of surprise and making early detection likely. The naval air arm was severely depleted because of costly plane diversions during the last two years to losing battles in the South Pacific.

Ozawa was charged with orchestrating a decisive Japanese victory in the uneven matchup. His plan was to supplement his carriers with land-based aircraft and capitalize on the advantage of Japanese carrier planes having a 210-mile range advantage over the American counterparts.[6] Ozawa's carrier planes could launch attacks against the American fleet, outside of their range, land, and rearm on Guam before hitting the American ships again on the return trip.

Spruance was under orders to "capture, occupy and defend Saipan, Tinian, and Guam" and his orders made no specific mention of pursuing an enemy fleet in battle.[7] He calculated the approaching Japanese ships would not be in a position to attack until June 18. Spruance went ahead with plans to attack various islands by carrier planes—Iwo Jima and Chichi Jima to the north (critical staging areas for planes moving south from Japan to the Marianas) along with Guam and Rota—removing a key component of the enemy battle plan in the process.

The First Mobile Fleet was deployed in three sperate task forces—a vanguard of light carriers and big surface ships followed by two separate groups of the large carriers moving about one hundred miles behind. A critical element of the Japanese plan was for land-based planes in the Marianas to attack and weaken the American fleet in advance of Ozawa's arrival. The Combined Fleet headquarters assured Ozawa the planes from Guam would sink a third of the American carriers ahead of the battle.[8] The admiral received false reports indicating these attacks were taking place with great success.

Ozawa also believed there were as many as 500 land-based planes available to support him. The devastating American air attacks reduced the number to about fifty.[9] Ozawa entered the battle not knowing only a small number of feeble attacks by land-based planes mounted against the American fleet caused no damage.

Spruance was concerned the Japanese commander could use some of his ships as a decoy to lure Task Force 58 away from the Marianas and then have a second group make an end-run attack on the invasion force. He believed it to be a sound strategy, even telling his flag secretary he would "take out the transports" if he were the

Japanese admiral. "I'd split my forces and send some of my fast ships to deal with the transports."[10]

Spruance met with Admiral Turner and General Smith off Saipan ahead of the confrontation. He looked at the helpless transports anchored off the beachhead. "The Japs are coming after us," he told his subordinates as he pledged to keep the enemy away from the landing zone.[11] The admiral's cautious approach proved wise during the Battle of Midway and he would follow the same strategy during the upcoming battle.

Spruance moved Task Force 58 about 180 miles west of Saipan into the Philippine Sea, with his fast battleships operating slightly father west of the aircraft carriers. He made clear to his commanders the priority was to defend the beachhead and transports no matter what transpired and quelled later requests to move the battle force directly toward the approaching enemy.[12] While the carriers could move west toward the enemy during the day, Spruance instructed the carrier force to turn around and travel east at night to ensure Japanese ships did not sneak past in the darkness. The orders galled Admiral Mitscher, who thought his airmen were being held back by a leader who was not an aviator.[13] Spruance, however, would not relent.

The great battle began early on the morning of June 19 with Ozawa taking advantage of his longer-ranged carrier planes to strike first. The American ships were steaming about 150 miles west of the Marianas at the time and had been spotted by an enemy scout plane. Ozawa launched a series of four air strikes throughout the course of the day.

A host of key advantages favored the Americans in the pending air battles. The fight pitted veteran American pilots against poorly trained and inexperienced Japanese counterparts. The Americans also developed more advanced fighter-control systems, since the last carrier battles were fought around Guadalcanal more than a year ago, allowing for fighters to better intercept the approaching enemy planes.

The first Japanese raid took place in the morning with about seventy planes from the light carriers manned by the least experienced pilots. The approaching enemy was picked up by American radar at 10:00 a.m. about 150 miles away. Radar-directed Hellcat fighters tore into the approaching Japanese formation, shooting down many attackers before the enemy even came into range of shipboard guns. Only twenty-eight Japanese planes—less than half of the attacking force—reached the battleship task force. The battleship *South Dakota* was the only ship hit when a lone bomb caused minor damage.[14]

The second Japanese attack, considered by Ozawa as his main strike, comprised about 128 planes from the large carriers. The formation was picked up by American radar shortly after 11:00 a.m. and was again broken up by fighters with only a small number of enemy planes reaching their intended targets. The planes failed to hit any American carriers. Ninety-seven enemy planes were lost.[15]

Lieutenant (Junior Grade) Alex Vraciu was piloting a Hellcat off the carrier *Lexington* during the action. He followed the vector to a position about thirty-five miles west of the American ships. "Spotgazing intently, I suddenly picked out a large, rambling mass of at least fifty enemy planes two thousand feet below, port side and closing," he recalled of the action. There were no Japanese fighter planes in view.

Vraciu tore into the enemy formation. The young pilot shot down five Japanese planes in seven minutes. He had a sixth in his sights just as anti-aircraft fire from nearby American ships started to explode close by. He decided to go in for the kill anyway. "Number six blew up with a tremendous explosion right in front of my face. I must have hit his bomb. I had seen planes blow up before but never like this!"[16]

The final two Japanese strikes took place during the afternoon. Both formations were misdirected and only a portion of planes found the targets. The Japanese again failed to damage any American aircraft carriers. The final strike suffered severe plane losses partly attributed to a failed attempt to land on Guam.

Ozawa's air fleet suffered devastating losses in a single day of action. Only 130 carrier planes returned intact out of the 373 aircraft launched throughout the day and about 50 more planes were destroyed on Guam and Rota.[17] No American ships were seriously damaged and operations around Saipan were not disturbed.

No American air strikes were launched on the first day of the battle. Spruance impatiently paced the flag plot aboard *Indianapolis*, concerned his carriers were too far away to strike the Japanese fleet. His reconnaissance planes were still searching for the exact location of the enemy carriers. The day was all defensive for the American airmen. Spruance also did not yet know the First Mobile Fleet already suffered serious losses from undersea attackers.

The submarine *Albacore* hit Ozawa's flagship *Taiho*—the largest aircraft carrier in the Japanese fleet—with a single torpedo shortly after 8:00 a.m. The carrier managed to continue air operations before a massive explosion due to leaking fumes sent her to the bottom of the sea in the early afternoon. The submarine *Cavalla* hit the carrier *Shokaku* with three torpedoes. The Pearl Harbor veteran sank at 2:01 p.m. with heavy loss of life after suffering a series of secondary explosions. Ozawa was down to only about one hundred operational planes on his remaining carriers.

Far-reaching American search planes finally found the First Mobile Fleet during the late afternoon of June 20. With only three hours of daylight left, Mitscher took the calculated risk of ordering a strike of more than two hundred aircraft. His planes would be traveling to their extreme range and have to return to the carriers in darkness—a risky undertaking in 1944. An abundance of inviting targets awaited the American fliers.

The attack sank the carrier *Hiyo* and two tankers. Three other carriers, the battleship *Haruna*, a cruiser, and a destroyer suffered varying degrees of damage.[18] Sixty-five Japanese planes were shot down.[19]

The American pilots endured a long return flight. Many were not trained in night landings. Risking revealing his position to any prowling enemy submarines, Mitscher ordered his aircraft carriers to turn on all their lights to aid the airmen. A total of eighty planes were lost to either landing accidents or ditching into the sea after running out of fuel.[20] All but forty-nine airmen were saved.[21] The extensive recovery and rescue operation delayed any attempt to pursue the Japanese.

Ozawa was down to only thirty-five operational aircraft as he retreated northwest toward Okinawa. The Japanese plan for a decisive battle to save the Marianas evaporated in defeat. The Battle of the Philippine Sea was the largest aircraft carrier action in World War II.[22] The one-sided American victory destroyed the remaining elements of the Japanese naval air arm and the losses were irreplaceable. A returning American fighter pilot exclaimed, "It was just like an old-time turkey shoot" when describing the air battles.[23] The name stuck, giving the battle a popular nickname—the Great Marianas Turkey Shoot.

Spruance faced criticism, even in the shadow of a great victory, over his handling of the battle. Mitscher lamented over the bulk of the Japanese fleet escaping. "The enemy had escaped," he woefully wrote in his battle report. "He had been badly hurt by one aggressive carrier strike at the time when he was within range. His fleet was not sunk."[24]

Nimitz remained a stout supporter of Spruance, although wrote "a decisive fleet air action could have been fought, the Japanese fleet destroyed, and the end of the war hastened."[25] Admiral King defended Spruance, noting he was "rightly guided by his basic obligation" to protect the amphibious operation. Only after the war, when Japanese naval records became available, was it determined Spruance's placement of Task Force 58 on June 19 was the best possible location to block the approach of Japanese forces.[26]

Chapter 25

RESCUE SHIP

THE LAST WEEKS BEFORE THE invasion of Guam found United States warships and planes continuing an unrelenting attack on Japanese positions across the island, George Tweed looked for a way to contact the Americans, and Antonio Artero hoped to find a way for him and his family to survive the upcoming battle. Tweed's hideout gave him a good view of any activity happening on the west side of the island. He watched as American ships hurled shells ashore at a furious pace. He made notes about the locations of Japanese gun positions and any other information he thought could help the liberators.

The sailor once waved to a low-flying American plane frantically enough to attract the attention of the pilot. The airman took notice and flashed his recognition lights as the plane sped past.[1] Nothing further became of the encounter. "On another occasion a plane was disabled, made a landing on the sea very near the shore," Tweed explained. "The pilot managed to climb out of the ship and began swimming for shore. When he was about fifty feet off shore a bunch of Japs lined up and opened fire on him and he was killed before he was able to reach shore."[2]

The navy man wondered how he could get aboard one of the American ships operating off the coast. He had, after all, spent much of his naval career in communications. "I considered swimming, but they were so far out that that was impractical because the ships probably wouldn't be there by the time I was able to swim that far." The next idea was to use signal flags. "So I took a large piece of gauze, cut it in half, fastened it to a couple of sticks to use as semaphore flags."

Flags were used by sailors in communications for more than a century. In the semaphore system, a sailor waved flags at various angles to represent letters of the alphabet and numbers. Combinations could be used to spell out words.

"I stood up on a high rock for more than a week," Tweed recalled. "Every time a ship would come in sight, or ships came near there, I stood up there waving these flags without any results. Apparently, they didn't see me."

He explained to Artero what he was doing during one of his visits. Artero warned him to be careful. Japanese soldiers were now manning a coastal lookout point down the coast about a half a mile south from his hideout. Attracting their attention could bring death to himself, Artero, and his family. They were too close to liberation to not see it actually happen.

The signaling came to an end after about a week. "I was bitterly disappointed," Tweed later wrote. "Only a few miles stood between me and the United States warships and I couldn't bridge that short distance."[3]

The next plan developed by the sailor was to paddle out to a warship. He began construction of a bamboo raft. "I intended to leave the island about two or three o'clock in the morning under cover of darkness and paddle out to sea," Tweed later explained. "I thought that by daylight I could be five or six miles off the coast and be picked up by the American ships coming there that day, coming there to shell the island." The plan was loaded with risk—Tweed could be stranded at sea and an easy kill for Japanese gunners if he was not picked up by a ship. The plan was never put into action.

A young officer named John Carroll likely never met Tweed. The thirty-year-old lieutenant commander was a native of Chicago. Tweed was already a long-standing veteran sailor by the time Carroll became an officer in the late 1930s. Lieutenant Commander Carroll assumed command of the destroyer *McCall* on May 2, 1944.[4] She sailed from Pearl Harbor for the Marianas operation shortly after Carroll became commanding officer.

The ship was assigned to Task Group 58.1, one of four groups of fast aircraft carriers making up Admiral Mitscher's Fast Carrier Task Force (Task Force 58).[5] The destroyer escorted the aircraft carriers during the Battle of the Philippine Sea before retiring for a brief visit to Eniwetok. She again sailed with the carriers during a raid on Iwo Jima in early July before resuming operations in the Marianas.

The daily orders for July 10 came to *McCall* at 12:20 a.m. The ship was directed to spend the day with the destroyer *Gridley* patrolling the waters around Guam. "A pair of destroyers were to be designated daily by Commander of the Screen to operate during daylight hours for patrol, rescue purposes, and silencing of shore batteries observed on Guam only," Carroll wrote.[6]

The paths of John Carroll and George Tweed were about to cross.

A worried Artero came to see Tweed with some distressing information one day before *McCall* arrived off Guam. "On the 9th of July, on Sunday, he came to me and told me that the Japs had ordered all natives on the island, men, women, and children, into concentration camps," Tweed later said. "He asked me what he should do. I told him that I didn't want to advise him because if it turned out wrong and it cost him his life, then I would always feel responsible."[7]

Tweed asked him if there was any way his family could hide in the jungle until the Americans arrived on the island. "He said that was almost impossible unless the Americans came within a day or two because he had eight children and he could not keep them quiet and also that he would have to go out and get food for them, in which case he would probably meet Japs and they would kill him." The rumor was the Japanese announced any islanders not in the camps by 4:00 p.m. on Sunday would be shot on sight. One of the camps was set up near an airfield—certain to be a target for American bombardment. Artero worried the civilians would be killed in the process.

Tweed later recalled Artero "felt that he would be killed regardless of what he did. So I asked him if something happened that he didn't go to the concentration camp, if he would come back the next day, which would be Monday and let me know." Artero agreed to the request. "But the next day, up until very late in the evening, he had not shown up," Tweed continued. "On that day, on Monday, the American ships came there and the heavy cruisers and destroyers bombarded the island very heavily."

The lone American sailor on Guam marveled at the vast array of United States warships attacking the island. Most of the ships departed at the end of the day. However, Tweed noticed that not all the ships sailed away. He soon learned the routine. "Along in the evening after they quit and had gone back seaward two destroyers were left to circle the island and harass the Japs at night," Tweed noticed. Ships also passed close during the daytime. "Two destroyers would pass my hideout everyday as they circled the island," he later recalled.

The *McCall* and *Gridley* were operating in the area all day. The destroyers set a course for Guam early in the morning, and by 6:33 a.m., they were firing at targets of opportunity off the island's northwest coast. Most of the day was spent alternating between anti-submarine patrols and shore bombardment.

The *McCall* sent 165 rounds of five-inch gunfire into targets near Agaña just after 8:30 a.m. Lookouts spotted a fire burning ashore because of their bombardment.[8] She then transitioned into an anti-submarine patrol about six miles west of the island before returning closer to shore late in the afternoon for a resumption of bombardment duty. At 5:40 p.m., the ship was straddled by shells from a shore battery. Carroll ordered an immediate response with the five-inch main battery guns and smaller anti-aircraft weapons. "Fire was returned and battery demolished," he reported. The ship was not damaged.

The action took place south of Tweed's position. The firing from *McCall* ended just after 6:00 p.m. Tweed was back in his cave for dinner when the engagement took place. The sound of gunfire aroused his attention. He rushed out to find the ships were suddenly moving toward his hideout. "They were very close in, closer than any ships had been so far," he noticed.

"I got a new idea, so in addition to the semaphore flags, I took a small mirror up on top of the rock with me." It was nothing more than a small three-inch mirror given to him by Artero. "The sun was very low in the sky and was just in the right position to cast a good reflection back seaward from the mirror," Tweed explained. "I flashed the reflection of the sun on the bridge of the leading ship to attract their attention."

The destroyer *McCall* underway shortly after her completion in 1938. The warship served throughout the Pacific before supporting the invasion Guam—and rescuing George Tweed—in July 1944. (US Navy / Naval History & Heritage Command)

He wanted to make sure his signal was seen. "In order to make it more visible I quivered the mirror back and forth, wiggled it back and forth, so that they could see it better or so that it would be more likely to attract their attention," Tweed said. "If a light could warn and rave and weep, mine did."[9] The tactics worked perfectly. Lookouts aboard *McCall* reported seeing a heliograph at 6:20 p.m.

Fire Controlman Third Class Thomas Quinn was on the bridge of the destroyer. "And all of a sudden we saw flashing of lights," he recalled of the moment.[10] Only later did Tweed learn the sailors initially thought his mirror flashes were a Japanese gun and were getting ready to open fire. "I dropped the mirror and started waving the white flags, just in time [for] them to hold their fire," Tweed said. "I don't remember all that I told them because I was so highly elated."

The men aboard the destroyer initially did not know what to make of the signals. "Investigation showed a man trying to send us a message by semaphore," Carroll recorded in *McCall*'s war diary.[11] Quinn remembered "it was fragmentary." Tweed gave them the location of a battery of Japanese coastal guns mounted close to Agaña. He knew the invasion was very close, possible even only days away, and felt the guns could be easily knocked out by a battleship. "Finally, I asked the ship by semaphore if they would take me aboard," Tweed said. "They didn't answer, so I felt rather dejected but still continued to watch them."

The sailors aboard *McCall* began to think it might be an American. "Finally, we had the signalman come up and it was Morse Code," Quinn explained. The signalman replied by blinking light and some rudimentary communications took place. "We figured it's an American and he wants, you know, to be rescued," Quinn continued.

Sending a boat to the shore of an enemy-held island was an extremely risky undertaking. Carroll ordered a motor whaleboat, manned by a volunteer crew, to be dispatched to rescue the signal sender.[12] He later described the group as "a heavily armed volunteer landing party."

Quinn boarded the whaleboat with eight other sailors while both destroyers stayed about 2,500 yards offshore. The volunteer party did not know what to expect as the whaleboat slowly moved closer to the island. There was still the possibility it could be a Japanese trap. One thing was for certain—the next few minutes were going to be critical.

Chapter 26

THE RESCUE

THE EFFORTS TO SIGNAL AND communicate with the American
destroyer *McCall* was successful and now George Tweed was hoping
to be rescued after about two and a half years on the run. "After about
five minutes I saw them drop a boat in the water," he remembered.
"That was sufficient answer for me." Time was now critical as it was
starting to get dark. Tweed scribbled out short letter and left it in the
cave for Antonio Artero. "I hurriedly gathered up a few things that I
wanted to bring with me, some pictures that had been salvaged from
my house by natives and brought to me out in the bushes, some
notes that I had made of my observations of the war, my machete,
my pistol belt and holster and dashed down the cliff to the edge of
the water," he later recalled.[1]

The eager sailor made it down to the coastline in record time.
"By that time the boat had approached the shore and was lying to,
looking for me," Tweed explained. "I walked along the water until

I found a place where the water was deep enough so that the boat could proceed right up to where I was standing, so that I wouldn't have to swim and get my pictures and notes wet. When they saw me, they approached my location, but when about 150 feet off shore they stopped, laid to."

The stopping started a cautionary conversation between the sailor and the destroyer men and somewhat of a tug of war. "Come on in. There's plenty of water here," Tweed shouted out. The response was a definite no and a request for him to swim out. "No, I can't swim out, I've got too much gear here to swim with, there's plenty of water here, there's eight feet of water right up to where I am standing," Tweed responded. "No, we're not coming in. You leave your gear there and swim out," was the response from a voice in the whaleboat.

"I said I can't leave the gear here, because if I do the Japs will find it and they will kill the man who owns this ranch," Tweed yelled. The same response came from the boat. The destroyer men were understandably cautious. "He came down to the water's edge and we weren't sure," Thomas Quinn later remembered. "We thought it might have been a trap from the Japs trying to get us."

A breakthrough finally came. "You leave the gear there and swim out and then if you're okay we'll come in and get the gear," a sailor shouted from the boat. Tweed found the arrangement agreeable. He now understood the sailors were afraid of him and with good reason given they were off an enemy-held island. Tweed began quickly peeling off his clothes. He overheard a voice from the boat "By gosh, it looks like an American."

"By then it was getting pretty dark so none of us could see very well," Tweed continued. "I took off my clothes, jumped in the water and swam out to the boat." A group of arms reached over the side of the whaleboat when Tweed arrived at the side. "They pulled me aboard and as soon as they saw that I was an American they went back to the beach and picked up my clothes." Tweed's rescue was completed without incident. "Fortunately, the landing party was not taken under fire by the enemy," Lieutenant Commander Carroll noted.

The rescue of George Tweed from Guam was finally over. "And we got him," destroyer man Quinn simply remembered.[2] A barrage of questions followed soon after Tweed was pulled aboard the whaleboat. The sailors were astounded to find out they just rescued a man who had been on the run since the start of the war.

Tweed was worried if the sailors had any weapons in case Japanese soldiers suddenly appeared on the shore. He was comforted when he saw they were heavily armed with submachine guns. The whaleboat quickly went back to *McCall*, arriving at the destroyer's side at 7:45 p.m.[3] The boat was hoisted aboard the destroyer along with all the men inside.

Tweed was given a nudge over the side of the whaleboat and caught by a group of sailors standing on deck. The rescued sailor was ecstatic to be out of the jungle and aboard a warship. "Needless to say that I was very very happy to get back in the navy again after hiding in the buses of Guam," Tweed recalled of the moment.[4]

Carroll was there to shake Tweed's hand. "I suppose I identified myself to them," Tweed later recalled. He remembered Carroll saying, "Welcome, Mr. Tweed."[5]

The skipper accompanied the new addition down below deck where a meal was about to be served. "I got on board and was taken down to the officers' mess room where they provided me with food," Tweed said. A ham dinner with all the accompaniments was served on fine China dishes and linen. "But the first thing I reached for was a slice of bread and some butter. I'd dreamed of it for two years."[6] The years of hiding in the jungle had taken a toll on Tweed's weight. He weighed 130 pounds, down from about 170 at the start of the war.[7]

Carroll told Tweed he was very lucky. His signal was initially thought to be flashes from a Japanese gun. The destroyer was getting ready to open fire until a sailor said it looked like someone was trying to send a signal.[8] Tweed passed along information about the Japanese. "He has information as to the strength, morale, pre-landing casualties, and disposition of the enemy on Guam," Carroll later wrote. "He informed us that we conducted our bombardment and rescue within range of six-inch coastal defense batteries."[9]

Tweed was later looked over by the medical officer and found to be in good condition. He was able to take a shower—a luxury years in waiting. A new set of clothes made him feel human again. He spent time talking with various sailors—telling of his experiences on Guam and hearing about the progress of the war—and also paid a visit to the radio room.

Radioman Third Class James Mills was among the volunteer members of the rescue party. He recalled the entire group was awarded the Navy and Marine Corps Medal. "The landing party was commanded by Lieutenant Robert Harold Shaw, who was especially commended for his direction of the party," Mills said.[10] Shaw's citation noted his "heroic forceful leadership…under conditions of great personal danger from enemy fire" in completing the rescue operation.[11]

The McCall's daily duty off Guam was concluded and Carroll ordered his ship away from the island. The two destroyers departed the island waters at 7:30 p.m. for a return to voyage Task Group 58.1. The ships rejoined the formation just before midnight.[12] The morning hours found McCall steaming with the other ships about eighty-five miles southeast of Guam.[13]

She pulled up alongside the aircraft carrier Hornet, then serving as the flagship of the group. The massive size of the aircraft carrier towered over the small destroyer. Tweed was transferred to Hornet at 7:00

a.m. The group's commanding officer, Rear Admiral Joseph Clark, sent a simple one-line message back to *McCall*: "Very well done."[14]

Some of the sailors aboard the carrier were astonished to see this strange-looking man. Tweed had not shaved for a few days prior to his departure. "I can still see him when they brought him aboard," remembered Seaman First Class James Armstrong who was serving on *Hornet* at the time. "With his long hair and beard, he looked like the wild man from Borneo or something."[15]

The sight of the large group of American ships and aircraft must have been an equally astounding sight for Tweed. Task Group 58.1 was a powerful armada of frontline ships, including four aircraft carriers carrying hundreds of planes, five cruisers, and thirteen destroyers.[16] Many of the ships, including the large carriers *Hornet* and *Yorktown*, were of a new design and not in service when the war started.

Tweed marveled at the new types of planes that he was not familiar with from before the war. "Wait until you are brought up to date on new models," a sailor told him.[17] The time aboard *Hornet* was a whirlwind of endless introductions, meetings, and questioning. A chief yeoman was assigned to accompany the visiting sailor and be his guide. Tweed spoke with intelligence people, top officers, and was taken to meet with Admiral Clark.

"Where did we ever get such a big navy?" he asked the admiral. "This is only part of it," was the reply with a smile. Clark promoted Tweed to chief radioman on the spot. He was soon outfitted a new set of clothes at the admiral's expense. As a side note, Tweed later found out he did pass the chief's exam taken back in late 1941. Although the time aboard the *Hornet* was frantic, and Tweed was enjoying his new freedom, he likely was also thinking about those he left behind on Guam.

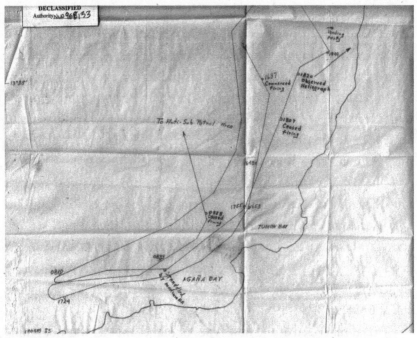

A hand-drawn map, enclosed as part of *McCall*'s action report, shows movements during the pre-invasion bombardment activities off Guam. The map includes the sighting of George Tweed's signals and launching of the rescue party on July 10, 1944. (US Navy / National Archives)

While Tweed was enjoying his newfound freedom, Artero was back on Guam trying to make sure he and his family could survive the upcoming battle. He arrived at Tweed's cave to find the sailor gone. Artero quickly found the letter Tweed wrote before departing. "A destroyer is sending in a boat to take me aboard. God bless you, my friends," Tweed wrote. The navy man was careful not to mention Artero by name in case the Japanese found the letter first. "If we live until the war is over, you will surely hear from me. Your true, life-long friend, George Tweed."[18]

Artero was subsequently warned the Japanese authorities were on his trail for helping Tweed. The occupiers were rounding up civilians ahead of the coming American invasion. He decided to go into hiding. The Artero family gathered up food and supplies and went to the very same cave used by Tweed. Once settled into the hiding place, they waited for the American liberators to arrive.

Chapter 27

GUAM PRELIMINARIES

ADMIRAL RICHARD CONOLLY WAS A colorful navy man known for thoroughness and enthusiasm. He began the war in command of the destroyer screen protecting Admiral Halsey's carriers. Conolly was transferred to the Atlantic Theater to lead the 1943 invasion of Sicily before returning to the Pacific for the Marshalls operation. He earned the nickname "Close-in Conolly" after maneuvering some battleships extremely close to shore for bombardment during one of the assaults in the Marshalls.[1] The Marianas operation found Conolly leading the Southern Attack Force. He was in tactical command of the Guam invasion using the amphibious command ship *Appalachian* as his flagship.

The admiral's counterpart on land was Marine Major General Roy Geiger. The officer's background was mostly in aviation, including becoming the fifth member of the corps to earn his wings as a naval aviator in 1917.[2] He commanded marine aviation on

Guadalcanal and was back stateside in Washington, DC, in 1943 when he rushed back to the Pacific to assume command of the invasion of Bougainville in the Solomon Islands after the unexpected death of the general who was to lead the operation.

Conolly and Geiger developed a good working relationship while planning the Guam operation. "At no time was there a conflicting opinion that was not settled to the entire satisfaction of all concerned," Geiger wrote.[3] Much of the planning took place at the general's headquarters on Guadalcanal.

The invasion plan featured two amphibious landings on the western coast of the island with the Orote Peninsula and Apra Harbor as key targets. The 3rd Marine Division was to come ashore near Asan Point—about midway between Apra Harbor and Agaña. The landing site for the 1st Provisional Marine Brigade was planned for Agat, just south of the Orote Peninsula.

Going forward, the landings near Asan will be referred to as the northern landings and those taking place close to Agat will be called the southern landings. Conolly divided his force into two smaller groups to work in the northern and southern sectors. The troops were to push inland to expand the beachheads before seizing Apra Harbor and the Orote Peninsula. The Japanese resistance was expected to be strongest around the beachhead and in the immediate surrounding areas. The ground forces were to move into the remainder of the island once the key objectives had been secured.

The invasion of Guam was originally planned to take place on June 18, a few days after the landing on Saipan. The timeline soon faced challenges. The early commitment of the floating reserve (27th Infantry Division) to the Saipan fight, coupled with the impending naval battle in the Philippine Sea, caused the postponement of the Guam portion of Operation Forager.

The transports of the Southern Attack Force, carrying soldiers of the 3rd Marine Division and 1st Provisional Marine Brigade, initially lingered in the waters east of the island in case they were needed for the Saipan battle. The ships loaded with the 3rd Marine Division eventually sailed back to Eniwetok Atoll—and its huge lagoon—in the Marshalls. At the same time, the distance reserve of the army's 77th Infantry Division set sail from Hawaii. Their arrival in the battle zone was critical before the landing on Guam could take place. The new invasion date, designated as W Day, was set for July 21.

The delay gave the navy an expanded opportunity to deliver one of the most thorough bombardments of an island to date in the Pacific. Admiral Spruance initially had hesitations about an extensive bombardment of Guam over concerns about the safety of the civilian population; after all, it was an American territory. He relented on the condition of developing a plan to target only Japanese positions and strongpoints.

Conolly was meeting with Admiral Turner in his sea cabin aboard *Rocky Mount* at the time. He decided to make the plan himself. He left the cabin, climbed down the ladder, climbed back up, and re-entered the cabin. "I have the fellow, Kelly," he told Turner, "and his name is Conolly."[4]

The Southern Attack Force included two groups of support ships for bombardment and local air support. Task Group 53.5 was the Southern Fire Support Group of three battleships, three cruisers, and twelve destroyers under the command of Rear Admiral Walden Ainsworth. The composition of the force changed as ships rotated between Guam, Saipan, and forward bases in the Marshalls. The Carrier Support Group (Task Group 53.7) included five small escort carriers equipped with fighters and bombers for use around and over Guam.

Admiral Richmond Kelly Turner was the overall amphibious commander
for the Marianas operation. The admiral is shown aboard Rocky Mount
off Saipan on June 17, 1944. (US Navy / National Archives)

The island was thus far only targeted by navy ships once—on
June 16—just before the initial invasion date was postponed. The
bombardment resumed at 12:20 p.m. on July 8 by a group of cruisers and destroyers under the command of Rear Admiral Turner Joy
in the heavy cruiser *Wichita*. The warships were supported by planes
from the escort carriers.[5] The island remained under regular bombardment until W-Day on July 21 with ships of all types shuffling in
and out of the surrounding waters. There was typically at least one
battleship on station every day. Conolly arrived off Guam on July 14
with a task force composed of his flagship *Appalachian*, battleship
Colorado, and four destroyers.

Admiral Ainsworth was a veteran of naval battles in the Solomon Islands and likely had no qualms about moving his ships close to shore to plaster the Japanese defenses on Guam. He arrived off the island with two cruisers and some destroyers on July 17. Much of the activity was focused on the western side of Guam. The operations included smaller ships making close reconnaissance of various beaches.

Conolly took an active role in overseeing what he termed the "softening up" period of bombardments before the invasion. Aerial reconnaissance photos were taken every day by carrier planes or land-based aircraft from Saipan. The film was air dropped to the *Appalachian* for development. "A target board composed of officers from the gunnery, air, and intelligence sections and a representative of the [landing force] was engaged in evaluating all reports of the bombardments and air strikes together with information from frequent photo interpretation," Conolly later wrote. "This board made up a daily list of profitable targets together with their priorities for assignment to Bombardment and Support Units."[6] The tempo of the bombardment increased as W-Day approached, with much emphasis placed on the landing beaches and inland areas immediately behind.

The heavy cruiser *Indianapolis*, with Admiral Spruance aboard, arrived off Orote Point with two escorting destroyers at 7:15 a.m. on July 20.[7] The small force steamed over from Saipan and reported for duty with the on-site commander. The cruiser contributed some eight-inch gunfire to the bombardment on the day before the invasion. Even Conolly's flagship *Appalachian* directed fire toward a target near Asan Point for twenty-five minutes during the late afternoon.[8]

The diaries of Japanese soldiers on Guam provide a glimpse of what life was like on the receiving end of the massive bombardment. Private First Class Teruo Kurokawa wrote, "the bombardment was almost unendurable."[9] Some openly wondered why the Combined

Fleet had not arrived. An army lieutenant wrote, "Our positions have been almost completed but have not been done as we had hoped… great effort was put into the construction, but we still have been unable to complete the cover. We are in a terrible fix."[10]

A critical step in the preparation for the landings was the arrival of the navy's Underwater Demolition Teams about a week ahead of the invasion date. The teams were developed in the aftermath of the bloody assault on Tarawa. They were responsible for reconnaissance of the invasion beaches and removal of any obstructions—natural or those placed by the Japanese. Beginning at sundown on July 17, these frogmen moved in close to the designated beaches to destroy any submerged obstacles with explosives to clear the way for the amphibious forces. The dangerous work was often completed under heavy cover fire from nearby warships.

The obstacles destroyed included palm log cribs filled with coral, barbed wire, and wire cages filled with cemented coral. A total of 640 obstructions were demolished off the beaches at Asan and about 300 at Agat, where some appeared to have been recently constructed.[11] Conolly noted the work of the underwater teams "exceeded that contemplated for the operation. The work of the teams was an inspiration for the entire task force."

Of all the resources available in the American arsenal at the time of the Guam invasion, there were two vehicles worthy of special highlight due to the important roles in the impending operation. The job of getting the assault troops safely to the beach would be done by an amphibious vehicle fated to become closely associated with the Pacific War. Officially designated as Landing Vehicle Tracked, or LTV in the alphabet soup list of American landing craft names, the part tank/part landing craft vehicle was better known as an amphibious tractor, or more simply, as the Amtrac.

The design was based on the "alligator" amphibious vehicle man-ufactured by the American Food Machinery Corporation for rescue work in Florida swamps.[12] Adapted for military use, the Amtracs were tracked vehicles, operated by gasoline engines, capable of operating in the water or on land. Small paddles on the tracks made movement through water possible. The tracks allowed the Amtracs to climb over obstructing reefs (a critical issue in many island invasions), drive through small obstructions, and crawl up beaches with armor pro-tecting the passengers. The vehicles measured twenty-five feet long by just over ten feet wide, weighed twenty-three thousand pounds, and carried twenty men. A small crew drove the craft and manned several machine guns. Larger landing craft often transported troops to a mid-point where they transferred to Amtracs for the final voyage to the beach.

Once ashore, the soldiers were to be supported by an awesome assortment of weapons, including artillery, mortars, bazookas, heavy machine guns, and the medium M4 Sherman tank. Over 50,000 Shermans were built during World War II.[13] The tank played a promi-nent role in providing mobile firepower for infantry in all theaters of the war. The armored vehicle was manned by a crew of five, armed with a seventy-five-millimeter cannon and three machine guns, and capable of a sustained speed of twenty-five miles per hour. The Sherman more than outclassed the smaller Japanese tanks on Guam.

The Japanese defense of Guam was led by Lieutenant General Takeshi Takashina. Little is known about the general's background other than he served in Manchuria before deployment to the Marianas in early 1944.[14] Also on the island was the commander of the Japanese 31st Army, Lieutenant General Hideyoshi Obata, who became stranded on Guam while trying to return to Saipan from Palau. Although Obata was the senior leader, he delegated the defense planning and actual leadership in battle to Takashina.

The forces available to Takashina numbered about 18,500 troops composed of the 29th Division, assorted independent army units, and various naval guard forces. The Japanese soldiers were supported by a few dozen tanks and a variety of coastal defense guns, field artillery, and anti-aircraft guns. American submarine attacks prevented the garrison from ballooning to a force of about 35,000 troops and more than a hundred tanks.[15]

The Japanese completed the airfield on the Orote Peninsula once planned by the Americans. The 3,600-foot runway made of coral and concrete became operational in January 1944. A second runway was constructed east of Agaña. A third was started, though never completed, near Dededo in the north-central part of the island.[16] Airpower on Guam was largely destroyed by American carrier planes during the preliminaries of the Philippine Sea battle. There were no naval forces available to the defenders.

The Japanese strategy to defend Guam was essentially the same as the battle plan on Saipan. The emphasis was to meet the invaders at the beaches. The defenders were to launch an organized counterattack if the Americans were able to push ashore and then fall back to the hills if all else failed.[17] The flawed strategy of placing strong forces at the beach significantly ignored the American strength of pre-invasion bombardments. A similar strategy largely failed a month earlier at Saipan.[18]

Defensive fortifications stretched across a large portion of the west coast from the Orote Peninsula to Tumon Bay northeast of Agaña, including underwater obstacles, concealed artillery positions, trenches, and bunkers. The extra month's delay in the invasion gave the Japanese more time to prepare—sufficient time to allow the defenders to install most of their coastal defense guns.

Takashina's defenders would be outnumbered more than two to one by the invading forces; his soldiers had to defend an island about double the size of Saipan with less men. He would likely not be able to stop the invaders, although the forces were enough to put up a strong fight. The general established defensive sectors and dispersed his troops around the island.

Takashina redeployed most of his assets in mid-June, stationing soldiers at the seaside fortifications, on the Orote Peninsula, and as part of a mobile reserve stationed in the central part of Guam. The general initially believed the Americans would land at Tumon Bay.[19] The location featured a wide beach spanning about two and a half miles. He learned the probable target beaches were actually at Asan and Agat in early July.[20]

Every Japanese soldier, sailor, and airman was deeply ingrained in the concept of total sacrifice for the emperor—surrender was forbidden. The belief was based on the Code of Bushido or the Way of the Warrior and originated with samurai warriors in feudal Japan.[21] Like so many other island battles, Guam was to be a fight to the death.

The day of July 20 ended with Conolly and his staff optimistic of the impending invasion set to begin the next morning. The forecast was for good weather conditions. The naval and air bombardments were believed to have caused extensive damage to the defenders. Some American officers thought the bombardment was so complete that only token resistance would occur once the assault started. Those overly optimistic beliefs proved to be far from reality. The Japanese defenses were not eliminated by the bombardment, and the marines were about to face a fierce fight for the island.

Marines and sailors attend a church service aboard a coast guard–manned transport on the eve of the Guam invasion. The initial landings took place in two locations on July 21, 1944. (US Navy / National Archives)

Chapter 28

GUAM INVASION

THE THUNDEROUS ROAR OF FOURTEEN-INCH guns on the battle-ship *New Mexico* sounded at 5:33 a.m. on July 21 to mark the start of W-Day on Guam. A stream of 1,500-pound shells went hurling toward land every time the battleship's main battery cannons roared. The shells spread a path of destruction across the invasion beach and surrounding area.

The *New Mexico* was just one of a powerful group of warships—including five battleships—positioned to support the landings on Guam. "The preliminary naval bombardment was an outstanding feature of the assault," General Geiger wrote. "Postponement of W-Day and the availability of supporting ships permitted the period of the preliminary bombardment to be greatly extended."[1]

All various naval units were in position around the island by 6:00 a.m., including Admiral Conolly aboard *Appalachian*. The transports carrying the assault troops assembled in designated areas off the northern and southern landing zones under the cover of darkness.

At 6:15 a.m., twenty-six planes from the carrier *Wasp*, a mixture of fighters and bombers, arrived over Guam to provide a roving patrol. A continuous stream of planes from various carriers flew over the island throughout the morning to support the landings.

The northern landing zone was a 2,500-yard stretch of beach wedged between two points of land jutted out into the sea—Asan Point and Adelup Point (known as the "devil's horns")—about halfway between Apra Harbor and Agaña. Marines aboard the transports were up early for what had now become a traditional invasion day breakfast of steak and eggs. Many of the men made last-minute checks of their weapons and gear while nervously waiting for the operation to start. The drone of planes flying over at mast-head height and the booming guns of the fire support ships made for a dizzying scene of action—a mixture of anticipation and sheer terror.

The fourteen-inch main battery guns of the battleship *New Mexico* fire during the pre-invasion bombardment of Guam. The photo was taken on July 18, 1944—three days before the invasion. (US Navy / National Archives)

The voice of Geiger suddenly sounded on loudspeakers aboard the transports. "You have been honored," he said in a final message to the troops. "The eyes of the nation watch you as you go into battle to liberate this former American bastion from the enemy," he said in part.[2] Small landing craft bobbed in the water off the sides of the transports. The assault troops began going over the rail and climbing down cargo nets hanging out over the side of the transport. Not an easy task as each soldier was weighed down by about forty pounds of gear plus the weight of their weapons.

The dawn ushered in the start of a clear day with a calm sea and light surf. The landing craft were to ferry the troops from the transport area to an outlying reef where Amtracs were waiting to take the men on the final run to shore. Four beaches—labeled Blue, Green, Red 1, and Red 2—were the destination for thousands of soldiers of the 3rd Marine Division.

American landing craft unloading off the northern beaches during the Guam invasion. The photo was taken near Asan Point on July 21, 1944. (US Navy / National Archives)

An intensive hourlong bombardment from air and sea began at 7:15 a.m. The terrific pounding included 312 carrier planes dropping 124 tons of bombs on the landing beaches and surrounding area.[3] The naval gunnery was carefully orchestrated to not interfere with the aerial bombing.

The landing took place in waves. Smoke and haze hung over the invasion beaches from the heavy bombardment as the first wave of craft moved toward the shore. Leading the way was a line of landing craft, modified for fire support, unleashing a barrage of rockets and gunfire at the shoreline. Next came a wave of amphibious tanks firing their guns ahead of the assault troops. An observation plane above used parachute flares to signal to the support ships the location of the approaching landing craft.

A series of steep hills, partially covered with jungle growth and caves, dominated the landscape behind the target beaches. There were some dry rice paddies not far from the beach. The terrain allowed the defenders to move men and guns forward into the prepared positions—at least to those sites surviving the bombardment. The high ground of Fonte Plateau was positioned further inland behind the beachhead area. General Takashina's headquarters was hidden behind the plateau. He started assembling reserve forces behind Fonte Plateau once the invasion was underway.

The towering Chonito Cliff dominated the left side of the landing beaches and featured a complex network of cave defenses. The high ground allowed the defenders a commanding view of the beaches and gave them the ability to pour mortar and artillery fire onto the low land below. The Amtracs slowly plodded toward land as shells splashed in the water all around. Some of the approaching craft suffered direct hits.

The first marines were on the beach at 8:29 a.m. The initial group was followed by successive waves of men throughout the morning hours.[4] "The unloading of ships was very effectively accomplished in the face of difficult reef and beach conditions," Geiger wrote.

Two US officers plant the American flag on Guam eight minutes after the first troops landed on the island. The exact location of the photo is unknown. (US Marines / National Archives)

Once ashore, the marines were in a difficult situation—wedged between the sea and high ground beyond the beaches. A group of tanks, landing about forty minutes later, provided cover fire as troops on Blue Beach swiftly advanced across dry rice paddies to take a ridge behind. The fast movement may have caught the Japanese defenders off guard. Taking the ridge secured the rice paddies, a designated location for artillery guns to move in and set up.[5]

Twenty-three-year-old Marine Lieutenant Jack Eddy, a St. Louis, Missouri native, was among the soldiers headed for the beaches. His platoon was crammed aboard a small Higgins land craft moving from the transport to the outlying reefs. "Some guys were on the bottom of the boat on their hands and knees throwing up; and then there are other guys cracking jokes," Eddy later recalled.[6] About 1,000 yards from the beach, out of range of many Japanese guns, the men transferred to Amtracs for transportation over the reefs and to the beach.

The situation worsened as Eddy's Amtrac approached land. "There were tractors being hit, being swamped," he later said. "We had some near misses with some big stuff...there were explosions in the water around us, but we made it to shore without being hit." The original destination, Green Beach, was clogged with marines, causing Eddy's platoon to be shifted to another beach.

Once ashore, Eddy was thrown into the violent and chaotic battle, on the beachhead and during the subsequent advancement of about 1,500 yards inland. He saw death firsthand. "Things happen... that's it...things happen, and there's nothing you can do about it," he later said. "People should look at it and say, realize it's supposed to happen. It's war. People kill each other in war."

Marines under the command of Lieutenant Colonel Ralph Houser rushed toward Chonito Cliff, despite suffering heavy losses. They were trying to wrestle control of the key high ground away from the Japanese. "Nearly half my old company lies dead on the barren slopes of Chonito Cliff," wrote Private First Class Cyril O'Brien, a marine war correspondent. "Four times they tried to reach the top. Four times they were thrown back." The exhausted men were advancing inch by inch. "They attacked up a 60-degree slope, protected only by sword grass, and were met by a storm of grenades and heavy rifle, machine-gun, and mortar fire."[7]

Flamethrowers and tanks later assisted by pouring fire directly into enemy caves and strongpoints. Houser committed his reserve units to the fight and the cliff was under American control by noon. Thousands of marines were ashore, along with all their field artillery, by the end of the first day. The marines captured additional high ground to expand the beachhead.

The beaches in the southern landing zone were bordered by Bangi Point, a small promontory of low elevation jutting out into the sea on the south and the town of Agat on the north. The landing was carried out in similar fashion as in the north, including a tremendous pre-invasion bombardment. The terrain in the area was mostly low hills and open ground, more favorable for the attackers than in the north. The abundance of open space gave the Americans room to maneuver and bring heavy firepower to the defenders. The initial assault was carried out by the 1st Provisional Marine Brigade.

The southern area was defended by Japanese infantry using a series of trenches and strongpoints. The marines came under fire as soon as the landing vehicles began approaching the beach. Small arms, machine guns, and cannon shells rained down on the attackers from a well-concealed Japanese position at Gaan Point in the approximate middle of the landing zone. A concrete blockhouse, with a four-foot-thick roof, somehow escaped targeting in the bombardment.[8] The guns on Gaan Point were thought to have knocked out nine landing craft.[9]

The marines were able to rapidly advance despite stiff Japanese resistance and were about 1,000 yards inland by 10:34 a.m., allowing for tanks and reserves to start coming ashore. A group of tanks and infantry knocked out the Gaan Point stronghold with an attack from the undefended rear. The marines then went about systematically destroying bypassed Japanese positions. Army soldiers of the 77th Infantry Division began coming ashore later in the day.

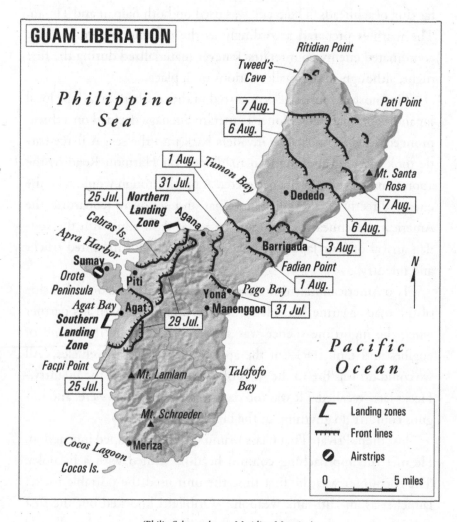

GUAM LIBERATION

Philippine Sea

Ritidian Point

Tweed's Cave

7 Aug.

6 Aug.

Pati Point

1 Aug.

Tumon Bay

31 Jul.

25 Jul. **Northern Landing Zone**

Cabras Is.

Agana

Dededo

▲ Mt. Santa Rosa

7 Aug.

6 Aug.

Barrigada

3 Aug.

Apra Harbor

Sumay

Orote Peninsula

Piti

Fadian Point

1 Aug.

Agat Bay

Southern Landing Zone

Agat

Yona

Manenggon

Pago Bay

31 Jul.

29 Jul.

Facpi Point

25 Jul.

▲ Mt. Lamlam

Talofofo Bay

Pacific Ocean

N

▲ Mt. Schroeder

Cocos Lagoon

Meriza

Cocos Is.

⌐ Landing zones

Front lines

⊘ Airstrips

0   5 miles

(Philip Schwartzberg - Meridian Mapping)

The Americans held two beachheads on Guam at the end of W-Day. The invaders were well-versed in the Japanese strategy of counterattacking beachheads. The tactic was used on both Saipan and Tinian. The marines prepared accordingly as the evening arrived. A large coordinated enemy counterattack never materialized during the first night, although some smaller actions took place.

The most serious attacks occurred in the southern area. The local Japanese commander Colonel Tsunetaro Suenaga decided on a three-pronged attack to push the invaders back into the sea. A fierce battle took place at an American roadblock on Harmon Road in the approximate center of the perimeter. A breakthrough would take the enemy directly to the village of Agat and seriously jeopardize the American beachhead. The attack began at 2:30 a.m. with the sudden arrival of four Japanese tanks followed by gun-mounted trucks and infantry.

Two American machine guns were set up with one on either side of the road. Marine Mel Heckt was manning one with his partner when the nighttime silence was suddenly broken by the sound of engines and tank tracks of the approaching Japanese vehicles. "All we could do was fire to the sides of them to keep back the infantry," Heckt later recalled. "It was too dark to see where they were, and our guns couldn't do anything to the tanks."[10]

Just then, Private First Class Bruno Oribiletti jumped into action. He met the approaching column head-on armed with a bazooka. The encounter was the first time the unit used the portable rocket launcher as an anti-tank weapon.[11] Oribiletti knocked out the first two Japanese tanks before return fire killed him. The delay allowed enough time for a group of American Sherman tanks to arrive on the scene and destroy the remaining enemy vehicles. The discouraged Japanese soldiers retreated.

The Americans were fortunate Takashina had no detailed plans for massive counterattacks during the first night. The general missed out on what might have been his best chance to inflict heavy casualties before the beachheads were substantially expanded and turn the tide of the invasion.[12] The American troops began to expand both beachheads the next day.

Marines in the northern zone met stiff resistance while attacking high ground through a rough landscape. Veterans from Guadalcanal said it was the worst terrain they ever encountered.[13] They ultimately succeeded in clearing out the Japanese from various ridges and strongpoints while suffering high casualties. Troops on the right flank of the beachhead seized the Piti Navy Yard and Cabras Island. The American territory was enlarged, and yet gaps remained in the lines.

The beachhead in the south expanded with the marines pushing inland. The full 77th Infantry Division landed with many of the soldiers having to wade ashore due to the shortage of landing vehicles. The army soldiers harmoniously operated with the marines and there were no major issues between the two services. Moving north from Agat allowed the invaders to seal off the entrance to the Orote Peninsula and trap about 2,500 Japanese remaining on the finger of land. The American forces from the north and south sectors first came in contact with each other at the base of the peninsula.

Chapter 29

GENERAL TAKASHINA'S COUNTERATTACK

GENERAL TAKASHINA WAS READY TO strike after several days of planning and redeploying his soldiers. He decided on the night of July 25–26, five nights after the initial landing. His plan was for a major counterattack in the northern sector to split marine positions before attacking the divided units. His men on the high ground were using high-powered binoculars, strong enough to see the facial features of individual marines below, to carefully study the American positions looking for gaps.[1] A coordinated assault was to be delivered by the men trapped on the Orote Peninsula. The counterattack was to be an all-out effort. The subsequent events are often considered to be the climactic battle for Guam.

The night found the units of the 3rd Marine Division defending a 9,000-yard frontline of difficult terrain and with few available reserves.[2] It was a firm, although somewhat precarious, position with various breaks in the American lines. The night was to feature a range of actions from the Japanese, including suicidal charges, sharp thrusts, infiltration tactics, high courage, and fanaticism.[3]

Marines were huddled under ponchos in their foxholes as a steady rain fell during the night. Some Japanese activity was noted during the last hours of July 25. Enemy troops began infiltrating and snooping at various points along the line around midnight to locate gaps and weak points. Cannon and mortar fire began to rain down on the left side of the marines' line during the night.

Occasionally, groups of Japanese troops rushed forward in a frantic attack as the enemy continued to probe for weak points. Desperate hand-to-hand combat broke out at various times. "It was the last stand of the second platoon," Marine Corporal Charles Moore said of the fight in his sector. "There were three attacks that night and by the third there was nobody left to fight, so they broke through. They came in droves throwing hand grenades and hacked up some of our platoons."[4]

The attack was bad timing for marine Jack Eddy's platoon. They fought an uphill battle on a slope for much of the day and were looking forward to some rest. Their position was on top of Fonte Plateau. "There we were, pretty beaten up and exhausted," he recalled of the night. The men were suddenly faced with an onrush of enemy soldiers. "Our problem was that there weren't that many of us. They came in a big group and we were spread out. A group of fifty would hit a spot where there were only seven or eight people—you're convinced that they're going to run right over you," he said.

The marines were quickly locked in a life-or-death struggle. "It was the most traumatic experience I ever had, it will live in my memory forever," Eddy continued. "I had expected to be in battle, but never anything like this. When you think about fighting, you think that you're 100 yards away, but this was pretty gruesome, fighting them from 20 feet away and they're running all around you and screaming."[5]

Private Frank Chuisano was dug in further west on the line. The New York City native and his fellow marines watched as an occasional Japanese illumination flare exploded in the sky. "We were beat—we were all trying to get some rest," Chuisano remembered. "Then a flare went up again, and like all of a sudden, I saw them. They were there, in front of us." When another marine shouted in fear they were going die, Chuisano could only tell him to keep shooting. The stream of enemy soldiers kept coming. "They crawled, they climbed over their dead. They were all on top of each other, two, three high," he continued.[6]

What seemed to be the main Japanese thrust began at about 4:00 a.m. slightly to the left of the perimeter center. A determined enemy attack overran a thinly defended portion of the line. Another breakthrough took place farther to the right where a group of Japanese moved through a gap to take a hill behind the frontline and began attacking a marine command post. A hastily assembled force of cooks, bakers, clerks, and mess attendants held off the attackers while a patrol attacked the Japanese from behind.

A group of about fifty Japanese soldiers, some heavily loaded with demolition charges, broke through the frontline and pushed all the way through to a field hospital in the rear area. Medical personnel quickly evacuated the most seriously wounded men. The walking wounded, clad in underwear and pajamas, banded together with an assortment of behind-the-lines personnel—including medical staffers and corpsmen—to defend the hospital with any weapons they could find. Some wounded fired right from their cots in the tents.[7] Sixteen Japanese were felled near the surgery tent alone, attesting to how close the hospital came to be overrun by the enemy.

Two companies of pioneers, under the command of a training officer, were quickly assembled at the beach. The pioneers served as the marine shore party and were typically responsible for unloading landing craft and moving supplies—not as frontline soldiers.[8] The ragtag force at the hospital were able to hold off the Japanese attackers until the pioneers arrived in force to chase the enemy away.

Artillery and naval gunfire hit enemy troop concentrations behind the frontlines and thwarted Japanese efforts to reinforce the counterattack.[9] Daylight on the morning of July 26 allowed the marines in the northern sector to begin the process of clearing out the remaining Japanese stragglers. Only later was the true scope of the attack realized. The Japanese appeared to have used more troops in the Guam counterattack than in the giant banzai charge on Saipan.[10]

A similar scenario played out in the southern area. Intermittent rain showers hid the final preparations of the Japanese for the attack from the Orote Peninsula. They were apparently using Guam as a liquor distribution hub for the whole Central Pacific area.[11] Marines in frontline positions reported hearing yelling, laughter, and the breaking of bottles as the enemy emptied their supply of sake.

A suicide charge of drunk Japanese began just before midnight. Many members of the horde were navy personnel armed with an assortment of weapons, ranging from rifles and pitchforks to bats and broken bottles. The attackers were led by sword-swinging officers. They rushed through mangrove swamps toward the frontline and immediately drew the attention of American forward lookouts. One drunken officer was later reported to have attacked an American tank with a sword.[12]

The marines opened fire with a fusillade of cannon, mortar, machine gun, and small arms fire. Pack Howitzers were quickly moved close to the frontlines to fire at point blank range. "Arms and legs flew like snowflakes," an American lieutenant commented. "Japs ran amuck. They screamed in terror until they died."[13] Occasional flares revealed the dizzying scene of the drunken attackers reeling about near the forward positions, falling into fox holes, and aimlessly throwing hand grenades.[14]

At least three waves of attackers lunged toward the American lines. The Japanese who made it through the barrage were fought off by the marines in close-quarter fighting. Some enemy survivors of a failed charge fled back to the swamp where they were later wiped out by artillery fire. The American lines held throughout the night. Morning light revealed about 400 Japanese bodies sprawled about on the ground.[15] The breakout from the Orote Peninsula failed and the Japanese still trapped on the finger of land were isolated and doomed.

The American lines did not suffer a wholesale collapse in either sector as Takashina had hoped. Survivors of the attack in the northern area began arriving at the general's headquarters shortly after dawn providing grim firsthand reports of the disaster. He quickly grasped the scope of the catastrophe.

The Japanese lost a sizable number of men, including some of their best soldiers and a large number of weapons in the attacks. Losses were particularly heavy among frontline officers—as much as 95 percent for some of the units involved in the counterattack. Numerous companies were down to just a few men.[16] About 3,500 Japanese were estimated to have been killed during the action on both fronts. The marines reported 166 men killed and an additional 645 wounded during the fighting.[17]

Both Chuisano and Eddy survived the night of terror in the northern area. Eddy remembered hearing about the staggering number of Japanese who were killed. Eighty dead bodies were counted in front of one of his machine gun positions. "I was just a platoon leader," he later recalled. "I was doing what I was supposed to be doing—I kept my men together and we stayed in the battle."

General Geiger came ashore at about 1:00 p.m. on July 26. He established a command post and assumed direct control of the land operations. The American flag was hoisted above his headquarters the next day.[18]

Takashina understood there were no reinforcements coming to Guam. His offensive capability was largely destroyed in the failed counterattack. He concluded there was no hope to expel the Americans from the island. His only viable option was to retreat with the remaining troops to the rugged northern half of the island and inflict as many casualties on the Americans as possible.

The general met with his staff on the morning of July 27 to review the existing operational plans. A defensive line was to be established across the middle part of the island stretching from Dededo to Barrigada with strongpoints further north around Mount Santa Rosa. Takashina issued orders for his scattered troops to begin the move north. A contingent of soldiers was left behind to fight a rearguard action. The directive was to be the last order he ever gave.

Chapter 30

AMERICAN DRIVE

THE AMERICAN FORCES IN THE southern sector were ready to go on the offensive on the morning of July 26. The troops held the line in the face of the Japanese counterattack the previous night. The arrival of additional troops allowed for a rotation on the frontlines. The soldiers of the 77th Infantry Division relived the marines manning the beachhead perimeter. The marines then launched a drive to dispel the remaining enemy from the Orote Peninsula and seize control of the airfield.

The terrain on the peninsula favored the defenders with the only entry point from the main part of the island requiring the attackers to pass through a constricted area. The low and dense ground vegetation was highly adaptable for the defenders to create concealed positions—a trademark of the Japanese tactics.[1] The enemy had ample time to prepare in-depth defensive positions throughout the peninsula. The Japanese soldiers trapped on Orote attempted a breakout as part of the failed counterattack. They only tried one other move—escape by the sea. A small number of barges full of soldiers put to sea from Sumay during the later afternoon of July 25. The foray into Apra Harbor, presumably to land behind the lines in the northern section, was immediately stopped by American artillery.

The American assault began with a thunderous barrage from army and marine artillery. Planes, naval ships, and anti-aircraft guns on Cabras Island across Apra Harbor combined to pound the Japanese positions.[2] Two separate groups of marines moved out to attack the left and right sides of the peninsula.

Dense underbrush and Japanese counter fire initially slowed the American advance while the soldiers moved through the dangerous narrow base of the peninsula. The attack continued the next day with marines on the right side the peninsula advancing toward the airfield against light resistance, while those on left were pinned down and suffering heavy casualties. The Japanese were dug in around the old marine barracks and rifle range. The defenses included an assortment of trenches and pillboxes. American tanks helped propel a surge forward. A total of twelve Japanese tanks were knocked out early in the fighting.

The enemy defenses began to break down late in the day on July 27 when a lone Japanese officer attacked a tank with his sword and another carrying a large battle flag led a group of soldiers to annihilation after marching directly in heavy American fire. Smaller groups of enemy soldiers, often numbering about a dozen, flung themselves forward in futile attacks. The various actions were more suicidal than any form of an organized counterattack.[3] The Japanese later abandoned their frontline position and began haphazardly running away—a rare happening in the Pacific War.[4] It was the turning point in the battle for Orote.

The marines continued to advance and were soon in control of the former barracks, rifle range, and the town of Sumay. The combined tank-infantry drive continued to push the defenders toward the end of the peninsula. When a platoon of army tanks, accompanied by some marine infantry, pushed to the outer tip of the peninsula, they only found two Japanese soldiers still alive.

The occasional sounds of booming artillery and sporadic small arms fire were in the background when a group Americans solemnly gathered at the skeletal remains of the former marine barracks on the afternoon of July 29. The group included high-ranking officers such as Admiral Spruance, General Smith, and General Geiger. They were joined by an assortment of lower-ranking officers and regular soldiers. At 3:30 p.m., a marine sounded "To the Colors" on a captured Japanese bugle as a United States flag was raised on the flagpole. Marine Brigadier General Lemuel Shepherd delivered a short message. "On this hallowed ground, you officers and men of the 1st Marine Brigade have avenged the loss of our comrades who were overcome by the numerically superior enemy three days after Pearl Harbor. Under our flag this island again stands ready to fulfill its destiny as an American fortress in the Pacific."[5]

The American flag raised was very different than the one lowered in defeat about two and a half years ago. It represented a nation seeking revenge and driving across the Pacific toward Japan. A nation with a navy so powerful, the force likely was beyond the imagination of Captain McMillin, his tiny garrison, and George Tweed back in 1941.[6]

The Orote area was declared secured on the early evening of July 29. Minor mopping-up operations continued the next day. Only a few remaining Japanese servicemen were found. A platoon of American soldiers was sent to investigate Fort Santa Cruz. They found six dead Japanese and took two live prisoners.

The marines wasted little time in getting the newly captured airfield operational. Engineering units quickly arrived to work on the runway. The first plane—a Navy TBF Avenger—landed about six hours later.[7] Additional planes quickly arrived, giving the Americans an operational airfield on Guam. What was commonly considered one of the best defensive positions on Guam was now under American control. An estimated 2,500 Japanese perished on the Orote Peninsula. The United States suffered 115 killed and 721 wounded in the operation.[8]

The first week on Guam for the Americans saw two successful landings, expanded beachhead perimeters, furious Japanese counterattacks beaten back, and the Orote Peninsula secured. The string of events concluded the assault phase of the Guam operation. Geiger now focused on securing the rest of the island.

Geiger suspected most of the remaining enemy was moving north. An established road system allowed for the movement of heavy equipment and the rugged terrain allowed the enemy to slip away to create strongpoints. The general could not discount the possibility of some Japanese soldiers moving to the southern part of the island, most likely only small numbers of soldiers with light infantry weapons. The terrain in the south also favored the defenders. However, the road system was far less numerous and many of the roads—not suitable for the movements of large numbers of troops and vehicles at any time—were often impassable for motorized traffic during the heavy rains of July and August.

The southern part of the island was mountainous and full of dense jungle foliage. Captured documents suggested the Japanese unit stationed in the south—the 10th Independent Mixed Regiment—had already moved north.[9] Aerial reconnaissance proved inconclusive; the thick jungle could easily conceal troop concentrations and hide movements.[10] Geiger needed to know the enemy's disposition in the south. Any sizable force could threaten the flank of the American advance north. The only viable option was a ground reconnaissance. The task fell to the 77th Infantry Division.

A total of five patrols, each consisting of five soldiers and a Guamanian guide, were assembled for the operation. The groups were to move south and east looking for any sign of the Japanese. The mission was a dangerous undertaking with the patrols lacking the usual advantage of numbers and firepower. Each group was to report in by radio every few hours and could call for artillery support if needed.

All the patrols departed on the morning on July 28. One group turned back after two soldiers and the guide were beset with fever. Another patrol moved east to the area around Ylig Bay. They only encountered a few Japanese and stayed out of their way. The group stayed overnight in a cave overlooking the eastern coast before returning to the American lines the next day. They encountered numerous Guamanians—some were surprised to see the Americans in the interior so soon after the invasion. They told of only small bands of Japanese, and in some cases, just individual soldiers, roaming through the area.[11]

The three remaining patrols ventured further south. Two reached the slopes of Mount Lamlan and turned back after encountering rifle fire. The third continued south to the coastal village of Umatac. They returned north on the coastal road and reported no sign of the enemy.

Two additional patrols set out on July 30 with one going east and the other moving far to the south. Both reported no Japanese contact. The patrols confirmed Geiger's assumption—the main concentration of the enemy retreated north. He was now free to pursue the Japanese.

Takashina and his chief of staff left their command post shortly after issuing the order for the retreat north. They were in the vicinity of Mount Macajna, possibly rallying soldiers to move, when spotted by an American tank.[12] A stream of machine gun bullets from the tank killed the general.

Tactical command of the remaining Japanese forces on Guam fell to General Obata. He reported the results of the failed counterattack to Imperial Headquarters in Tokyo. The general noted "our forces failed to achieve the desired objectives, losing more than 80% of the personnel, for which I sincerely apologize."[13] The Imperial leaders urged the defense of Guam to continue as long as possible.

Obata decided to keep Takashina's withdrawal and defensive plans intact. He was facing a desperate situation with a dwindling number of men and resources. His largest concentration of forces was in the area east of the northern beachhead. The numbers included about 1,000 infantry men, 800 naval soldiers, 2,500 service and support troops, an artillery unit down to six cannons, and two complete tank companies.[14] Thousands more Japanese were scattered around various locations on the island. Some would eventually join the units moving north. His battered forces began an organized move north across the island's middle section on July 30.

The retreating Japanese moved into defensive positions beginning near Tumon Bay and stretching southeast. A second line was prepared further northeast close to the village of Ipapao. A final last stand was to take place around Mount Santa Rosa if both lines fell. Obata moved to a new command post at Mount Mataguac, just west of Mount Santa Rosa. A hastily formed unit, composed mostly of naval personnel and laborers, was assembled on August 1 and began work immediately on establishing positions in the Mount Santa Rosa area—including dummy positions to fool he Americans.[15]

The same strategy—retreat to the island's interior—was effectively used by the Japanese defenders in Saipan. However, Obata had less troops to work with on a bigger island and most of his best soldiers were lost in the failed counterattack. The odds were stacked against him, but the general was determined to make the final capture of Guam as painful as possible for the Americans.

Chapter 31

MOVING NORTH

THE MEN OF THE 77TH Infantry Division and the 3rd Marine Division spent much of July 29–30 resting and adjusting their lines. The units dispatched patrols to survey the enemy situation near the fronts. The latter included the small army teams sent to reconnoiter the southern part of the island.

General Geiger was ready to pursue the retreating Japanese. He knew the rugged territory of northern Guam favored the defenders. Although aware of the general route of the Japanese retreat, he was not entirely certain where his advancing troops would meet strong resistance. The main fighting was likely to take place somewhere in the fifteen-mile long by five-to-eight-mile wide area in the northern portion of the island. Mount Santa Rosa was to be the likely location of a big fight. A large amount of supplies had been accumulated back on the beaches to support the drive north.

Geiger's plan was to swing north with his two full divisions, pivoting on the left flank until his forces occupied the central part of the island. The units were to then drive into the northern part of Guam. The 3rd Marine Division was to advance on the left, or western side of the island, and the 77th Infantry Division on the right. A combination of artillery and naval gunfire pounded selected targets and known or suspected enemy assembly points in advance of the operation—including a last-minute barrage the night before of 1,600 shells from ships and nearly 500 rounds fired by artillery.[1] The 1st Marine Provisional Brigade was to safeguard the advance and continue to patrol the southern part of the island.

The advance north was to be done in a controlled manner with neither side advancing too far ahead of the other. Geiger established two initial lines as advancement objectives. The first, designated O-1, began just east of Agaña and followed the Agaña-Pago Road south and east to the eastern coast. The second line, O-2, was further north, running from the end of Agaña Bay in the west to Fadian Point to the east. Additional lines were to be established once the initial objectives were met.

The offensive began at 6:30 a.m. on the morning of July 31. The marines on the western side of the island quickly moved into Agaña after meeting only token resistance during their advance. The once-beautiful Plaza de España, along with much of the city, lay in ruins. The marines slowly advanced, carefully searching the buildings for enemy snipers. Searching house to house was a dangerous undertaking. In one instance, a marine opened a closet door to find a Japanese officer hiding with sword in hand. The American quickly closed the door, riddled it with gunfire, and then moved on to continue his search without looking at the outcome of his fusillade.[2]

The Japanese did not defend the city in their haste to retreat north. The only enemy soldiers found were the wounded left behind and a few stragglers. The marines entered the plaza at 10:45 a.m. All Agaña was under American control by noon.[3]

The advance of other marines was slowed by rough terrain. Scattered small groups of Japanese were occasionally encountered throughout the day. The only real battle occurred directly south of Agaña near the town of Ordot where a party of enemy soldiers was left behind to defend a supply dump. The American infantry attacked with overwhelming force only to be slowed by the sudden appearance of two Japanese tanks. There was no friendly armor close enough to intervene. A bazooka man knocked out both Japanese tanks, allowing the assault to be completed. No further resistance was met and the marines continued to advance to the O-1 line.

The wider of part of the swing fell to the 77th Infantry Division, operating on the right side of the island. The soldiers needed to move about 10 miles to reach the O-1 line. Few roads existed in the area and the narrow trails were not suitable for heavy traffic. The infantrymen slowly trudged through foothills and steep slopes while moving toward the eastern coast. Men tried to move in columns as best they could under the difficult circumstances. They sometimes slid down the slopes of steep ravines and pushed through thick underbrush. Units often lost visual contact with each other. Jeeps were initially able to follow along, but the rugged terrain eventually no longer allowed the vehicles to accompany the men.

Individual soldiers carried heavier than normal loads, making for an exhausting journey in the humid summer heat. "The flies and mosquitos have discovered your route of march and have called up all the reinforcements including the underfed and undernourished who regarded us as nothing but walking blood banks," one soldier later wrote. "We continued to push on..."[4]

The troops reached the high ground overlooking the Pago River late in the day after an advanced reconnaissance patrol reported seeing no Japanese in the immediate area. The enemy was encountered when the Americans approached the village of Yona. Two Japanese men ran across the trail, disappearing into the jungle, as the first soldiers approached the village. Some small arm fire was then heard in the distance.

The Americans quickly formed a skirmish line and swept into Yona. The enemy in the town, who may have been acting as a rear guard, appeared to have been caught by surprise. Five were killed in a brief fight. The majority of the estimated fifty to one hundred Japanese soldiers slipped away.[5]

The advancing American soldiers dug in for the night along the O-1 line after the long agonizing march. However, the day was not without some rewards. One of the highlights occurred when a patrol came across a civilian camp holding about 2,000 Chamorros near the town of Asinan. The camp was unguarded, but the civilians were too frightened to leave even after the Japanese departed. They were quickly liberated. The overjoyed civilians were not sure if they were to kiss, bow, or shake hands with their liberators; some tried to do all three at once. Many carried tiny American flags they had kept hidden from the Japanese during the occupation.

The American soldiers passed out cigarettes and rations. "We were told by the Japanese that the USA was being defeated, that Japan had control of the Hawaiian Islands, and that the Americans had only one ship left as the rest had been sunk," one civilian reported.[6] The liberators learned that about 800 Japanese soldiers had been stationed near Yona and they recently departed northward toward Barrigada.

The advance to the second objective, the O-2 line, was swiftly accomplished on August 1. The marines' stopping point was just short of the Tiyan Airfield. Further to the east, the soldiers of the 77th Infantry Division also reached their section of the O-2 line without difficulty. The marines took control of the airfield and army troops seized the Pago River bridge intact.

The main problem facing the Americans was their extended supply lines. The ability to keep the flow of supplies moving through the rough terrain was extremely difficult. The situation was particularly acute on the army side with a supply line stretching as long as sixteen miles. Engineers began work on cutting out a new road from the south. The advance eventually outpaced their ability to complete the new supply route.

The Agaña-Pago Road was now firmly in American hands. However, it was in poor shape and greatly congested with supplies, artillery, and troops all vying for the limited space. Shipments of ammunition were given top priority, although it was not an issue early in the advance owing to the limited contact with the enemy.[7] As a result, many units did not receive a timely resupply of rations and water.

Geiger notified his troops on the night of August 1 to be ready to move out in the morning. The main Japanese force was reported to have fallen back to positions about eight miles northeast of the O-2 line. Geiger wanted to keep the pressure on the enemy to prevent them from having sufficient time to organize and prepare strong defenses around Mount Santa Rosa. He ordered the offensive to continue on the morning of August 2 to a new objective—the O-3 line about four miles north of the American positions.

Two naval forces were assembled on each side of the island to support the two prongs of the offensive. Admiral Ainsworth moved off the eastern coast with his flagship light cruiser *Honolulu*, heavy cruiser *New Orleans*, two battleships, and six destroyers to begin working over Japanese positions with gunfire. The guns on the battleship *Colorado* were the first to open fire on Mount Santa Rosa. Ainsworth noted "there is a reported large concentration of disorganized and disheartened" Japanese soldiers.[8] The fire support continued throughout the day and into the night with the help of star shells when needed.

Most of the fighting during the advance to the O-3 line took place on the army side of the offensive. The major objective of 77th Infantry Division was the town of Barrigada, located about two miles from the current O-2 line position, followed by Mount Barrigada, only a mile further. The town was important for two reasons—a critical road junction to help the supply line situation and a water reservoir. The reservoir was in the center of the town and was capable of providing 20,000 gallons of water per day. With no streams in the area and the ongoing supply problems, the water shortage was reaching a critical stage for some units.

The move began on the morning of August 2 with about a dozen light tanks pulling out to provide reconnaissance as a spearhead for the operation ahead of the infantry. The armor headed up Price Road, a northern branch of the Agaña-Pago Road, in a column formation. The tanks battled a series of improvised roadblocks during various forays out and back to determine the strength of the enemy.

The tanks cautiously approached the town of Barrigada during the late morning. The lead tank became hung up on a tree stump, causing the whole column to grind to a stop. About 150 Japanese suddenly appeared out of the jungle. They attacked the tanks with machine guns, twenty-millimeter cannons, and hand grenades. A frenzied melee ensued in which the tanks successfully fought off the attackers without suffering any casualties themselves.

The Japanese seemed determined put up a fight for Barrigada. Although surrounded by thick foliage, the town itself was in a large clearing, making the area easy to defend. The American tanks and infantry were met with a torrent of fire when approaching the town. The enemy was hidden in well-concealed positions throughout the greenery behind the village, giving them a commanding view of the open areas—positions so good that American fire had little effect.[9] Early attempts to flank the Japanese positions were unsuccessful due to the effectiveness of the enemy fire.

The slow advance—only a few yards at a time in some cases—eventually yielded results. The Americans were in control of the town, the reservoir, and the crest of the mountain by August 4. The town, though, lay in ruins. Army engineers worked quickly to establish a working water station for the thirsty soldiers. The water break offered a brief respite for the weary men. The battle was not over and there was much more fighting to be done on Guam.

Chapter 32

FINAL BATTLES

THE END GAME OF THE American sweep north were two points representing the farthest extremes of Guam—Ritidian Point in the northwest and Pati Point in the northeast. Only mopping up operations and tracking down enemy stragglers was likely to be left once the points were reached. The American troops were steadily gaining territory as the Japanese were pushed into an increasingly smaller portion of the island.

A variety of intelligence was gleaned from captured documents and interviews with enemy prisoners. The information allowed General Geiger to conclude the Japanese were withdrawing to the Mount Santa Rosa area.[1] The location of the presumed enemy's last stand was about six and a half miles northeast of Mount Barrigada and close to the eastern coast. The area was thick jungle with rugged terrain and many crevasses. Some well-armed enemy outposts, including one at Finegayan, first needed to be cleared out before American troops could assault the Mount Saint Rosa area.

Geiger wanted to keep the enemy on the run and under constant pressure. He ordered his forces to remain in pursuit before the Japanese had sufficient time to build strong defensive positions. His ground forces were to close on the enemy as fast as possible.[2]

The marines on the west side of the front moved to attack Finegayan. The town was almost directly north of Tiyan Airfield. The Finegayan operation was to be the last major battle for the 3rd Marine Division on Guam. The marines moved out on the morning of August 3 after artillery dropped almost 800 shells into their area of advancement the night before.[3] The Americans encountered roadblocks and strong resistance as they moved closer to the town. The terrain favored the defenders as was usually the case in northern Guam. Tanks eventually overran the Japanese positions and close fighting followed—hand-to-hand at times.

The 737 Japanese around the Finegayan area were cleared out by nightfall on August 6. The operation opened an important road junction connecting the main road to the network of trails extending to the northeast, giving the Americans the ability to move vital supplies north to be closer to the front. The operation also broke the outer defensive ring of Mount Santa Rosa.[4]

The seizure of the town yielded a surprise find of a hundred cases of Japanese beer. The loot was quickly placed under guard before it could be consumed. The beer was later moved to storage for use after the island was fully secured.

The marines continued to advance north in columns along trails meandering through the thick jungle. Separate patrols operated about 200 yards off each side of the trails to handle any possible Japanese soldiers hiding in the underbrush.[5] Direct contact with the enemy was avoided except in areas where roads or open spaces made battle feasible.

The Americans hoped there was now a clear path north on the western side of the island. An armored reconnaissance patrol was dispatched toward Ritidian Point. The group wisely turned back after encountering stiff resistance on the trails, including attacks from hidden anti-tank guns.[6]

Geiger's next designated advancement line stretched across the island about a mile south of Yigo.[7] The town was located northeast of Barrigada and directly west of Mount Santa Rosa. The first elements of the 77th Infantry Division reached the line on August 6 after battling pockets of Japanese resistance in the vicinity of Barrigada.

The terrain north of Barrigada became even more difficult for movement. The dense vegetation prompted American units to break into smaller groups. Each of the groups advanced out of sight of the others. Patrols often had to be dispatched to locate adjacent units. Small pockets of Japanese were often bypassed by the leading units and left to be dealt with by those further behind. Inaccurate maps and aerial photos—the latter often taken when clouds obscured key areas—only added to the soldier's problems.[8]

The American soldiers experienced the full spectrum of operating in the jungle under these challenging conditions. Thick vegetation, rain, mud, heat, humidity, cold nights, and bugs all combined to create misery. The last weeks of the fight on Guam became a war of small encounters, ambushes, and close contact fighting.

Staff Sergeant John Kane was running through the brush during an ambush when he fell into a hole containing two Japanese soldiers. "Bring me a bayonet," he yelled to a comrade.[9] One of the enemy soldiers tried to grab his leg, prompting Kane to give him a swift to kick to the face before quickly jumping out. One of the Japanese then detonated a hand grenade, just as the American raised his light machine gun to fire, instantly killing both enemies.

When Staff Sergeant Benjamin Szafasz found a lone Japanese soldier hiding in a clump of vegetation, he quickly tossed a white phosphorous grenade into the enemy's position. The Japanese was able to throw it out before the explosion, yelling, "Me no wanna die!"[10] Szafasz ordered him to come out only to have the Japanese commit suicide by exploding his own grenade upon himself.

The thick undergrowth and narrow trails made for the use of some new tactics for tank-infantry advances developed by members of the 77th Infantry Division. A pair of Sherman tanks, one on each side of the path, spearheaded an advance on a trail. The remaining tanks of the platoon followed about one hundred yards behind in a column formation, moving in the center of the trail. The American logo of white stars was painted over on all tanks to eliminate an easy aiming point for the enemy.[11]

Four soldiers were assigned to walk with each of the two lead tanks to provide close protection and act as spotters. One soldier walked in front of each tank to watch for suspected mines and any obstructions. A field radio mounted on the back of the tanks allowed for communication between the tankers and soldiers. The key feature—somewhat controversial at the time—was having infantrymen preceding tanks instead of the men following the armor into action.[12]

The two lead tanks advanced through the vegetation to bust a wider path for the soldiers who followed. The arrangement of having a pair of tanks forward allowed for twice the fire to be poured onto the enemy, who often hid in ambush positions. The tanks could mutually support each other with machine gun fire if swarmed by Japanese soldiers in a tactic known as "back scratching."[13]

The Japanese deployed their dwindling number of tanks in a piecemeal fashion during the fight with the Americans in the north.

However, the vehicles were not used *en masse*, but rather in scattered small actions. A wild incident took place on the American line during night of August 5–6. The strange episode involved two enemy tanks.

A unit of American army soldiers were cautious over the possibility of a Japanese suicide night attack when they dug in for the night near the right side of the front. The enemy night tactics were well-known. The men were exhausted after a long day of moving through the jungle where the thick foliage separated them from other nearby friendly forces. An evening downpour only added to their misery. What happened next could not have been expected by anyone on the American side.

The sound of moving tanks was heard around 2:00 a.m. coming from the direction of another American unit. The soldiers had been warned about friendly tanks operating in the area, but the guards nonetheless remained vigilant. Moonlight revealed two Japanese tanks with a group of machine gun-equipped infantrymen. The Americans quickly opened fire with small arms and grenades, stopping the infantry and prompting the tanks to veer away. A Japanese soldier perched on top of the first tank yelled out, "American tank— OK, American tank—OK," even as the tank unleashed a stream of fire from its turret.[14]

The two tanks, void of their infantry support, separated for a time while pushing through the perimeter with their guns blazing. Terrified American soldiers scattered. Some nearby American tanks could not fire for fear of hitting friendly soldiers. Small arms fire was ineffective against the armored vehicles. An excited bazooka man forgot to pull the safety pin on his ammunition before firing, rendering his shot useless. Anti-tank gunners turned their cannons to get a better aim only to have the enemy tanks shift course.

One Japanese tank collided with a Sherman before it backed off, ran over a jeep, and disappeared into the darkness before the

Americans even had time to react. The two tanks eventually rejoined before moving north through the perimeter. The vehicles eventually encountered the same group of soldiers who initially sighted them. The Americans were poised for an attack from the outside and were not expecting one from behind. One wounded soldier staggered to his feet only to be run over and killed. The tanks passed close to two others, crushing their rifles.

All throughout the ordeal, the lone Japanese soldier remained firmly perched on top of the one tank. He was killed by a parting rifle shot from an American soldier as the marauding tanks vanished outside the perimeter. The tanks made good their escape seemingly unscathed.

The plundering Japanese tanks left behind a trail of destruction. Equipment of all sorts was bullet-ridden or damaged and at least one jeep was crushed. Fifteen Americans were killed and forty-six were wounded.[15] An artillery observation party was nearly wiped out.

The tanks were last seen moving north on a trail into the jungle. One subsequently broke down, prompting the Japanese to stop to work on it. A fierce firefight started when the tanks were later discovered by an American patrol. The Japanese held more favorable positions and were able to pour fire toward the Americans, causing heavy casualties. The enemy eventually slipped away into the jungle. The two tanks were later found abandoned with three dead crewmen nearby.[16] The odyssey was a uniquely strange episode as the Japanese days on Guam were fast coming to an end.

Chapter 33

TWEED AFTER GUAM

AFTER SPENDING YEARS ON THE run while waiting for American forces to return to Guam, George Tweed was not on the island when the liberators finally arrived. The sailor was sent back to the United States after his rescue by the destroyer *McCall* and short stay aboard the aircraft carrier *Hornet*. He later wrote of the departure as "the disappointment of my life."[1]

Tweed was put ashore on Saipan to catch a flight to Hawaii. He likely did not know Japanese stragglers were still hiding on the island even though major combat operations ended. Tweed's life almost ended abruptly during the brief visit when the navy uniform caught the attention of an enemy sniper. The soldier took a single shot and missed. Tweed subsequently traveled from the Marianas to Pearl Harbor and then on to California.

Much of the news coming out of the Pacific at the time was about the fighting in the Marianas and the liberation of Guam. The general public did not yet know about Tweed's story—but it would not remain a secret much longer. Reporter Robert Sherrod, a war correspondent for *Time* and *Life* magazines, sat next to Tweed on the long flight from Saipan to Hawaii. The veteran reporter spent time embedded with American troops and covered island invasions in the Aleutians, Tarawa, and Saipan.

The sailor was interviewed and talked at length about his time on the run and his rescue from the island. His voice was hoarse by the time he arrived at Pearl Harbor and met Admiral Nimitz. He apologized to the admiral for his rasping voice. "I've talked more in the past three days than I have in the past 31 months put together," Tweed said.[2]

The home-bound sailor spoke with reporters while in Hawaii before traveling on to California. The story ran in major newspapers about a month after his rescue, appearing on the front pages of the *New York Times*, *Chicago Tribune*, and other big city papers on August 11, 1944. Sherrod was among the reporters to publish a story on the Tweed episode. His article appeared in the August 21, 1944 issue of *Life* with a smaller news article in *Time* during the same week.

The navy gave Tweed a thirty-day furlough. The sailor used the time to reunite with his family. He first stopped by to see his mother-in-law, Mrs. W. H. Sudderth, in Santa Paula, California. Tweed's appearance was drastically different than before the war. He lost weight and still looked haggard from the ordeal on Guam. "He knocked at the door and when I answered I didn't recognize him," Sudderth said.[3] She described him as "so gray haired."[4] His brown hair was now about half gray.

Tweed then went to see his wife Mary and their two sons in San Diego for about two weeks. "Ronald knew me right away, and just the next day Robert called me Daddy," Tweed said of his children. "I sure got a kick out of that."[5]

He subsequently traveled to Oregon to visit his mom on her farm near Portland. "It has been such a long time since I had him with me I had forgotten just what he did like, but I seemed to remember mashed potatoes and gravy," his mother said. Tweed jokingly replied, "Don't ever ask me to eat rice."

While in Oregon, the sailor mused to a reporter about possibly going back to Guam as a civilian. "But after the war is over, I think I'd like to go back to Guam," he said. "I have a hunch I can cash in on something I've learned in the navy radio. The climate there isn't too good on radio sets, and someone could have a swell job there as a radio repairman."[6]

Tweed filed for divorce shortly after his return in a surprise development. The sailor later testified he and Mary agreed to separate while still on Guam before the war.[7] The court quickly granted the divorce. He married Dolores Kramer about a year later in Washington.[8]

The end of the furlough found the sailor traveling east to Washington, DC. Per his official navy record, Tweed was assigned to the Bureau of Naval Personnel until February 19, 1945. He was then attached to the Naval Training School in Del Monte, California, for about four months before duty again sent him back to Washington.[9]

Tweed was interviewed by a representative of the Office of Naval Records and Library in Washington on August 25, 1944. The interview was mostly about his time hiding on Guam. The conversation was recorded and later transcribed into a twenty-one-page transcript.

It was only a matter of time before some type of decoration was bestowed upon the serviceman for his actions in the Pacific. Tweed was awarded the Legion of Merit by Secretary of the Navy James Forrestal on September 9, 1944 in recognition of his actions of eluding the enemy and providing pre-invasion intelligence. The citation noted he was "courageous and resourceful under relentless stalking by the Japanese."[10]

A bevy of newspaper and magazine articles were published in late 1944 and the stream continued into the following year. The stories told of Tweed's life and exploits on Guam. He soon became well-known around the country and earned the name "Ghost of Guam." At war bond rallies, interviews with reporters, speeches at war material factories, and events of all types, Tweed spoke of his time on Guam.

"For months I wandered through the brush, ragged, hungry, [utterly] fatigued—a hunted animal," he related on one occasion. "Sometimes the Japs were only a few yards from me, pistols ready. There was a price on my head—1,000 yen, dead or alive. Eventually fifty men were assigned to seek me out."

The sailor regularly gave credit to the civilians who helped him hide and survive. "I could not have survived one week if it had not been for the loyalty of the Chamorros," he later said. "Virtually every one of them who fed me or gave me a bed during my bitter wanderings within the Jap lines was tortured. Not one betrayed me."[11]

The Museum of Modern Art in New York City was the setting in late October 1944 for an advance showing of the Navy newsreel *Return to Guam* set to be released to the public. Tweed was among the invited guests, having recently returned from Guam himself. The newsreel, about the American liberation of the island, also depicted a reenactment of Tweed's rescue.

The audience was full of war plant industrialists and labor representatives. Tweed addressed them in a low voice. He spoke of when he first saw the island, the lack of defenses in the first days of the war, and his departure. He talked in a serious tone about the many Guamanians who helped him survive. "When I left them it was like leaving home, I'd been there so long."[12]

The George Tweed story was too much for book publishers to resist. The tale had everything publishers were looking for during wartime—heroism, adventure, true to life, and a tropical setting. Tweed collaborated with veteran newspaper reporter Blake Clark on a book. *Robinson Crusoe, USN* was released in the spring of 1945 to good reviews. The story follows Tweed from the start of the war through his time in hiding—including the help he received from various Guamanians—to his ultimate rescue and aftermath. Clark told the story in Tweed's own words as much as possible. One reviewer described the book as "a fast moving, breathless true story of adventure—a chronicle on one of the war's most unusual feats of valor."[13]

Tweed's time in the United States included incentive talks at war plants and other public relations activities. He was, after all, viewed by many as a war hero. The Pacific War ended with the Japanese surrender while Tweed was stateside. He longed to know about the Guamanians who helped him elude the enemy—did they survive the war? He was given permission to make a short return trip to the island and left Washington in the middle of September.

Landing in Guam was like arriving in a strange place. Gone were many of the recognizable landmarks—most had been destroyed during the fighting and replaced with tent cities. There were new roads and military activity was everywhere. He found Agueda Johnston at a Red Cross facility. She didn't recognize the clean-shaven sailor at first but was elated to see him once she knew it was Tweed.

Tweed was eventually reunited with Antonio Artero and met his family for the first time. They returned to the hideout—with an armed escort because of Japanese stragglers still on the loose in the northern part of the island. He spent about three weeks on Guam and met up with various Guamanians who helped him stay one step ahead of the Japanese—helped him stay alive. Tweed heard the stories of how they survived the brutal last days of the occupation before the American invasion. They occasionally shared a drink and talked about lost friends who did not live to see the liberation.

The sort of homecoming eventually came to an end. When Tweed's plane took off on October 15, he looked down on the island. The view reminded him of the Guam he knew back in 1939. "But they meant a lot more to me," he wrote of the sites. "I knew that island now."[14]

Chapter 34

PLIGHT OF THE CIVILIANS

THE LIBERATION OF GUAM BROUGHT an end to the long ordeal endured by the civilians during the occupation of the island. Conditions for the Guamanians began to steadily deteriorate once the Japanese realized the island would be a target for an American invasion. The schools and churches were closed, food rationing became harsher, and punishments were more severe.[1] Civilians were already forced to work on airfield construction and in agriculture for little compensation. The large influx of Japanese troops in early 1944 added to the critical food shortage and increased the demand for labor.

The rapid build-up of defensive fortifications began with work by construction units composed mostly of Korean laborers and Japanese engineers. The situation changed on February 23, 1944 when all able-bodied Guamanian men sixteen and older were mobilized for work.[2] The assignments were unrelated to one's skills or background and was often without regard for personal safety. The construction of defenses included digging out caves, building pillboxes and bunkers, working on the airfield at Tiyan, and erecting beach defenses.

The agricultural work was then mostly shifted to women. The Japanese planned to greatly increase Guam's food production. The occupiers wanted to be able to sustain up to 30,000 soldiers for the duration of the island's defense.[3]

The arduous cave and tunnel work was mostly done by hand with sledgehammers, shovels, and picks used to break out rocks. Laborers then carried out the rubble in sacks slung over their backs. The conditions were poor both inside and out. The dusty interiors of caves and tunnels often had no airflow, creating suffocating conditions. The men faced blazing sun and tropical humidity once outside.

The men building the beach defenses faced a different set of hazards. "Those of us working on the barricades were under extreme pressure," Ben Blaz later wrote. "We were pressured by the Japanese to get the project completed and completed right." The Guamanians knew the obstructions were meant to stop their liberators. "Adding to our plight was the physical danger. We had to carry the logs, rocks, and barbed wire across slimy, jagged coral, more slippery than ice covered by water."[4] He was heartened to learn after the liberation of the American demolition teams destroying the barricades just ahead of the landing.

The defensive work continued right up until the start of the American bombardment. A new hazard emerged for civilians just prior to the start of the invasion when the Japanese recruited Guamanian men and boys work as ammunition carriers. Their duty was to keep the dug-in soldiers supplied with bullets, cannon shells, mortar rounds, and hand grenades. The job was a virtual death sentence with open exposure to bombardments, air attacks, and crossfire. Those lucky enough to survive were often killed by the Japanese who feared the islanders would give away their positions to the Americans.[5]

The Japanese atrocities against the civilian population steadily increased in the time leading up to the American invasion and subsequent land battle. Many Guamanians already endured forced labor in harsh conditions, working in agriculture or building airfields and defenses. Now, with liberation so close, they faced a struggle for survival as the occupiers went on a killing frenzy.

"It is a day in my life that cannot be compared to any other," Joaquin Manibusan later wrote.[6] The civilian was part of a work party when he and another were given a sudden task by a Japanese officer. "It was late in the afternoon when we were ordered to dig a four-foot-deep hole. We did not know what the purpose of the hole, and others were ordered to dig two more holes."

The men were digging the graves for three Guamanians. They were undoubtedly accused of some minor offenses and were now to be put to death by sword. Manibusan remembered two of the men were from Piti and members of the Insular Guard Force.

He already felt the sharp blade of an officer's sword rub against the back of his neck when he and some others had their hands tied behind their backs and made to think they were about to be beheaded. "The interpreter told me that I was supposed to have my neck slashed twice, but I escaped death," he added.

The end of life for the condemned was severe and swift. "The sword was always cleaned before a beheading and then wiped off afterward," Manibusan explained. "One other command from the Japanese, part of their ritual was to have the people in the camp surround the holes and witness what would happen if anyone would be found in disobedience."

Some victims had direct ties to George Tweed, including Juan Pangelinan. The husky retired US Navy man and World War I veteran previously assisted the radioman. The American bombardment was already under way when he was ordered to report to Japanese authorities in Dededo, ostensibly to be compensated for the large amount of farm goods turned over to the occupiers.

He did not heed the advice of family members who told him not to go. "I had warned him to flee from his ranch and hide out in the jungle and wait for the return of the Americans," his brother Ben later said.[7] Pangelinan was tied up and beaten upon his arrival at the Japanese post. He was then placed on the hood of a car and driven to an agricultural area where he was beheaded.

Catholic priest Father Jesus Baza Duenas opposed the brutal techniques of the Japanese from the start of the occupation. He came under suspicion from authorities as a result. The clergyman later criticized the Japanese for using the church altar to praise Japan and eventually refused to have his sermons censored and to insert official announcements.[8] He lived in the southern village of Inarajan for most of the occupation.

Father Duenas was part of network of Guamanians who knew the movements of the American fugitives and the names of those who assisted them. He was also known to have ministered to Al Tyson and Clarence Johnston in the hopes of converting them to Catholicism.[9] The priest kept up on the progress of the war through regular visits to individuals with secret radios.

The priest and his nephew, Eduardo Duenas, were arrested on July 8, 1944—within days of George Tweed's rescue and only weeks away from the American invasion. The men were tied up and paraded through the village streets in front of civilians, who were ordered by the Japanese to remain silent. Three days of brutal beatings and torture followed. They were accused of being American spies and helping Tweed. Their bodies were badly bruised, faces swollen, and clothes splattered with blood when the ordeal was over.[10]

Father Duenas was subjected to a form of water torture. "That morning...there was Father Duenas laid on a bench, being scourged," recalled Francisco Naputi who witnessed the dreadful events. "He was made to open his mouth while half a gallon of water was being poured into his mouth until he finished it. So many people there were crying, and whoever cried was scolded by the Japanese."[11]

The pair was taken to the village of Tai, southeast of Agaña. They were joined by two other Guamanians, one of whom was Juan Pangelinan, and forced to kneel with their hands tied behind their backs in front of freshly dug graves. The men were executed by sword. The priest's body was exhumed after the island was freed from the Japanese. He is widely considered by Guamanians to be a war hero and martyr.[12]

Among the most heinous of Japanese atrocities took place at the very end of their rule. With the American invasion looming and word spreading of the fall of Saipan, General Takashina ordered all Guamanians throughout the island to be force-marched to campsites in the southern interior portion of Guam. The reason for the order was never entirely clear, although it was probably not humanitarian. The Japanese may have wanted to isolate the civilians to keep them from taking up arms in support of the Americans or to use them as hostages.[13] Another possibility is the move was part of a larger plan for wholesale murder.

The largest camp was in a valley near the Ylig River. The location has often been referred to as the Manenggon Concentration Camp.[14] Long columns of humanity, ranging in age from babies to the elderly, poured out of villages for what was often a long and strenuous march to Manenggon. They carried what few possessions they were able to take along. The civilians were frequently accompanied by Japanese soldiers who wielded bayonets to keep the people moving.

Young Blaz and his family were among the thousands making the journey. "We had not been given time to pack, so we had only what we could grab and carry," he later wrote. "My mother and father had told us to get food."[15] His family was soon walking to the camp.

"Thousands of people arose slowly from their makeshift camps and prepared to move out," wrote Ricardo Bordallo, who participated in the trek as a teen with his family. "Precious belongings—pathetic bundles of every size and description—were carefully lashed onto bull carts or shouldered by their owners. Fear filled the faces of every man, woman, and child."[16]

Soldiers were barking orders as the long column of people slowly moved toward the camp. Accounts are plentiful of people becoming sick, some too exhausted to continue, with beatings and other cruelties committed by the Japanese soldiers.[17] A heavy rain began to fall, only adding to the misery.

The civilians found little more than an open space once the people arrived at the destination. The site did not really qualify as a camp. "The Japanese had bulldozed the worst of the jungle and undergrowth, and they had constructed watchtowers for their guards," Blaz explained. "But that was all."

There were no buildings, toilets, or food—just open space. The Guamanians were on their own for survival. Some built temporary shelters using sticks and coconut leaves. They foraged for food and obtained water from the river. Survival seemed like a constant struggle. "One day melted into the next," Blaz added. "We lost all concept of time."

Women wash clothes in a creek near Agaña on August 12, 1944. The fierce battle
to liberate Guam left thousands of Guamanian civilians homeless and led to a large
reconstruction in the years after the war. (US Navy / National Archives)

A sense of fear hung heavily over the camp. The sound of distant explosions from the bombardment could occasionally be heard in the background. The Japanese guards warned anyone trying to escape would be killed. Men and boys were recruited to become laborers and ammunition carriers—many of those selected did not return. "We didn't know why we were being concentrated or how long we were to be held. We didn't know if we would survive," Bordallo recalled. Both Bordallo and Blaz survived the American invasion.

★　★　★

The first American patrols reached the outskirts of the Manenggon camp late in the afternoon of July 30. Soldiers from 77th Division overran the main camps the next day and found no sign of the enemy. The Japanese guards just simply disappeared one day ahead of the liberators. The Guamanians mostly stayed in the camp not knowing where the Japanese went. Some feared they were hiding in the nearby woods waiting to shoot anyone trying to leave.

People stared in disbelief when a small group of American troops suddenly showed up. "Hey, we're friends," said one soldier after cautiously approaching.[18] The situation suddenly changed—liberators finally arrived!

Bordallo was in the woods when the Americans arrived. "We ran down the hillside and into the frenzy in camp," he later wrote. "People were laughing and crying, hugging and kissing, shouting and jumping, dancing and singing."[19] The Americans passed out rations, candy, and cigarettes. The Guamanians later left the camp en masse.

Similar scenes of the liberators meeting the liberated took place all throughout the island. Marine Corporal Maury Williams Jr. first encountered civilians when leaving the frontlines for a rear area. "The youngsters ran alongside of us holding on to our rifles," he later recalled. "Old men held our hands and the women cried and cheered and patted our backs. All the hardship and misery and wounds we had suffered melted away at that moment and I said to myself—it has been worth it all." The encounter really struck a chord with the young marine. "I will never forget how grateful the people were."[20]

Antonio Artero and his family ran out of food after more than twenty days of hiding in the cave formerly used by Tweed. He had a critical decision to make—leave the safety of the hidden shelter to forage for food and risk being caught by the Japanese or have his family starve. He ventured out to his home and was surprised from behind by some soldiers—American soldiers. Artero learned the main battle for Guam was over. The Americans arranged for the family to move to a safe location until the Japanese stragglers were cleared out of the area around his ranch.

Chapter 35

GUAM SECURED

THE FINAL DEFENSIVE LINE THE Japanese attempted to stretch across northern Guam was broken by the end of the day on August 6. American ground forces breached the line in so many places it no longer represented a front. The enemy now controlled less than a third of the island. Organized resistance was starting to break down as the Japanese, increasingly operating in small groups without leaders, were lacking sufficient weapons. The enemy was facing the same difficult jungle conditions as their attackers.

"They were obliged to fight in the jungle and communicate with each other," Lieutenant Colonel Hideyuki Takeda later reported of the Japanese soldiers in northern Guam. "Therefore, they could not fight satisfactorily to show their whole strength. And as the American armored troops drove along the highways and trails in the jungle to cut off the front line into several pockets, our troops were forced to be isolated."[1]

General Geiger ordered an all-out attack, beginning on the morning of August 7, with the goal of defeating the remaining Japanese on the island. The bulk of the fighting fell to the 77th Infantry Division. The army unit was largely responsible for seizing the residual areas in the northeastern part of the island. The marines, operating further west, were to drive north all the way to the sea at the same time.

The final major American attack was to dislodge the Japanese from Mount Santa Rosa and nearby Yigo, both located in the army area of operations. The town was just west of the mountain and featured a key road junction from which jungle trails sprang in three directions. The Japanese area of operations would be even further limited once the town fell to the Americans.

The attack on Yigo began with a devastating artillery barrage. Hundreds of shells rained down on the road juncture and trails heading out of town to cut off any possible escape routes. Some enemy soldiers frantically ran toward the American lines, while others tried to escape north into the jungle. "My god, this is a slaughter!" an artillery officer in an observation plane cried out over the radio circuit after seeing Japanese running and falling in all directions amid the explosions.[2]

The ground attack followed the artillery lambasting with Stuart light tanks advancing ahead of infantry units. The smaller Stuarts were able to better navigate jungle trails but lacked the heavier armor and firepower of the Sherman tanks. Skillfully concealed Japanese defenses were built around a pair of tanks, two anti-tank guns, an assortment of lighter guns, and a makeshift group of infantrymen.[3] American infantrymen attacked pillboxes and strongpoints bypassed by the initial line of tanks.

The Stuarts headed directly toward the town. The attack slowed when the armor came under heavy enemy fire after moving up a slight rise and into an open area. The larger Sherman tanks were called forward as reinforcements.

The tank under the command of Sergeant Joe Divin was among those coming under withering enemy fire. An anti-tank shell hit the left side of his vehicle causing it to stall. Divin was badly wounded on both legs as he stood in the turret of his Stuart. He was blocking the escape route of his crew below him. The two other hatches were locked shut due to the turret having been turned off center. The mechanism to turn the turret had been damaged, preventing it from moving back to center.

Divin was rapidly losing strength due to blood loss. He put a tourniquet on his leg before painfully lifting himself out of the turret and onto the back deck of the tank. The move allowed his men to evacuate. The sergeant stayed in the exposed position long enough for his crew to reach cover. A burst of machine gun fire killed Divin before he could make good on his own escape.[4]

The Sherman tanks arrived on the scene only to have their crews initially unable to find the source of the enemy fire. Shrapnel and bullets ricocheting off the left side of the tanks quickly revealed the direction of the enemy fire. The tanks turned to pour fire into the forest where the Japanese were hiding.

Some of the larger tanks also fell victim to Japanese shells. One Sherman was hit in the gas tank and quickly became enveloped in a torrent of flames. The crew scrambled out and ran for safety. Another stalled under heavy fire, prompting its crew to abandon the tank. A third Sherman lost a track.

The enemy positions eventually proved vulnerable to flanking moves by American infantry. One troublesome Japanese pillbox withstood repeated fire, including a hail of machine gun bullets and six grenades. The position was silenced for good only after a flame-thrower man carefully moved into position to pour the searing flaming liquid into the box. The attackers eventually prevailed after a vigorous fight.

The seizure of Yigo secured the western side of Mount Santa Rosa. American soldiers dug in for the night of August 7–8, facing the mountain slopes, under warnings from their leaders to expect an enemy counterattack. No large-scale Banzai charges materialized.

The 900-foot-tall Mount Santa Rosa was under a nearly constant bombardment for almost a week. Naval guns were dropping shells around the clock since August 3. Flights of B-26 medium bombers and P-47 fighters operating from Saipan made daily attacks. Land-based artillery guns joined the pummeling in the days leading up to the final assault.

The Americans were preparing for a tough fight. A report from a Japanese prisoner indicated about 3,000 enemy soldiers were stationed in the immediate area.[5] The morning of August 8 marked the beginning of the attack on Mount Santa Rosa. The final prelude included a tremendous bombardment. Army units staged an enveloping attack. Soldiers simultaneously advanced up the north and south slopes, while other units held the approaches.

The American soldiers mounted a steady advance. Although some resistance was encountered on the approaches to the mountain, there was no opposition on the bare slopes of the large hill. A line across the summit was in place by early afternoon—Mount Santa Rosa was in American hands. Patrols were quickly dispatched toward the sea with orders to investigate all caves and other possible places where Japanese troops could be hiding.

Fears of heavily fortified defenses proved to be unfounded. Only about 500 bodies were counted after the battle, indicating the others—if the intelligence numbers were accurate—slipped away into the jungle to fight another day.[6] The enemy actually withdrew from the mountain during the heavy bombardment, leaving only a rear-guard unit behind.[7]

The capture of Mount Santa Rosa brought an end to the major fighting on Guam. Geiger issued a simple directive: "Push all Japanese from Guam."[8] Only a small swath of land in the northeast remained unoccupied. The troops began looking into caves and scouring the beach areas. The entire northwest portion of the island was soon under American control. Elements of the 3rd Marine Division pushed northeast toward Pati Point, even as army units were fighting on Mount Santa Rosa. The marines in the west moved all the way to Ritidian Point.

General Obata knew the end of the battle for Guam was drawing near. He sent a message to Imperial Headquarters in Tokyo on August 10: "most of the island is lost and we are without weapons, ammunition, or food," he stated. "The achievement of the original mission is now hopeless. I do not know how to express my apology."[9] Even Radio Tokyo conceded most of the island was lost and reported nine-tenths of Guam was under the control of American troops.[10]

The marines operating in the northwest encountered scattered pockets of Japanese defenders during their advance. Only minimal resistance was initially found during a light sweep around Mount Mataguac. The location of Obata's hidden headquarters, set up in a cave, at first remained undetected.

The headquarters was not to stay concealed for long. The end for Obata began when some Guamanians pointed out the location of a defensive zone or some type of headquarters position. The area was where the army and marine sectors joined. A marine patrol spotted a small jungle-covered hill in the army's zone and scouts came under immediate fire when they approached.[11] The marines backed off and notified the army.

Reconnaissance soldiers discovered a basin or "fortified depression" measuring about one hundred yards long and forty feet deep.[12] The thick brush concealed entrenched soldiers, armed with machine guns, mortars, and small arms, who were likely going to fight to the death. A violent fight developed after a flamethrower man came under fire when he approached the position. The American soldiers withdrew late in the day after suffering heavy casualties.

A larger attack began the next morning with tanks and mortars providing an opening barrage. American infantrymen formed a skirmish line and walked into the depression to root out any Japanese who survived the bombardment—few were found alive. On the side of the basin, where explosions blew away foliage, a series of small tunnels were found leading to caves.

The soldiers had unknowingly stumbled across Obata's headquarters. Gunfire was coming out from the tunnels, making it clear an unknown number of enemy soldiers were inside. White phosphorous grenades were tossed into a cave, prompting two Japanese soldiers armed with rifles rush to out. The pair were quickly shot down.

Obata remained hidden inside his command post. Knowing his headquarters had been discovered, he sent a final message to Tokyo reiterating the situation on Guam was hopeless. "Our souls will defend the island to the very end. I am overwhelmed with sorrow for the families of the many officers and men. I pray for the prosperity of the Empire."[13]

Singing or some type of chanting was heard from deep within the cave when American demolition teams were called in to close the entrances with explosives. Four 400-pound blocks of high explosives eventually sealed the caves shut. The move condemned those hiding inside to the fate of a suffocating death.

The odor of death was so great the men needed gas masks when the entrances to the caves were dug open four days later. An elaborately constructed interior was found with four-foot concrete walls and a large radio transmitter.[14] Over sixty bodies, including Obata, were discovered. The general either committed suicide or was killed near the end of the fighting.

The main battle for Guam was now over. The fighting was reduced to the Americans clearing out small pockets of scattered resistance. The American commanders were planning a public statement. An official announcement came at 11:31 a.m. on August 10 when Geiger declared the end of organized resistance on Guam.[15]

The proclamation coincided with the arrival of a group of senior American military personnel, including admirals Nimitz and Spruance, marine generals Smith and Alexander Vandegrift. The leaders inspected frontline units and discussed the future role of the island in the ongoing drive toward Tokyo.[16] The work of the soldiers and marines, however, was far from finished.

The brutal Japanese atrocities against the civilian population continued right up to the end of the active fighting. A marine patrol near Chaguian on August 8 found a Japanese truck filled with the beheaded bodies of thirty Chamorro men. Their hands were tied behind their backs.

Another patrol found additional bodies dumped in the jungle close to the same village the next morning.[17] The men were thought to range in age from thirteen to seventy-six. They were likely taken from a concentration camp near Manenggon to bring supplies north to the Japanese command post.[18] The Guamanians were likely murdered to prevent giving away information to the Americans.

Chapter 36

HUNTING FOR STRAGGLERS

THE END OF ORGANIZED ENEMY resistance on Guam did not mean the end of the fighting. There were an estimated 7,500 Japanese personnel unaccounted for on the island at the time it was declared secure.[1] The large number of missing enemy fighting men came about in various ways. Many small pockets of defenders were bypassed—or missed altogether in the thick jungle—during the drive north. Some of the enemy soldiers simply slipped away, as was the case with many of the Mount Santa Rosa defenders.

The military leadership on Guam switched from the combat group to a new Island Command after the island was declared secure. The new leader was Marine General Henry Larsen, who assumed command on August 15. The general already completed months of preparation after his appointment to the role in April. "The important members of my staff proceeded to Guadalcanal where the Corps staged out from and went in with the assault," he later said.

"I landed personally with key members of my staff on the first day of the assault."[2] Larsen quickly became the central leader on Guam, responsible for hunting down the remaining enemy, providing security, resuming the civilian government, and overseeing a massive construction and rebuilding project.

The final phase of the military portion of the invasion operation began immediately after the secure declaration—hunting down the remaining Japanese soldiers until the island was free of the enemy. The at-large Japanese were now labeled as stragglers. The options of surrender or be killed were the only two real choices for the remining enemy.

The centuries-old Code of Bushido, meaning the way of the warrior, has been described as a "complex set of Japanese values stressing honor and loyalty to country and family above all else."[3] The concept was widely taught in schools and in the military. The Bushido was later used to fuel Japanese nationalism. By World War II, the code included the idea of death before surrender. The code still held sway over the defeated Japanese soldiers on Guam. Many servicemen were too proud to dishonor their emperor by surrendering.[4]

Finding enemy personnel willing to give up was hard to come by during the initial weeks after the end of the major fighting, although it was not for a lack of effort on the part of the Americans. Various methods were deployed to convince the stragglers to give up.

The soldiers of the 77th Infantry Division spread leaflets in the jungle around Mount Santa Rosa in an early attempt to persuade those in hiding to surrender. The leaflet began with the simple statement "It is Not a Disgrace to Take a New Lease on Life" and told of the Japanese naval defeat in the Battle of the Philippine Sea, explaining "as a result at the present time, your planes and submarines cannot come to your aid." The document noted the US government treats prisoners fairly and the Japanese who surrendered on Saipan were "living under very pleasant circumstances."[5] The handouts were not very successful in convincing stragglers to turn themselves in to American authorities.

An occasional straggler eventually began to give up, "and after interviewing them for two or three days we find that he is willing to go out and encourage some others to come in," Larsen later said. Some of the willing prisoners spoke through loudspeakers mounted on trucks traveling along the narrow jungle trails, while others did the same in landing craft sailing close to the coast. "That met with considerable success," Larsen added.[6]

The hunt for the Japanese unwilling to surrender was meticulous and relentless. A "straggler line" was established east to west across the island from Tumon Bay to Fadian Point, encompassing about the northern third of Guam. The line was an effort to prevent enemy soldiers from trying to infiltrate south where they could raid supply depots and cause havoc in rear areas.[7] Unlike George Tweed, the Japanese fugitives would not be getting help from the local population. Many Guamanians greatly suffered at the hands of their captors during the occupation and had no qualms about conveying information on suspected Japanese movements and hideouts.

The area north of the line was divided into zones with a combat unit assigned to each area. Their mission was to hunt down and eliminate any Japanese stragglers. Strong patrols were quickly dispatched wherever enemy activity was reported. An occasional fierce firefight developed when small groups of Japanese were located. The enemy groups were typically about ten to fifteen men. The result always favored the Americans.

The thick jungle terrain made for a long mopping-up period. The American tactics proved to be very successful. Over eighty Japanese, on average, were killed or captured daily from August 10 through the end of the month.[8]

The remaining Japanese were for the most part disorganized, lacked weapons, short on food, and leaderless. Most of the stragglers eventually fell into survival mode with the need for finding food supplanting everything else. The dwindling number of weapons and small amounts of ammunition were saved for hunting food, not Americans. Some scrounged supply dumps looking for food or weapons and stole American military clothes to camouflage their appearance.[9] A steady stream of hungry survivors, some of whom may have forgotten caution, were killed close to supply stations.[10]

Indiana native Robert Amstutz was among the marines searching for stragglers. "They had a lot of snipers on Guam," he later recalled of the enemy holdouts. He remembered the dangers of crossing through a clearing while on patrol in the jungle. "Maybe you would watch a guy and he would take off and it might be 25 or 30 yards or up to 50 yards you would have to go," Amstutz explained. "You would zigzag and stay low. Run fast, zigzag and stay low. That was the secret to staying alive. Maybe the guy in front of you would get hit or maybe he wouldn't and maybe you would."[11]

The problems with Japanese stragglers continued while his unit later conducted patrols and tried to train. "There would be a big valley of jungle and the fellows would split and they wouldn't even go down through there. Then we set up and started training," Amstutz remembered. "We were always getting shot at, anytime we went out." The group then tried something different after assembling for a patrol. An officer barked, "Now we are going to go down through the jungle. If you see anything, don't take the easy route around it. You go through it." The orders were to investigate anything they see as potential enemy soldiers. The marine remembered many Japanese were found and killed after the tactics were changed. "Then things kind of calmed down," he said.

The stragglers were not a major threat from a military stand-point. However, they occasionally caused disruptions and had dangerous encounters with civilians.[12] The encounters only reinforced the need to clear the island of all remaining Japanese.

A Japanese navy corpsman was killed by an American patrol in November 1944. Sample entries from his recovered diary provide a glimpse of what life was like for a straggler:

> August 23: "All around me are enemies only. It takes a brave man, indeed, to go in search of food."
>
> September 19: "Our taro is running short and we can't afford to eat today."
>
> October 2: "These days I am eating only bread fruit. Went out in search of some today but it is very dangerous."
>
> October 15: "No food."[13]

Many of the remaining stragglers were in failing health or outright sick. Some died of dysentery and other tropical diseases. Others were too weak to fight for survival and blew themselves up with hand grenades instead of giving up. The American Island Psychological Warfare Unit convinced some to surrender.

A group of armed volunteer civilians was organized to assist American soldiers in the hunt for stragglers. The group was mostly members of the police force and known as the Guam Combat Patrol. The Guamanians combed jungle areas on foot looking for any traces of human activity such as footprints and broken brush. They questioned civilians to gather information while hunting for the holdouts and their hideouts.

The mission was a dangerous undertaking—two members of the group were killed in action and three were wounded.[14] Some members remembered the horrific atrocities endured by the Guamanians during the occupation and preferred to take no prisoners.[15] The group killed at least 117 Japanese stragglers and captured five before the Combat Patrol was disbanded in November 1948.[16]

Two Japanese army officers—Lieutenant Colonel Takeda and Major Kiyomachi Sato—tried to organize the scattered survivors to fight a sustained guerilla war with little success. Sato led a group of about one hundred soldiers in the southern part of Guam. In February 1945, they killed six visiting American sailors who were exploring the jungle. Sato surrendered on June 11, 1945, after his force was reduced to about thirty-five men and he concluded further resistance was futile.[17]

Takeda led a group of about sixty-seven men in the north. He surrendered at the end of the war on September 4, 1945. About a week later, Takeda ordered another group of almost fifty to do the same—the last known sizable group of Japanese hiding out on Guam.[18] Thereafter, only many small groups and individuals remained at large.

The experiences of Kazuo Hoshi may have been typical of long-term stragglers. He was a civilian attached to the Japanese navy's meteorology unit and arrived on Guam in 1944. Hoshi was given crash training on survival tactics and rudimentary weapons before the American invasion. He traveled to northern Guam with other meteorology workers and some wounded soldiers after the Japanese counterattack failed to turn back the invaders.

An officer later directed the group to flee into the jungle, telling them, "You guys are young. Go in the jungle and try to survive."[19] They dodged American gunfire while making their escape during a rain storm. Hoshi was quickly thrown into the new reality of life as a straggler. He ended up with a wounded navy chief petty officer and a young civilian meteorology staffer.

The men hid in caves and frequently moved around while mostly staying in the northwestern part of the island. They occasionally encountered other Japanese fugitives. The men scrounged up food any way they could—foraging, fishing, eating livestock from abandoned ranches, and even stumbling across some discarded American canned food. Although the group came across some guns, they wisely chose not to fire the weapons knowing the noise would give away their position.

Surrender was never considered, even though the Americans dropped leaflets. Hoshi concluded the war was over when he saw a large number of American planes and ships around the island. He thought of coming out of the jungle when he turned twenty-five. "I'd rather breathe freedom at least once than live in the jungle forever, even if I get killed," he later recalled thinking.[20]

The time on the run came to an end when a hunter stumbled across the three stragglers one night. Although Hoshi escaped into the jungle, another companion chose to surrender. The other person later left a note saying the war is over, urging the two remaining men to surrender, and leaving instructions on to how do so. Hoshi and his companion decided to give themselves up. They walked to the place designated in the instructions and found a lone American soldier waiting with a dog. He returned to Japan a few weeks later.

Evidence of people hiding in the Guam jungle occasionally surfaced in the decades after World War II. A joint US military–Japanese operation named Operation Straggler took place in 1953. Authorities distributed leaflets, hung posters on trees, and left packages in caves, but no Japanese came forth to surrender.[21]

Press reports in March 1955 told of a haggard Japanese soldier breaking into a home to steal food.[22] A straggler named Bunzo Minagawa was eventually captured on May 21, 1960 by Guamanians in the southern part of the island. He later helped convince his partner, Masashi Ito, to surrender. The pair was thought to be the last remaining holdouts on Guam.[23]

There was one last straggler hiding out and was found on January 24, 1972—twenty-seven years aftter the end of World War II. Army Sergeant Shoichi Yokoi was apprehended by two local fishermen near the Talofofo River in southern Guam. He arrived on the island on March 4, 1944, as part of the Japanese pre-invasion build-up, after his ship survived a torpedo attack by an American submarine en route.[24] His platoon did not participate in the disastrous counterattack on the American beachhead and became isolated in the southern part of the island after the fighting moved north.

The number of Yokoi's companions dwindled until he was eventually alone. He emerged to a very different world from 1945 with an amazing story of survival. "I would like to be reunited with my family and then go up a mountain and meditate for a long time," he said shortly after his capture.[25] Yokoi returned home to Japan and was greeted with a hero's welcome. He later made a return trips to Guam. "The only thing that gave me the strength and will to survive was my faith in myself and that as a soldier of Japan, it was not a disgrace to continue on living," Yokoi said more than a decade later.[26] Yokoi's episode might be considered the real end of straggler activity on Guam.

Chapter 37

BUILDING NEW BASES

THE FINAL TOLL IN LIVES for the battle for Guam was stagger-ing. Of the more than 55,000 American servicemen participating in the operation, 1,440 were killed and 5,650 were wounded.[1] The total Japanese dead can only be estimated. An unknown number were buried in caves and destroyed fortifications or killed in bom-bardments, their bodies never to be found. By the end of the war, 18,337 Japanese were known to have died and about 1,250 became prisoners.[2]

Rapid changes started happening on Guam immediately after the end of organized Japanese resistance. The activity transitioned from combat to construction as the fighting began to wind down. The August 10 meeting of top American commanders, including Admiral Nimitz, set the stage for rebuilding the island and turning it into a major forward operating base for the ongoing drive to Japan.

The key American commanders during the invasion quickly began departing the island.

General Geiger and his staff left for Guadalcanal to begin planning his next operation—the invasion of Palau. Most of the major combat ships and naval commanders also left the area. Admiral Conolly took his flag down from *Appalachia* on the afternoon of August 10. He flew to Pearl Harbor. By the end of the day, no warships larger than a destroyer remained in the Marianas except for Admiral Spruance's flagship *Indianapolis*. Spruance sailed aboard the cruiser for Pearl Harbor on August 26.[3]

The assault troops were gradually replaced with the garrison forces of General Larsen's Island Command. Extensive work was needed to convert Guam into a major forward operating base for the United States. The progress was underway even as soldiers continued to hunt down Japanese stragglers. "The development of a naval base at Guam has been the dream of naval officers for some forty-five years and is now in the process of being realized," Larsen said. He viewed the potential of the island as immense, later noting "there is reason to believe that Guam will become a household term like Pearl Harbor, Gibraltar, and other terms synonymous with military power."[4]

The construction was a joint venture between units of the three service branches involved in the island's liberation—Navy Seabees, army engineers, and marine engineers. There was great cooperation among the services with the Seabees completing about 75 percent of the actual construction. Very little local labor was initially used as many Guamanians were working in the agricultural area or focused on rebuilding their own homes.

Most projects were built for military purposes. However, many of the developments later benefitted the civilian population. Initial construction initiatives included new roads, water systems, and various civilian projects.

The building of roads began while the final stages of the liberation battle was still raging. The constructions of a network of permanent roads were considered a substantial undertaking due to the numerous rocky outcroppings. It was to be the most difficult started to date in the Pacific. Specifications were like those in the United States, with main arteries to be four lanes wide and made of asphalt. Secondary roads were generally two lanes and made of packed coral.

The first major road project was a highway connecting Agaña and Sumay. Construction began a few weeks after the American landings. Progress was slow due to rains and the constant need for supplies to move inland as the front pushed north. Once completed, the four-lane highway was twelve miles long and included nine bridges. The Guam road network eventually reached a total of 103 miles.

No large-scale development can take place on any island without a good supply of water. The water system on Guam was heavily damaged during the pre-invasion bombardment and subsequent battles. The existing resources would have been inadequate for the number of people on the island post-liberation. Various methods were used to develop a new water system—shallow wells in areas near the coast, deep wells inland, and the tapping of springs and rivers. The new system used sixty-seven sources to produce 12 million gallons of water per day.[5]

Much of the civilian housing was destroyed during the liberation battle. There were few inhabitable buildings left in Agaña, Asan, Agat, and Sumay. Lightweight prefabricated structures made of corrugated steel known as Quonset Huts sprang up across the island.

About 15,000 Guamanians needed housing. The Island Command set up three camps in Agaña, Agat, and close to the Ylig River. Each was equipped with a hospital, food preparation area, water, and sanitary systems.[6] The facilities were primitive and crowded, but served as a bridge for civilians needing a place to stay before eventually returning to their own homes or farms.

The announcement by Nimitz about using Guam as a forward base came on August 9, one day before the meeting of the top American commanders. On the same day, he also announced plans to use the island as his forward headquarters.[7] A high priority was quickly given to the development of military facilities of all types.

The building of airbases was a key strategic reason for the seizure of the Marianas. A total of five airfields were constructed on Guam with paved runways and supporting facilities. The airstrip on the Orote Peninsula was initially started by the Americans before the war and completed by the Japanese during their occupation. Marine engineers and Navy Seabees lengthened and rebuilt the existing runway for use by fighters. Various adjacent buildings were constructed, including workshops and warehouses. Orote Field began operation in early August and remained in constant use thereafter.

The almost-complete Japanese airstrip at Tiyan, a few miles northeast of Agaña, was rebuilt into Agaña Field. The base was primarily used for transport planes. The Japanese finished the clearing of land for a runway north of Tiyan, but no additional work was completed at the time of the American invasion. The site was developed into Depot Field (later renamed Harmon Field) with extensive taxiways and a series of large hangars. The base was mostly used for maintenance and repairs of bombers rather than combat missions. Operations began in late October 1944. The base eventually became the largest repair facility for B-29 bombers in the Pacific.[8]

Work on the largest airfield construction project on Guam began in early 1945. Two large airbases for B-29s were carved out of the jungle on the northern side of the island, an area Larsen noted "constitutes an immense potential unsinkable aircraft carrier." North Field and Northwest Field were constructed near Ritidian Point and Pati Point, respectively. Each featured two 8,500-footrunways, taxiways, hardstands, and operations buildings. The first combat flights to Japan took place on February 25, 1945 from North Field. Northwest Field began operation on June 1, 1945. Guam-based bombers operated against Japan for the remainder of the war.

A high urgency was given to the development of port facilities at Apra Harbor. Piers were constructed on Cabras Island, the harbor bottom dredged, and the lengthy breakwater was extended to provide more complete protection for the harbor area. A setback occurred when a large typhoon hit the island in early October 1944. Much of the initial construction work was destroyed, but the rebuilding process started immediately.

A large tank farm, supply depot, naval hospital, and administrative buildings were added. The island eventually became a major naval operating base, with a cargo port, repair facility, and submarine base. The Guam naval base was large enough to be able to support about one-third of the Pacific Fleet by the end of the war.[9] Nimitz moved from Hawaii to his new advanced headquarters built on the Fonte Plateau in early 1945. His command remained on the island until the end of the war.

Along with the bases came the people to operate the facilities. The number of service personnel on the island ballooned. Various types of support facilities were built across Guam, with everything from living quarters and administrative building to supply dumps. One supply depot was spread across 250 acres and contained 369 buildings.[10] The total population of Guam, both military and civilian, swelled to over 220,000 before the end of the war.[11]

Chapter 38

END OF THE WAR

THE AMERICAN VICTORY IN THE Marianas campaign was a dagger thrust deep into the Japanese inner defensive line. The campaign marked the first time in the war an American flag was planted on Japanese territory in the islands of Saipan and Tinian. The defeat was a devastating blow to Japanese leadership. Emperor Hirohito exclaimed, "Hell is upon us" when told the Saipan invasion was underway.[1] The Marianas defeat directly led to the replacement of Prime Minister Hideki Tojo and his entire cabinet.

Aside from the shame, loss of face, and establishment of new American air bases, the defeat had significant military ramifications for the Japanese. The Imperial Navy suffered tremendous aircraft losses in the disastrous Philippine Sea battle. The Americans now possessed a forward operating base, ever closer to Japan, to be used as a staging area for more large invasions.

The war was far from over for the battled-hardened veterans who fought to take Guam back from the enemy. Many received a period of rest before participating in future battles. The United States conducted multiple large amphibious invasions in the year after the Guam operation, including the liberation of the Philippines, Iwo Jima, and Okinawa. The latter two islands further destroyed the Japanese inner defensive ring and tightened the noose on the Home Islands. A significant part of the remaining Japanese fleet was destroyed during the Battle of Leyte Gulf in the Philippines in October 1944.

The 3rd Marine Division remained on Guam until moving north on February 1945 to participate in the battle for Iwo Jima. After initially held in reserve, the division landed on February 24. The unit faced heavy and well-organized resistance while battling the Japanese in difficult terrain. The marines made slow progress and sustained heavy casualties before eventually pushing the enemy back in early March. The unit later returned to Guam to train for the invasion of Japan and were still on the island at the time of the Japanese surrender.

Indiana marine Robert Amstutz was among those on the island after the fighting ended. He remembered the difficult attempts to coax the remaining Japanese holdouts to surrender. "They dropped leaflets in the jungle that the campaign was over and they should come in and surrender," he later recalled. "They weren't going to lose face by doing this. They got very few of them like that."

One day, he received orders to pick up five Japanese stragglers who surrendered near the village of Talofofo in the southeastern part of the island. "Me and [kids] named Bums and Mugan went up there. We had a recon, kind of an oversized jeep that was probably three seats on each side and two bucket seats up front. It could carry eight people," Amstutz recalled.[2] They arrived to find a total of nine prisoners. Eight were stripped from the waist up to prevent any hiding of weapons. One was in full uniform and still carrying a pistol.

"He wanted to surrender to an officer," Amstutz continued. "Mugan was a PFC and was the biggest ranked guy that we had. Mugan took his sidearm off of him, kicked him in the rear end and said, Get your butt in there. I don't even like American officers." The vehicle traveled about fourteen miles across Guam to get back to base with some of the prisoners hanging over the sides. "I had carbines, but you couldn't watch them or anything. You just slung the carbine. They weren't going to do anything. They were glad to get out of that place."

The 1st Provisional Marine Brigade left Guam for Guadalcanal in September 1944. The unit was formally deactivated, and its men became the nucleus for the new 6th Marine Division. The unit participated in the brutal fight for Okinawa starting in April 1945.

The soldiers of the 77th Infantry Division fought in the liberation of the Philippines after departing Guam. The unit landed on the island of Leyte in late October 1944 and participated in the campaign until early 1945. The division later fought in the Battle of Okinawa before returning to the Philippines to prepare for the invasion of Japan.[3]

The end game in Marianas and Guam was the strategic bombing of Japan. The air offensive aimed to cripple industrial production on the enemy's Home Islands. The first B-29 bomber raid from the Marianas took place on November 28, 1944 with the planes making the long haul from Saipan to Japan—a one-way flight of about 1,350 miles.[4] The first months of the bombing missions were plagued by poor weather conditions, the inability to hit the primary targets due to clouds and altitude, and plane losses—amounting to about 6 percent of the total force in one month alone. The losses were equally attributed to operational issues and Japanese countermeasures of fighters and anti-aircraft fire.[5]

Army Major General Curtis LeMay took over command of the bombing offensive in January 1945. He later established his head-quarters on Guam. LeMay implemented new tactics and began fire-bombing major Japanese cities. He ordered a series of massive night-time raids against some of the largest industrial cities—Tokyo, Kobe, Nagoya, and Osaka. The flimsy wooden structures in the densely packed urban areas proved to be no match for American incendiary bombs. One raid on Tokyo during the night of March 9–10 created a massive firestorm. At least 83,000 people were killed and 267,000 buildings destroyed in the conflagration.[6] The bombers were run-ning out of viable targets in the big cities by the summer of 1945. The planes were then turned loose to strike secondary cities.

President Roosevelt did not live to see the end of World War II. Stricken by polio before he became president, he died in Warm Springs, Georgia on April 12, 1945.[7] Vice President Harry Truman became his successor. The new president quickly faced critical deci-sions on the war effort. Germany surrendered in May 1945, bringing the fighting in Europe to a close and allowing President Truman's war focus to shift to the Pacific.

The summer of 1945 found the Japanese empire in a grave posi-tion. The American offensive operations moved the war front on the doorstep of the Home Islands. The aerial bombing campaign, cou-pled with ongoing carrier raids, mining of harbors, and the contin-ued submarine offensive brought critical shortages of food, fuel, and other important strategic materials. Both the Japanese military and civilian populations were in a dire situation.[8] Fuel shortages grounded planes and kept the dwindling number of remaining Imperial Navy ships in port.

An invasion of the Home Islands was only a matter of time. The highest circles of the Japanese government were bitterly divided over negotiating a peace or fighting to the bitter end. The humiliation of an unconditional surrender, the publicly stated goal of the Allies, appeared to be too much for most leaders to accept.

The American Joint Chiefs of Staff issued a directive on April 3, 1945 for General MacArthur to "make plans and preparations for the campaign in Japan."[9] Operation Downfall was the overall name given to the two-phase invasion of Japan designed to bring the Pacific War to a close. The plan was composed of Operation Olympic, an invasion of the southwestern home island of Kyushu in November 1945, and Operation Coronet, a landing in the Kanto Plain region near Tokyo in the spring of 1946. The operations were to be expanded and continued until all organized Japanese resistance in the Home Islands ceased. The invasion forces included those already fighting in the Pacific and an additional American army to be transferred from Europe.

The operation would have been the largest campaign in the Pacific War. American planners envisioned the operation to be bloody beyond any previous campaign in the Pacific and more difficult than the invasion of Normandy in France.[10] The invaders were sure to face suicidal defenders, intent on fighting to the last man. Japanese military and civilian casualties would have been staggering. Planners grappled with the possibility of the fighting continuing into 1947.[11]

The Pacific War was ultimately ended not with a bloody invasion, but by the atomic bomb. The weapon was the product of the Manhattan Project, a secret undertaking to convert uranium into a fission bomb capable of destroying an entire city. President Truman approved the use of the weapon against Japan shortly after the first successful atomic bomb test took place in New Mexico on July 16, 1945.[12] Allied leaders issued the Potsdam Declaration on July 26, 1945. The ultimation called for Japan to unconditionally surrender or face "prompt and utter destruction."[13] The declaration made no specific mention of the atomic bomb.

A B-29 operating from Tinian dropped an atomic bomb over the Japanese city of Hiroshima on August 6, 1945. The detonation obliterated the city in a matter of seconds. More than 80 percent of the buildings in Hiroshima were destroyed and 71,379 people were killed.[14] Thousands more later died of radiation exposure. The Japanese leadership refused to surrender in the face of the massive destruction.

A second atomic bomb was dropped on Nagasaki on August 9. The events were the only time nuclear weapons were used in a conflict. Within days, Emperor Hirohito made the decision to accept the terms of unconditional surrender. His recorded message was broadcast after a failed last-minute coup by radical militarists wanting to keep fighting.[15] The Empire of Japan formally surrendered on September 2 in a ceremony held aboard the battleship *Missouri* in Tokyo Bay.

AMERICAN PRISONERS

THE END OF THE WAR brought liberation for another group of servicemen from Guam—the American garrison captured in 1941. The prisoners endured a forced departure from the island in early January 1942 for a voyage to Japan. Back in the United States, no information was available as to the fate of the Guam prisoners in the weeks immediately following the fall of the island.

The official Japanese news agency Domei aired an interview with Captain George McMillin on January 17, 1942. The former governor stated he had been moved to Japan and reported "satisfactory" treatment by his captors.[1] The interview was the first public news about the Guam men and offered a confirmation that at least some were still alive. The Red Cross sent the US State Department an accurate list of the prisoners about a week later.

The Guam captives subsequently descended into the hellish nightmare of life as prisoners of the Japanese. They were to spend over three-and-a-half arduous years in Japan. Some were moved to different locations as prisoner camps were set up across the Home Islands. Many eventually mixed with prisoners sent from the Philippines and various other conquered territories. The group including British, Australian, and Dutch servicemen. The captives were forced to work in various capacities, including agriculture, factories, and loading food aboard trains.

Navy nurse Leona Jackson was among a small group of civilians moved to Kobe in the middle of March 1942. The party was met by a Japanese man who spoke nearly perfect English. "I don't believe he was American born, but he certainly was American educated, at least in part," Jackson later said. "He was working with the Japanese immigration office, and throughout our whole stay at the detention house in Kobe he was considerate of us and went out of his way to do many things that were nice to us. I think that his people too were still in the United States, and he realized that they would receive decent treatment at our hands and was trying in his own way to give us the sort of treatment he felt his own people were getting."

The quarters for the nurses and civilians were in an old hotel with many amenities not available to the other Guam prisoners—real beds, hot water, and a good amount of food. "Life was reasonably uneventful here, except for one thing," Jackson explained. "That was Doolittle's raid." She was working in the garden with a priest when three American planes flew past with one momentarily veering off to drop bombs on the Kobe docks before rejoining the others speeding away. "We didn't know that it was General Doolittle until we were on the way home, but whoever it was—the bombing was certainly a welcome visitor as far as we were concerned."

By the middle of 1942, there were growing rumors of a civilian prisoner exchange between the United States and Japan. Jackson did not except to be included. "We were military personnel, and we had no expectation of coming back."[2] She was wrong. Jackson and the other Guam nurses were included and departed Japan aboard *Asama Maru* in late June. The transport made stops in Hong Kong, Vietnam, and Singapore to pick up more passengers before proceeding across the Indian Ocean to Lourenco Marques in southeastern Africa. She was met by MS *Gripsholm*, a Swedish ship chartered by the United States carrying Japanese civilians and diplomats.

The actual exchange took place on July 23, 1942.[3] "Once docked, we were home, we were back in the hands of the navy," Jackson later recalled of the end to her ordeal. "Of course, there was the little item about our getting back into the States." The *Gripsholm* then set sail for New Jersey after making a short stopover in Brazil.

Little news was initially available to the prisoners about the progress of the war beyond the guard's constant assurances that the Japanese were winning. Marine Garth Dunn was sent to the Hirohata prison camp west of the city of Osaka. He arrived in October 1942. Prisoners from the camp worked at the nearby Seitetsu Steel Mill or as stevedores unloading ships on the docks at the port. Their only connection to the outside world was when a Chinese ship came into port.

"There were always Chinese who spoke English on the ships, but they had to be careful speaking to us because they couldn't let the Japanese find out what was going on," Dunn remembered. "They would slip somebody an American newspaper, or maybe talk with one or two people, who in turn spread the word. We weren't absolutely sure, but we thought they were telling us the truth, and we certainly wanted to believe what they were saying—that the Americans were getting close, especially a month or so before the war ended."[4]

Marine Don Manning was among those who worked at the docks near Osaka. "All through those years, we kept hoping we'd get out," he recalled. "We had nothing but soup and rice with a piece of rancid fish or meat once a month. Everybody was weak from the diet, but nobody could stop work unless he wanted to be beaten to death."[5] Manning's weight dropped from 160 to 121 pounds during his time as a prisoner.

Conditions for the prisoners gradually worsened as the war progressed. The decline became especially pronounced after the Americans won key victories in 1944. The already-meager daily diet of food was reduced as shortages rapidly spread across Japan. The men began to suffer from exhaustion, malnutrition, and disease. On multiple occasions, the guards lined up the prisoners in front of soldiers with bayonets, though the situation never escalated further.

Later in the war, the prisoners began to see the B-29 bombers and knew the Americans were moving closer to Japan. The captives at the Hirohata prison camp were able to get a clear view of the bombers hitting the nearby town of Himeji on July 4, 1944. "We were looking out from underneath the eves of the barracks, watching them bomb it, cheering the fireworks, shouting and hollering," Dunn recalled. "For us, it was the greatest Fourth of July we ever had."[6] The Japanese guards eventually put a stop to the cheering.

The planes appeared as little sliver specks in the sky, leaving streaking white contrails to Guam sailor Edward Hale. "The guards would beat us if we looked up and were seen to smile," he later wrote. "But we surely smiled inside."[7] He later told comrades, "Someday soon we'll look out towards the Inland Sea and see more warships than the Japanese think there are in the world!"[8]

Rumors were spreading in early August 1945 about a new type of bomb dropped by the Americans capable of destroying an entire city. Marine Captain Charles Todd remembered the Japanese ranting about an "inhuman bomb."[9] The prisoners knew nothing about atomic bombs and had no idea what the weapon could be.

The end of the war seemed to be getting closer. "We had a hunch that the end was near because of the fact that several of the meanest guards suddenly disappeared right after Hiroshima," sailor Robert O'Brien recounted.[10] Then the Japanese surrendered.

The news of the capitulation was not formally revealed to many of the prisoners. "Although no announcement had been made, so many strange things were taking place that we felt sure the war must be over," Navy Commander Donald Giles wrote. "Cigarettes were issued; more rice was provided; some fruit, which we hadn't seen for a long time, appeared."[11] Guards were soon laying down their weapons.

Todd emembered the camp commander gathered the prsioners together. "He told us that Japan had quit fighting in the interest of world peace," he later recalled.[12] The American captives knew better than to believe such propaganda.

"To me, it seemed as if a huge window had suddenly opened, as if fresh air and sunshine had burst in upon us," recalled Hale. "I shook hands with the man on my right and asked him if he thought it was over. He agreed."[13]

Manning remembered "all hell broke loose" after the news arrived of the Japanese surrender. "The prisoners screamed themselves hoarse and nearly tore the place to pieces," he continued. "We got ahold of the instigators of the beatings and terrible treatment we had had. We practically beat them to shreds." Manning later left the camp with others in search of food and clothing.

American flags suddenly began to appear in prison camps. Throngs of American ships and planes shifted from preparing to invade Japan to rescue operations. Planes crisscrossed Japan, Korea, China, and elsewhere, searching for prisoner of war camps. The operations were part of a concerted effort to locate all the Allied prisoner camps on mainland Japan. The process actually began months before the surrender. A list of known prisoner and civilian internment camps had been compiled. The coordinates were provided to the appropriate commands to prevent the sites from becoming targets of American bombers.[14]

General MacArthur ordered the Japanese to account for all prisoner camps after the surrender. The letters "PW" were painted on the roofs of all camps for identification purposes. Through various methods, including the dropping of leaflets and radio broadcasts, American prisoners were directed to stay in their camps until help arrived.

Back on Guam, an endless stream of ships flowed into Apra Harbor dropping off loads of supplies. Various supplies and provisions were packed into drums rigged with parachutes. The B-29s were soon flying missions of mercy dropping cargoes of food, medicine, and clothing to the prisoners.[15] The United States carried out Operation Swift Mercy from August 30 to September 20 to provide aid and supplies to the prisoners until they could be evacuated.[16]

The evacuation of American prisoners from Japan became a high priority in the weeks after the formal Japanese surrender. Most liberated prisoners of the Guam garrison were sent back to the Unites States. The trek was often a long trip with many stopovers and transfer points. Many never returned to Guam.

The surviving Japanese military leaders were held accountable for their actions in the years after the war. MacArthur ordered the arrest of key Japanese leaders one week after the capitulation. The list included the former prime minister, General Tojo. Eleven Allied countries formed the International Military Tribunal for the Far East on April 29, 1946.[17]

The tribunal focused on high-profile cases and national leaders. Japanese war criminals stood trial for a variety of horrific crimes perpetrated against military prisoners and civilians. Most defendants were found guilty and sentenced to prison terms or death. Tojo was sentenced to death and was hung in 1948.

The groundwork for addressing Japanese war crimes specifically committed on Guam and other islands began in late 1944. The US Navy War Crimes Commission on Guam—or the Guam Commission as it became known—was established under the direction of Rear Admiral John D. Murphy. The commission was one of many taking place at various locations around the Pacific. It was separate from the larger war crime trials held in Tokyo and the Philippines. The group operated much like a court and jury combined. Commissioners presided over cases with a prosecution and defense before deliberating and recommending punishment.[18]

Operating in a large Quonset hut near Agaña, the Guam Commission tried 144 military and civilian war criminals.[19] Charges included murder, permitting subordinates to commit atrocities, mistreatments of prisoners, and torture. The crimes took place on various islands. A total of 136 defendants were found guilty.[20] Ten of the convicted men were hung on Guam.

The atrocities related to Guam included charges against Chamorros from Saipan recruited by the Japanese during the occupation. Other crimes were related to the search for George Tweed. Additional charges encompassed the senseless rape and murders taking place in the final weeks before the American invasion.[21] The work of the Guam Commission concluded in May 1949.[22]

Chapter 40

AFTER THE WAR

THE PROCESS OF REBUILDING GUAM from the devastation of World War II took many years. Aside from the physical damage to the island, the war had also been costly for the local population—at least 1,170 Guamanians, representing about a tenth of the civilian population—died by the end of the Japanese occupation.[1] The aftermath of war was a long process of rebuilding an island and civilian lives.

The Civilian Affairs Section of General Larsen's Island Command was responsible for working with the Guamanians. "These were the people who had suffered all manner of atrocities under Japanese rule," Larsen later said. Many civilians were initially brought to the beachhead areas. "Careful preliminary planning and organization had made it possible…to provide with all essentials these thousands of destitute people whose home and property had been destroyed, who were suffering with overworked and under-nourished bodies in poor health."[2]

Some infrastructure work began immediately after the liberation to support the construction of the airfields and naval bases. The rebuilding of civilian areas followed. Most of the larger cities—including Agaña—were heavily or completely destroyed. A large amount of building debris from Agaña was pushed into the ocean to form Paseo, a small peninsula jutting out into the water.

The residents of the village of Sumay on the Orote Peninsula were initially displaced by the Japanese during the occupation. The people were subsequently moved inland to the new town of Santa Rita-Sumai. The land area of the former Sumay was incorporated into the American naval base.

Structures of all types were built—government buildings, churches, homes, and schools. The Guam Bank re-opened for business. "Wholesalers and retailers were set up in business with merchandise from naval stocks," Larsen explained. Workers from the Philippines came to the island to provide labor for the construction projects. Initially staying in large camps, some Filipinos later stayed on Guam and started their own families.

The local population had deep Catholic roots dating back to the days of Spanish colonial rule. "From the flames and ashes of war, organized Catholic life was destined to emerge with unaccustomed vigor," wrote Father Julius Sullivan, a priest who served on Guam after the war.[3] Fifteen new churches were constructed in the post-war years. Nuns arrived from the United States to assist in the development of a Catholic school system.[4]

The government of Guam reverted to navy control for about five years after the war. The island was never reunited with the remainder of the Marianas and remained a territory of the United States.

The other Mariana islands, and various other formerly Japanese-controlled islands, were placed into a trust by the United Nations. The Trust Territory of the Pacific Islands was administered by the United States. Some of the islands later became an independent nation—the Federated States of Micronesia.[5]

Political changes came to Guam when the Organic Act of Guam was passed by Congress and signed by President Truman on August 1, 1950. The law made Guamanians American citizens and solidified the island's status as an unincorporated territory.[6] Oversight of the island was transferred to the US Department of the Interior. The act was amended in 1968 to provide for the popular election of a governor and lieutenant governor.[7] Later changes allowed for an elected legislature and for sending non-voting congressional representation to Washington. Later efforts to move Guam to commonwealth status were unsuccessful.

Economic expansion began in earnest during the 1960s and 1970s after President John F. Kennedy lifted the World War II-era restrictions for traveling to and from Guam.[8] Visitors to the island were previously limited to military personnel with a security clearance. Any non-residents wishing to visit the island needed to apply to the navy for authorization. The easing of travel restrictions was followed by the gradual construction of hotels, restaurants, banks, and shopping centers, leading to job opportunities and a more diversified economy. The removal of travel restrictions, an influx of Japanese commercial investment, and air travel all combined to give birth to a tourist industry.

The growth of post-war commercial air travel connected Guam to the rest of the world. The first commercial airport opened in 1967. The Antonio B. Won Pat International Airport is located a few miles east of Agaña. It is named after the first Guamanian delegate to the United States House of Representatives and is commonly known as

Guam International Airport. The airport originated as a Japanese airfield and became Naval Air Station Agaña after World War II. Today it provides connections to worldwide destinations—including Hawaii, mainland United States, and various Asian cities. It is the only international airport on the island.

The anti-Japanese sentiment on Guam remained strong in the immediate years after World War II. The feelings began to gradually fade when Japanese investment started flowing into the island after the visitor restrictions were lifted. The island was initially marketed in Japan as a closer and cheaper alternative to Hawaii, an enormously popular destination for Japanese tourists in the decades after the war.

The Tumon Bay area eventually became the main tourist area with the construction of entertainment venues, restaurants, duty-free shopping, and high-rises. A list of well-known resort names—including Hyatt Regency, Sheraton, and Westin—line Tumon Beach today. Prior to the Covid-19 pandemic, about 1.2 million people visited in Guam every year. The tourist industry provides the bulk of the island's non-government income. It supports nearly 18,000 jobs and contributes about $1.4 billion annually to the overall economy. Visitors from Japan and Korea currently comprise over 80 percent of the tourist market.[9]

Urbanization and the modernisms of the American way of life slowly began to take shape across Guam in the post-war years. The term Guamanian replaced Chamorros for the local population. Some of the World War II-era names, many dating back to Spanish colonial rule, have changed; the capital of Agaña is now known as Hagatña. The challenge of striking the right balance between the Chamorro culture, history, and Americanism remains. The 2020 United States Census put Guam's total population at 153,836.

The large US military presence on Guam remained indefinitely after World War II. The build-up was not without controversy as many families were forced to give up their land for use by the military without adequate compensation from the United States.[10] About 63 percent of the total land space on the island was retained for military use through purchases or leases in the early post-war years. About 11,000 Guamanians were displaced—about half of the indigenous population.[11]

The town of Sumay was absorbed into US Naval Base Guam. The Fonte Plateau, scene of brutal fighting during first days of the American invasion, was renamed Nimitz Hill in honor of the admiral using the location as his headquarters late in the war. The area remains a military annex with housing and administrative facilities.

North Field was renamed Andersen Air Force Base on October 7, 1949.[12] The sprawling base, on the northeastern part of the island, played a major role throughout the Cold War and beyond. The base served in an administrative and supply capacity during the Korean Conflict. The Vietnam War saw Andersen home to massive Boeing B-52 Stratofortress bombers. The planes flew missions to Southeast Asia during the almost-a-decade span of the Americans' direct involvement in the conflict. The island later served as a staging point for Vietnamese refugees heading to the United States.

The B-52 bombers remained at Andersen after the Vietnam War as part of the global nuclear deterrence force. The military facilities on Guam continued to play an important role in the post-Cold War world. The bases assisted in deploying troops and supplies to the Middle East during the 1991 Gulf War and housed American evacuees after the eruption of Mount Pinatubo in the Philippines later in the same year.[13]

Although the military bases on Guam have expanded and contracted at various times based on needs, a strong military presence remains a fixture on the island. The naval facilities there continue to support naval operations throughout the Pacific.[14] The Joint Region Marianas Command today oversees both the US Naval Base Guam, Andersen Air Force Base, and nearby areas in the Pacific. Military bases continue to be a major source of employment for Guamanians.

Many generations have passed since World War II, but the battle for Guam has not been forgotten. The date of July 21 is celebrated every year as Liberation Day on the island. The public holiday commemorates the day American forces landed in 1944 to begin the battle to free Guam from the brutal Japanese occupiers. Festivities have included the crowning of a queen, parade, carnival, fireworks, and solemn remembrances at massacre sites. Liberation Day continues as the largest celebration on Guam.

GEORGE TWEED AND GUAM: A COMPLICATED LEGACY

THE STORY OF GEORGE TWEED and Guam was just one of many heroic tales to emerge from the bitter fighting of the Pacific War. The story was regularly cast in a patriotic light during the last year of the war—loyal Guamanians seeing the sailor as a symbol of America. The civilians refusing to aid the Japanese occupiers in their search for the fugitive and often paying dearly for their silence in the form of torture and beatings.

General Henry Larsen of the Island Command heard the stories of how the Japanese tried to pressure the island residents into giving up information on Tweed. "But they still they refused to give the Japanese any information where Tweed was in hiding, not because it was Tweed, but because he is an American citizen and it was through their patriotism that they refused to tell the Japanese where Tweed was in hiding," he said at the time.[1] The story may very well be true, to some extent. However, different views of the narrative began to emerge after the war.

Tweed made a second post-rescue expedition back to Guam in September 1946. It turned out to be very different from his first visit. The main purpose of the trip was to present Antonio Artero with a new Chevrolet car, compliments of General Motors. The act was the fulfillment of a promise he made to Artero during one of their many conversations in the cave. Tweed secured the vehicle after writing to the president of General Motors about his ordeal on Guam after his return to the United States. The navy provided the transportation of the car to the island.

Tweed was now a well-known figure with a book published along with many completed speaking engagements and his story appearing in articles of all sorts. Events took a dramatic turn when the sailor was met by a group of protesters, reported to have numbered about a hundred people, led by Father Oscar Calvo. The Guamanians were upset over controversial and unsubstantiated writings in the book *Robinson Crusoe, USN*. The comments indicated Catholic priest Father Jesus Duenas may have openly spoke about Tweed's whereabouts with information given to him in a confessional. The accusation of essentially breaking the sacred seal of confession violates an absolute rule within the Catholic church.

Father Duenas was accused of aiding Tweed and was brutally executed by the Japanese just before the American invasion. The priest's image as a hero and martyr endures to this day for many Guamanians.[2] Also at issue was the idea of Tweed refusing to give himself up to end the suffering and killings of Guamanians who were brutalized in the desperate Japanese search for the fugitive.

An event was held in Agaña to formally turn over the car to Artero. Navy Captain Milton Anderson introduced Tweed, only to be met by about five minutes of booing and jeers. Some of the protesters held signs uncomplimentary to the visitor. Press reports wrote of a white-faced Tweed tearing up a protester's sign reading, "What about Tweed's desertion in the face of the enemy?" muttering, "You bunch of lousy rats."[3]

The protesters eventually moved away, allowing the event to continue—albeit with a much smaller crowd. Tweed made a formal presentation of the car before Artero gave a short acceptance speech. Several Guamanians came forward to shake Tweed's hand. Amalla Mariano gave him some flags given to her by Al Tyson and Clarence Johnston before their deaths.

Tweed later admitted the part in the book about Father Duenas was incorrect. "I repeated a story someone else told me and I mentioned that Father Duenas broke the seal of confession." He said the story was "untrue in all details" and he was "terribly sorry."[4] The sailor also attempted to find others who provided help during his visit to the island.

The matter of Tweed not surrendering periodically came up in the decades after the war. Comments made by businessman and politician B. J. Bordallo were typical of how some Guamanians felt. "What I could not understand was while many of our people were being brutalized on account of him, Tweed was moving from place to place, attending parties, and generally enjoying himself," Bordallo later said. "Knowing that people were being killed or maimed, if Tweed had really been a hero, he would have come out and turned himself in so that the wholesale brutalization of our people would cease."[5]

Looking back many years after the war, Adolfo Sgambelluri also could not understand why Tweed did not surrender. The former police officer was forced to work for the Japanese during the occupation while secretly helping Guamanian civilians to keep the occupiers from finding Tweed. He later stated he always knew of the fugitive sailor's whereabouts during the occupation.[6] Sgambelluri noted the sailor had no radio capable of sending messages and no way to pass along any information to the approaching Americans.

"When they started looking for him and having people tortured, that's the time he should come in before it becomes so serious that finally everybody's a spy because Tweed is still at large," Sgambelluri later explained. He also spoke of the repeating cycle of terror with Guamanians giving up names of people, whether they were involved with Tweed or not, under duress to Japanese interrogators in an effort to save themselves. "And they keep beating the guy up until naturally...he will just give up names and then they're going to pick up the other guy."[7]

Tweed saw the issue as one of self-preservation. "Well, I was just committing suicide if I did because of the fact that the Japs announced right at the start that they didn't want any more American prisoners," he later said about the option to surrender. "That any Americans left in the jungles would be killed."[8]

Later on, Tweed gradually spoke less of the patriotic angle and more of appreciation. He never seemed to forget those who helped him. "I greatly appreciate these people who did help me, those besides Antonio," Tweed told an interviewer many years later. "If it hadn't been for them, I wouldn't have lived until I got to Antonio's place. So naturally I give them part credit for the fact that I'm still alive and I appreciated it immensely."[9] Separated by generations from World War II makes it is easy for me to see both sides of the issue.

The end of the war saw throngs of servicemen leaving the military and returning to civilian life. George Tweed was among them. He remained on active duty for a few years before moving to the Naval

Reserve. Tweed retired from the navy with the rank of lieutenant on March 23, 1953, with thirty years of service to his credit.[10]

The longtime sailor returned to his native Oregon, eventually settling in Grants Pass. He later operated a television and radio repair business. The story of his World War II exploits slowly faded away until the saga was resurrected in the 1962 movie *No Man Is an Island.* The role of Tweed was played by actor Jeffrey Hunter. Film critics described the low-budget movie as "fairly good" and one noted "it aims at a modest dramatic goal and achieves it with a likable simplicity."[11]

Tweed remained friends with Artero long after the war even though he never visited Guam again. They were two individuals connected by time and place during a desperate period for both. News reports indicated that Artero and his wife Josefa visited Tweed's ranch in Oregon. The couple and the sailor exchanged letters over the years, updating each other on the progression of their lives and sharing family photos.[12]

The American government awarded Artero the Medal of Freedom, the highest civilian honor, for his help in saving Tweed. His son later stated his father "loved the medal dearly. It stood for freedom...."[13]

Artero's relationship with the American government later soured. The family was forced to sell a large part of their land holdings to the United States military when what later became Andersen Air Force Base was developed in the northern part of Guam after the war. Antonio Artero passed away in May 1984 at the age of seventy-nine. Tweed told a reporter the news "really breaks me up."[14]

The George Tweed story largely slipped away from the public's eye as the years passed. The tale occasionally surfaced in a news article, often in Guam and sometimes in relation to an anniversary of the liberation. Tweed again recounted his experiences in an interview broadcast on Guam television in 1984, perhaps bringing his story to a new generation of Guamanians. George Tweed died in a car accident in northern California on January 18, 1989.[15] He was eighty-six years old.

ENDNOTES

Prologue

1   "Secretary of the Navy John D. Long to Captain Henry Glass." Naval History and Heritage Command, https://www.history.navy.mil/research/publications/documentary-histories/united-states-navy-s/the-capture-of-guam/secretary-of-the-nav.html (accessed March 29, 2020).

2   Leslie Walker. "Guam's Seizure by the United States in 1898." *The Pacific Historical Review* vol. 14, no. 1 (March 1945), 3.

3   Gordon L. Rottman. *World War II Pacific Island Guide: A Geo-Military Study*. Westport, CT: Greenwood Press, 2002, 388.

4   Mairin Mitchell and Francisco Contente Domingues. "Ferdinand Magellan." *Britannica*, https://www.britannica.com/biography/Ferdinand-Magellan (January 12, 2000).

5   Philip Crowl. *Campaign in the Marianas*. Washington, DC: Office of the Chief of Military History, Department of the Army, 1960, 21.

6   Doug Herman. "A Brief, 500-Year History of Guam." Smithsonian Magazine, https://www.smithsonianmag.com/smithsonian-institution/brief-500-year-history-guam-180964508/ (August 15, 2017).

7   Laura Thompson. *Guam and Its People*. Princeton: Princeton University Press, 1947, 58.

8   Crowl, *Campaign in the Marianas*, 21.

9   Captain Lucius W. Johnson. "Guam - Before December, 1941," *U.S. Naval Institute Proceedings* vol. 68, no. 473, https://www.usni.org/magazines/proceedings/1942/july/guam-december-1941 (July 1942).

10   Herman, "500-Year History of Guam."

11   Ibid.

12   Frank Portusach. "History of the Capture of Guam by the United States Man-Of War 'Charleston' and Its Transport," *U.S. Naval Institute Proceedings* vol. 43, no. 170, https://www.usni.org/magazines/proceedings/1917/april/history-capture-guam-united-states-man-war-charleston-and-its (April 1917).

13   Marcus J. Thompson. "Revisiting the U.S. Capture of Guam During the Spanish-American War." Naval History and Heritage Command, https://www.history.navy.mil/browse-by-topic/wars-conflicts-and-operations/spanish-american-war/us-capture-of-guam.html (June 2017).

14   Ibid.

15   Walker, "Guam's Seizure," 10–11; Oscar King Davis. *Our Conquests in the Pacific*. New York: Fredrick A. Stokes Company, 1899, 74.

Chapter 1

1   George Horne. "Radioman, Rescued after 2-1/2 Years, Reveals in Graphic Detail Story." *New York Times* (August 11, 1944), 7.

2   Robert Sherrod. "Radioman George Tweed on Guam." *Life* (August 21, 1944), 44.

3   Roger Mansell. *Captured: The Forgotten Men of Guam*. Annapolis, MD: Naval Institute Press, 2012, 11.

4   Center for Research Allied POWS Under the Japanese. "Roster of Guam Personnel," http://www.mansell.com/pow_resources/guam/guamroster.html#anchor189970; Leo Babauta. "George Tweed." Guampedia, https://www.guampedia.com/george-tweed/ (accessed February 15, 2020).

5   George R. Tweed and Blake Clark. Robinson Crusoe, *USN: The Adventures of George R. Tweed*, RM1C on Jap-Held Guam, As Told to Blake Clark. New York: McGraw-Hill Book Company, 1945, 9.

6   Layla Raymanova. "George Tweed Interview Pt1." YouTube, https://youtu.be/k4ChrqynmGs (September 1, 2009). Hereafter cited as "George Tweed Interview Pt1."

7   "Plaza de España (Hagåtña)." Wikipedia, https://en.wikipedia.org/wiki/Plaza_de_España_(Hagåtña) (last edited January 30, 2022).

8   Donald T. Giles. *Captive of the Rising Sun: The POW Memoirs of Rear Admiral Donald T. Giles, USN*. Annapolis, MD: Naval Institute Press, 1994, 16.

9   Sherrod, "Radioman George Tweed," 44.

10 Horne, "Rescued after 2-1/2 Years," 7.

11 "Survivors: The Rescue of George Tweed." *Time*, August 21, 1944, 72.

12 "Narrative by George Ray Tweed, CRM, USN." World War II Interviews. College Park, MD: National Archives. August 25, 1944, 1. Hereafter cited as "Narrative by George Ray Tweed."

13 Horne, "Rescued after 2-1/2 Years," 7.

14 Ibid.

Chapter 2

1   Gordon Rottman and Howard Gerrard. *Guam 1941 & 1944: Loss and Reconquest*. Oxford, England: Osprey, 2004, 15.

2   "George Ray Tweed: Dates of Service" in "George R. Tweed Service Record." National Personnel Records Center, St. Louis, MO. Hereafter cited as "Tweed Service Record."

3   George Tweed, to Chief of the Bureau of Navigation. "Duty at San Juan, PR, Request For." April 29, 1939 in "Tweed Service Record."

4   Western Union Telegram of June 30, 1939 in "Tweed Service Record."

5   R. W. Robson. *The Pacific Islands Handbook*. New York: The Macmillan Company, 1946, 155; Rottman, *Pacific Island Guide*, 385.

6   Robson, *Pacific Islands Handbook*, 155.

7   Crowl, *Campaign in the Marianas*, 307.

8   Edward E. Hale and Helen Heightsman Gordon. *First Captured, Last Freed: Memoirs of a POW in World War II, Guam and Japan*. Sebastopol, CA: Grizzly Bear Press, 1995, 12.

9   Rottman, *Pacific Island Guide*, 385.

10   Crowl, *Campaign in the Marianas*, 308.
11   Rottman, *Pacific Island Guide*, 387.
12   Crowl, *Campaign in the Marianas*, 308.
13   Rear Admiral G. J. Rowcliff. "Guam." *U.S. Naval Institute Proceedings* vol. 71, no. 509, https://www.usni.org/magazines/proceedings/1945/july/guam (July 1945).

Chapter 3

1   Lieutenant (J.G.) William Thompson. "The Guam Story." *U.S. Naval Institute Proceedings* vol. 77, no. 578, https://www.usni.org/magazines/proceedings/1951/april/guam-story (April 1951).
2   "Treaty of Peace Between the United States and Spain; December 10, 1898." Yale Law School Lillian Goldman Law Library, https://avalon.law.yale.edu/19th_century/sp1898.asp (2008).
3   Crowl, *Campaign in the Marianas*, 22.
4   Timothy P. Maga. "Democracy and Defense: The Case of Guam, U.S.A., 1918–1941." *The Journal of Pacific History*, July 1985, 156.
5   Henry P. Beers, Robert G. Albion, E J. Leahy, and W N. Franklin. *American Naval Occupation and Government of Guam, 1898–1902*. Washington, DC: Office of Records Administration, Administrative Office, Navy Dept, 1944, 18.
6   Robson, *Pacific Islands Handbook*, 153.
7   Ibid.
8   Thompson, "The Guam Story," 2.
9   Beers, *American Naval Occupation and Government of Guam*, 22.
10   Herman, "500-Year History of Guam," 2–3.
11   Rottman, *Pacific Island Guide*, 388.
12   Thompson, *Guam and Its People*, 138–139.
13   Thompson, "The Guam Story," 5; Robson, *Pacific Islands Handbook*, 155.
14   "All the Way to Guam." Pan Am Historical Foundation, https://www.panam.org/pan-am-stories/622-all-the-way-to-guam-2 (accessed June 9, 2020).
15   Mansell, *The Forgotten Men of Guam*, 3.
16   Commanding Officer to Chief of the Bureau of Navigation. "Tweed, George Ray—Change of Beneficiary." January 7, 1939 in "Tweed Service Record."
17   C.D. Leffler to Mrs. George Tweed. "Transportation" (October 26, 1939), in "Tweed Service Record."
18   Rottman and Gerrard, *Guam 1941 & 1944*, 13.
19   Samuel Eliot Morison. *History of United States Naval Operations in World War II, Volume III: The Rising Sun in the Pacific*. Edison, NJ: Castle Books, 2001, 184.
20   "Gold Star." Dictionary of American Fighting Ships, https://www.history.navy.mil/research/histories/ship-histories/danfs/g/gold-star.html (accessed June 11, 2020).
21   Robson, *Pacific Islands Handbook*, 155.
22   Rottman, *Pacific Island Guide*, 389.
23   Mansell, *The Forgotten Men of Guam*, 11.
24   Dominica Tolentino. "Guam Echo and Guam Eagle." Guampedia, https://www.guampedia.com/guam-echo-and-guam-eagle/ (accessed June 21, 2020).

25 A. David Middleton. "The Ghost of Guam—KB6GJX." *QST Magazine* (March 1945), 38.

Chapter 4

1   Edward S. Miller. *War Plan Orange: The U.S. Strategy to Defeat Japan, 1897–1945*. Annapolis, MD: Naval Institute Press, 1991, 70–71.
2   Earl S. Pomeroy. "American Policy Respecting the Marshalls, Carolines, and Marianas, 1898–1941." *Pacific Historical Review* (February 1948), 51.
3   Dan Van Der Vat. *The Pacific Campaign*. New York: Simon & Schuster, 1991, 14.
4   John Costello. *The Pacific War*. New York: Rawson, Wade Publishers, Inc., 1981, 25; Ronald H. Spector. *Eagle Against the Sun: The American War with Japan*. New York: Vintage Books, 1985, 37.
5   Dirk Ballendorf. "Secrets without Substance: U.S. Intelligence in the Japanese Mandates, 1915–1935." *The Journal of Pacific History* (April 1984), 84.
6   Paul S. Dull. *A Battle History of the Imperial Japanese Navy*. Annapolis, MD: Naval Institute Press, 1978, 4.
7   Morison, *Rising Sun in the Pacific*, 17.
8   Costello, *The Pacific War*, 32.
9   Ibid., 71.
10 Spector, *Eagle Against the Sun*, 68.
11 Harry Gailey. *The War in the Pacific: From Pearl Harbor to Tokyo Bay*. Novato, CA: Presidio, 1997, 69.
12 Morison, *Rising Sun in the Pacific*, 63.
13 Gordon W. Prange, Katherine V. Dillon, and Donald M. Goldstein. *At Dawn We Slept: The Untold Story of Pearl Harbor*. New York: McGraw-Hill, 1981, 169.
14 Lewis Morton. *U.S. Army in World War II: The War in the Pacific: The Fall of the Philippines*. Washington, DC: Center of Military History, US Army, 1989, 52.
15 Dull, *Imperial Japanese Navy*, 7.
16 Morison, *Rising Sun in the Pacific*, 65.

Chapter 5

1   Rottman, *Pacific Island Guide*, 387.
2   "Naval Era Governors of Guam." Guampedia, https://www.guampedia.com/naval-era-governors-of-guam/ (accessed June 17, 2020).
3   Mansell, *The Forgotten Men of Guam*, 11.
4   Maga, "Democracy and Defense," 170.
5   Rottman, *Pacific Island Guide*, 389.
6   Maga, "Democracy and Defense," 170.
7   Ibid.
8   Rottman and Gerrard, *Guam 1941 & 1944*, 19.
9   Giles, *Captive of the Rising Sun*, 24.
10 "Surrender of Guam to the Japanese: The Report of George J. McMillin, Captain, USN." U.S. National Park Service, https://www.nps.gov. Hereafter cited as "Guam Surrender Report."

11 *Astoria* Deck Log, October 16, 1941.
12 Giles, *Captive of the Rising Sun*, 25.
13 Prange, Dillon, and Goldstein, *At Dawn We Slept*, 406.
14 Rear Admiral Edwin T. Layton, with Captain Roger Pineau and John Costello. *And I Was There: Pearl Harbor and Midway—Breaking the Secrets*. New York: William Morrow and Company, 1985, 215.
15 Mansell, *The Forgotten Men of Guam*, 14.
16 Giles, *Captive of the Rising Sun*, 27
17 Mansell, *The Forgotten Men of Guam*, 14.
18 Ibid., 26.
19 Horne, "Rescued after 2-1/2 Years," 7.
20 "George Tweed Interview Pt1."
21 Dull, *Imperial Japanese Navy*, 10.
22 Ibid., 11.

Chapter 6

1   Crowl, *Campaign in the Marianas*, 23.
2   Eric Lacroix and Linton Wells. *Japanese Cruisers of the Pacific War*. Annapolis, MD: Naval Institute Press, 1997, 751.
3   Glen Williford. *Racing the Sunrise: Reinforcing America's Pacific Outposts, 1941–1942*. Annapolis, MD: Naval Institute Press, 2010, 209.
4   "Guam Surrender Report," 3.
5   *Penguin* Muster Roll, September 1941.
6   Hale and Gordon, *First Captured, Last Freed*, 12.
7   Mansell, *The Forgotten Men of Guam*, 18.
8   War Diary, Sixteenth Naval District, December 8, 1941.
9   Giles, *Captive of the Rising Sun*, 28.
10 "Guam Surrender Report," 2.
11 Mansell, *The Forgotten Men of Guam*, 17.
12 "Narrative by Miss Leona Jackson, Lieutenant (jg), Navy Nurse." World War II Interviews. College Park, MD: National Archives. March 31, 1943, 1. Hereafter cited as "Jackson Narrative."
13 "Penguin." Dictionary of American Fighting Ships, https://www.history.navy.mil/research/histories/ship-histories/danfs/p/penguin-ii.html (accessed July 24, 2020).
14 Giles, *Captive of the Rising Sun*, 34.

Chapter 7

1   Horne, "Rescued after 2-1/2 Years," 7.
2   "Narrative by George Ray Tweed," 2.
3   Horne, "Rescued after 2-1/2 Years," 7.
4   Tweed and Clark, *Robinson Crusoe, USN*, 21–22.
5   Ibid., 23.
6   Horne, "Rescued after 2-1/2 Years," 7.

7   Naval Security Group Detachment. "US Naval Radio Station Libugon, Guam." Crane, IN, 1981, 24.
8   War Diary, Sixteenth Naval District, December 8, 1941.
9   "US Naval Radio Station Libugon, Guam."
10   Mansell, *The Forgotten Men of Guam*, 20.
11   War Diary, Sixteenth Naval District, December 9, 1941.
12   Dull, *Imperial Japanese Navy*, 22.
13   Rottman and Gerrard, *Guam 1941 & 1944*, 19.
14   US Army Historical Division. *Japanese Monograph Number 48: Operations in the Central Pacific, Volume 1*. Washington, DC: Department of the Army, 1946, 5.
15   Morison, *Rising Sun in the Pacific*, 185.
16   Williford, *Racing the Sunrise*, 209.
17   US Army Historical Division, *Japanese Monograph Number 48*, 3.

Chapter 8

1   Wakako Higuchi. *The Japanese Administration of Guam, 1941–1944: A Study of Occupation and Integration Policies, With Japanese Oral Histories*. Jefferson, North Carolina: McFarland & Company, 2013, 162–163.
2   Ibid., 5–6.
3   Giles, *Captive of the Rising Sun*, 41.
4   Williford, *Racing the Sunrise*, 209.
5   Giles, *Captive of the Rising Sun*, 43.
6   Mansell, *The Forgotten Men of Guam*, 27.
7   Giles, *Captive of the Rising Sun*, 45.
8   Ibid.
9   Morison, *Rising Sun in the Pacific*, 185.
10   Hale and Gordon, *First Captured, Last Freed*, 18.
11   "Guam Surrender Report," 5.
12   Giles, *Captive of the Rising Sun*, 48.
13   "Guam Surrender Report," 2.

Chapter 9

1   Ibid., 3.
2   Higuchi, *The Japanese Administration of Guam*, 163.
3   Rottman, *Pacific Island Guide*, 390.
4   "Jackson Narrative," 2.
5   Mansell, *The Forgotten Men of Guam*, 33.
6   "The death of Private Kauffman, USMC Sumay Barracks, Guam Island, December 10th, 1941." https://www.oocities.org/dutcheastindies/kauffman.html (accessed August 4, 2020).
7   Ibid.; Giles, *Captive of the Rising Sun*, 50.
8   Giles, *Captive of the Rising Sun*, 51.
9   Hale and Gordon, *First Captured, Last Freed*, 21.

10 Office of Public Relations, US Navy. *Navy Department Communiques 1–300 and Pertinent Press Releases.* Washington, DC: US Government Printing Office, 1943, 2.

11 Giles, *Captive of the Rising Sun,* 64.

12 Mansell, *The Forgotten Men of Guam,* 41.

13 Giles, *Captive of the Rising Sun,* 53.

14 Hale and Gordon, *First Captured, Last Freed,* 24.

15 Mansell, *The Forgotten Men of Guam,* 40.

16 "Marine Survives Imprisonment, Beating." *Ogden Standard-Examiner* (UT), October 18, 1945, 11.

17 Giles, *Captive of the Rising Sun,* 55.

18 Ibid., 59.

Chapter 10

1 "Great Shrine Island: The Japanese Occupation of Guam." US National Park Service, https://www.nps.gov/parkhistory/online_books/npswapa/extContent/wapa/guides/first/sec4.htm (accessed August 5, 2020).

2 Hale and Gordon, *First Captured, Last Freed,* 27.

3 Giles, *Captive of the Rising Sun,* 54–55.

4 "Jackson Narrative," 5.

5 "Argentina Maru Class." Combined Fleet, http://www.combinedfleet.com/Argentina_c.htm (accessed March 29, 2021).

6 Gavan Daws. *Prisoners of the Japanese: POWs of World War II in the Pacific.* New York: William Morrow, 1994, 285.

7 Higuchi, *The Japanese Administration of Guam,* 44.

8 "Marine Survives Imprisonment, Beating," 11.

9 Craig Smith. *Counting the Days: POWs, Internees, and Stragglers of World War II in the Pacific.* Washington, DC: Smithsonian Books, 2012, 57.

10 Thomas Saylor. "Oral History Project World War II Years, 1941–1946 – Marvin Roslansky," https://digitalcommons.csp.edu/oral-history_ww2/64 (June 25, 2004) .

11 "IJN *Argentine Maru*: Tabular Record of Movement." Combined Fleet, http://www.combinedfleet.com/Argentina_t.htm (accessed March 29, 2021).

12 Mansell, *The Forgotten Men of Guam,* 44.

13 "Great Shrine Island: The Japanese Occupation of Guam."

14 Boyd Dixon, Laura Gilda, and Lon Bulgrin. "The Archaeology of World War II Japanese Stragglers on the Island of Guam and the Bushido Code." *Asian Perspectives* (Spring 2012), 111; Higuchi, *The Japanese Administration of Guam,* 44.

15 D. Colt Denfeld. *Hold the Marianas: The Japanese Defense of the Mariana Islands.* Shippensburg, PA: White Mane Publishing Company, 1997, 152.

16 Higuchi, *The Japanese Administration of Guam,* 173.

17 "Great Shrine Island: The Japanese Occupation of Guam."

18 Ben Blaz. *Bisita Guam: Let Us Remember.* Guam: Richard F. Taitano Micronesian Area Research Center, University of Guam, 2008, 51.

19 Wakako Higuchi, PhD. "Japanese Military Administration of Guam." Guampedia, https://www.guampedia.com/japanese-military-administration-of-guam/ (accessed March 29, 2021).
20 Blaz, *Bisita Guam*, 48.
21 Tony Palomo. *An Island in Agony*. Annandale, VA: T. Palomo, 1984, 123.

Chapter 11

1 "Narrative by George Ray Tweed," 2.
2 Babauta, "George Tweed."
3 Middleton, "The Ghost of Guam," 39.
4 Layla Raymanova. "George Tweed Interview Pt2." YouTube, https://youtu.be/1o4EVSFJwmA (September 1, 2009). Hereafter cited as "George Tweed Interview Pt2."
5 Sherrod, "Radioman George Tweed," 44.
6 Babauta, "George Tweed."
7 *Penguin* Muster Roll, September 1941.
8 Palomo, *An Island in Agony*, 102.
9 Giles, *Captive of the Rising Sun*, 49.
10 Tweed and Clark, *Robinson Crusoe, USN*, 46.
11 "Narrative by George Ray Tweed," 10.

Chapter 12

1 Guy Nasuti. "The Forsaken Defenders of Wake Island." Naval History and Heritage Command, https://www.history.navy.mil/browse-by-topic/wars-conflicts-and-operations/world-war-ii/1941/philippines/defenders-of-wake.html (July 8, 2019).
2 Morison, *Rising Sun in the Pacific*, 227–228.
3 John Toland. *But Not in Shame: The Six Months After Pearl Harbor*. New York: Random House, 1961, 81.
4 "IJN *Hayate*: Tabular Record of Movement." Combined Fleet, http://www.combined-fleet.com/hayate_t.htm (accessed June 21, 2020).
5 Costello, *The Pacific War*, 162; Dull, *Imperial Japanese Navy*, 25.
6 Morison, *Rising Sun in the Pacific*, 248.
7 Spector, *Eagle Against the Sun*, 108.
8 Clayton Chun and Howard Gerrard. *The Fall of the Philippines 1941–42*. Oxford, UK: Osprey, 2012, 15.
9 Dull, *Battle History*, 29.
10 Chun and Gerrard, *The Fall of the Philippines*, 48.
11 Ibid., 57.
12 Costello, *The Pacific War*, 197.
13 Ibid., 202.

Chapter 13

1 Tweed and Clark, *Robinson Crusoe, USN*, 29.
2 Palomo, *An Island in Agony*, 105.

3   "Narrative by George Ray Tweed," 8–9.
4   Babauta, "George Tweed."
5   Palomo, *An Island in Agony*, 107–115.
6   Jasmine Stole Weiss. "George Tweed, Controversial War Hero, Refused to Surrender when Japanese Forces Invaded." Delmarva Now, https://www.delmarvanow.com/story/beyondliberation/2019/07/14/liberation-george-tweed-controversial-war-hero-survived-chamorus-guam/1722324001/ (accessed May 10, 2020).
7   Palomo, *An Island in Agony*, 116.
8   Quentin Reynolds. "These Are Americans." *Reader's Digest*, August, 1945, 36.
9   Babauta, "George Tweed."
10   Rene Mahone. "William G. Johnston 1880–1943: A Bibliography." Center for Research Allied POWS Under the Japanese, http://www.mansell.com/pow_resources/camplists/osaka/futatabi/JOHNSTON_Wm_G_bio_Futatabi.pdf (accessed September 21, 2020).
11   Reynolds, "These Are Americans," 35.
12   "Agueda Iglesias Johnston: Patriot." US National Park Service, https://www.nps.gov/parkhistory/online_books/npswapa/extContent/Lib/liberation6.htm (accessed September 21, 2020).
13   "George Tweed Interview Pt2."

Chapter 14

1   "Ernest Joseph King 23 November 1878 – 25 June 1956." Naval History and Heritage Command, https://www.history.navy.mil/research/histories/biographies-list/bios-k/king-ernest-j.html (August 11, 2008). Hereafter cited as "Ernest Joseph King."
2   "Fleet Admiral Ernest J. King: Ninth Chief of Naval Operations." Naval History and Heritage Command, https://www.history.navy.mil/browse-by-topic/people/chiefs-of-naval-operations/fleet-admiral-ernest-j--king.html (accessed June 23, 2020). Hereafter cited as "King: Ninth Chief of Naval Operations."
3   "Ernest Joseph King."
4   "King: Ninth Chief of Naval Operations."
5   Ibid.; Spector, *Eagle Against the Sun*, 126.
6   Clark G. Reynolds. "Admiral Ernest J. King and the Strategy for Victory in the Pacific." *Naval War College Review* vol. 28, no. 3 (Winter 1976), 57.
7   "Chester William Nimitz: 24 February 1885 - 20 February 1966." Naval History and Heritage Command, https://www.history.navy.mil/content/history/nhhc/research/histories/biographies-list/bios-n/nimitz-chester-w.html (accessed June 23, 2020). Hereafter cited as "Chester William Nimitz."
8   Edwin P. Hoyt. *How They Won the War in the Pacific: Nimitz and His Admirals.* New York: Lyons Press, 2000, 43.
9   "Chester William Nimitz."
10   Toland, *But Not in Shame*, 89.
11   Hoyt, *How They Won the War in the Pacific*, 44.
12   Van Der Vat, *The Pacific Campaign*, 149.
13   Hoyt, *How They Won the War in the Pacific*, 35; Spector, *Eagle Against the Sun*, 146.
14   Toland, *But Not in Shame*, 132.

Chapter 15

1 Van Der Vat, *The Pacific Campaign*, 153.
2 Spector, *Eagle Against the Sun*, 144.
3 Costello, *The Pacific War*, 236
4 Toland, *But Not in Shame*, 335.
5 Dull, *Imperial Japanese Navy*, 133.
6 Samuel Eliot Morison. *History of United States Naval Operations in World War II, Volume IV: The Coral Sea, Midway and Submarine Actions*. Edison, NJ: Castle Books, 2001, 63.
7 "Battle of the Coral Sea." Naval History and Heritage Command, https://www.history.navy.mil/content/history/nhhc/our-collections/photography/wars-and-events/world-war-ii/battle-of-the-coral-sea.html (accessed June 21, 2020).
8 Van Der Vat, *The Pacific Campaign*, 177.
9 Dull, *Imperial Japanese Navy*, 129.
10 Morison, *The Coral Sea, Midway and Submarine Actions*, 70.
11 Ibid., 75.
12 Dull, *Imperial Japanese Navy*, 133.
13 Ibid., 139–140.
14 Hoyt, *How They Won the War in the Pacific*, 88.
15 "Battle of Midway: 3–7 June 1942." Naval History and Heritage Command, https://www.history.navy.mil/browse-by-topic/wars-conflicts-and-operations/world-war-ii/1942/midway.html (accessed June 26, 2020). Hereafter cited as "Battle of Midway."
16 Morison, *The Coral Sea, Midway and Submarine Actions*, 94.
17 "Battle of Midway."
18 Van Der Vat, *The Pacific Campaign*, 199.
19 Spector, *Eagle Against the Sun*, 186.
20 Costello, *The Pacific War*, 319.
21 Dull, *Imperial Japanese Navy*, 179.

Chapter 16

1 Tolentino, "Guam Echo and Guam Eagle."
2 Middleton, "The Ghost of Guam," 39.
3 Palomo, *An Island in Agony*, 90.
4 Middleton, "The Ghost of Guam," 40.
5 "International Broadcast Station KGEI: 1939–1994: History Courtesy of FEBC International." http://www.theradiohistorian.org/kgei.htm (accessed September 23, 2020).
6 Jim Clifford. "KGEI: A Forgotten WWII Radio Story." https://www.smdailyjournal.com/news/local/kgei-a-forgotten-wwii-radio-story/article_4f8f263e-8062-11e7-bf9e-fbf338cf40e3.html (August 14, 2017).
7 Tweed and Clark, *Robinson Crusoe, USN*, 93–94.
8 "Narrative by George Ray Tweed," 19.
9 Tolentino, "Guam Echo and Guam Eagle."

10 Adam Lynch. "Deadly Game of Hide and Seek." *World War II*, June 2005, 18.
11 "Narrative by George Ray Tweed," 20.
12 Lynch, "Deadly Game of Hide and Seek," 16.
13 Babauta, "George Tweed."
14 "George Tweed Interview Pt2."
15 Eric Forbes. "Monsignor Oscar Calvo." Guampedia, https://www.guampedia.com/monsignor-oscar-calvo/ (accessed September 24, 2020).
16 Reynolds, "These Are Americans," 35.
17 Tweed and Clark, *Robinson Crusoe, USN*, 134–136.
18 Palomo, *An Island in Agony*, 109.

Chapter 17

1 Jasmine Stole Weiss. "Sgambelluri's (Almost) Secret Legacy as a WWII Double Agent." Pacific Daily News, https://www.guampdn.com/story/news/local/2019/03/03/wwii-veteran-marine-japanese-italian-sgambelluris-almost-secret-legacy/3038451002/ (March 4, 2019).
2 Raj Sood. "Sgambelluri's Secret Life." US National Park Service, https://www.nps.gov/parkhistory/online_books/npswapa/extcontent/lib/liberation29.htm (accessed September 25, 2020).
3 Weiss, "Sgambelluri's (Almost) Secret Legacy as a WWII Double Agent."
4 Palomo, *An Island in Agony*, 116.
5 Mansell, *The Forgotten Men of Guam*, 57.
6 Palomo, *An Island in Agony*, 110.
7 Mansell, *The Forgotten Men of Guam*, 56.
8 Palomo, *An Island in Agony*, 112.
9 Ibid., 115.
10 Mansell, *The Forgotten Men of Guam*, 57; Tweed and Clark, *Robinson Crusoe, USN*, 160.
11 "Narrative by George Ray Tweed," 11.

Chapter 18

1 Paul J. Borja. "Symbol of Hope, Controversy." US National Park Service, http://npshistory.com/publications/wapa/npswapa/extContent/Lib/liberation5.htm (accessed September 24, 2020).
2 "Narrative by George Ray Tweed," 12.
3 Lynch, "Deadly Game of Hide and Seek," 16.
4 Tweed and Clark, *Robinson Crusoe, USN*, 150.
5 Higuchi, *The Japanese Administration of Guam*, 195.
6 Palomo, *An Island in Agony*, 175; Tweed and Clark, *Robinson Crusoe, USN*, 151.
7 Tweed and Clark, *Robinson Crusoe, USN*, 152.
8 "Narrative by George Ray Tweed," 12–13.
9 Dominica Tolentino. "Pascual Artero y Saez." Guampedia, https://www.guampedia.com/pascual-artero-y-saez/ (accessed October 2, 2020).
10 Ibid.; Babauta, "George Tweed."

11 "Antonio Cruz Artero, Papers 1943–1946." UOG University Libraries Digital Repository, http://rfk2.edu.gu:8080/jspui/handle/20.500.11751/15 (accessed October 3, 2020).
12 "Narrative by George Ray Tweed," 14.

Chapter 19

1   Sherrod, "Radioman George Tweed," 44.
2   Horne, "Rescued after 2-1/2 Years," 7.
3   Lynch, "Deadly Game of Hide and Seek," 20.
4   Ibid., 18.
5   Tweed and Clark, *Robinson Crusoe, USN*, 162.
6   "Narrative by George Ray Tweed," 13.
7   Layla Raymanova. "George Tweed Interview Pt3." YouTube, https://youtu.be/aX1jBKGJe8s (September 1, 2009). Hereafter cited as "George Tweed Interview Pt3."
8   Tweed and Clark, *Robinson Crusoe, USN*, 165.
9   "Survivors: The Rescue of George Tweed," 72; Sherrod, "Radioman George Tweed," 44.
10 "Narrative by George Ray Tweed," 20.
11 Sherrod, "Radioman George Tweed," 44.
12 Ibid.
13 Babauta, "George Tweed."
14 "George Tweed Interview Pt3."
15 "Narrative by George Ray Tweed," 13.
16 "Father Duenas' Execution Site." US National Park Service, https://www.nps.gov/parkhistory/online_books/wapa/hrs/hrsf2.htm (accessed October 14, 2020).
17 Palomo, *An Island in Agony*, 119.
18 Tweed and Clark, *Robinson Crusoe, USN*, 209.

Chapter 20

1   Hoyt, *How They Won the War in the Pacific*, 207.
2   Craig L. Symonds. *World War II at Sea: A Global History*. New York: Oxford University Press, 2018, 489.
3   Victor Brooks. *Hell Is Upon Us: D-Day in the Pacific: Saipan to Guam, June–August 1944*. Cambridge, MA: Da Capo, 2007, 15.
4   Reynolds, "Admiral Ernest J. King and the Strategy for Victory in the Pacific," 60.
5   Walter R. Borneman. *The Admirals: Nimitz, Halsey, Leahy, and King—The Five-Star Admirals Who Won the War at Sea*. New York: Little, Brown and Company, 2012, 361.
6   Ibid.
7   Evan Mawdsley. *The War for the Seas: A Maritime History of World War II*. New Haven, CT: Yale University Press, 2019, 377.
8   Van Der Vat, *The Pacific Campaign*, 262–263.
9   Samuel Eliot Morison. *History of United States Naval Operations in World War II, Volume VIII: New Guinea and the Marianas*. Edison, NJ: Castle Books, 2001, 12.

10 Samuel Eliot Morison. *History of United States Naval Operations in World War II, Volume VII: Aleutians, Gilberts, and Marshalls.* Edison, NJ: Castle Books, 2001, 114.
11 Costello, *The Pacific War*, 431; Spector, *Eagle Against the Sun*, 259.
12 Van Der Vat, *The Pacific Campaign*, 300.
13 Ibid.
14 Gailey, *The War in the Pacific*, 261.
15 Ibid.
16 Morison, *Aleutians, Gilberts, and Marshalls*, 206.
17 Morison, *New Guinea and the Marianas*, 7.

Chapter 21

1 Crowl, *Campaign in the Marianas*, 55.
2 Dull, *Imperial Japanese Navy*, 302.
3 Rottman and Gerrard, *Guam 1941 & 1944*, 39.
4 Morison, *New Guinea and the Marianas*, 168; Crowl, *Campaign in the Marianas*, 329.
5 Crowl, *Campaign in the Marianas*, 19.
6 Gailey, *The War in the Pacific*, 301.
7 Crowl, *Campaign in the Marianas*, 39.
8 "Raymond Ames Spruance 3 July 1886 - 13 December 1969." Naval History and Heritage Command, https://www.history.navy.mil/content/history/nhhc/research/library/research-guides/modern-biographical-files-ndl/modern-bios-s/spruance-raymond-a.html (February 19, 2015). Hereafter cited as "Raymond Ames Spruance."
9 Gailey, *The War in the Pacific*, 156.
10 "Raymond Ames Spruance."
11 Borneman, *The Admirals*, 110.
12 Morison, *Aleutians, Gilberts, and Marshalls*, 86.
13 Borneman, *The Admirals*, 350.
14 Ibid., 350.
15 Morison, *New Guinea and the Marianas*, 160.
16 Ibid., 233.
17 Crowl, *Campaign in the Marianas*, 33.
18 Spector, *Eagle Against the Sun*, 301.
19 Morison, *New Guinea and the Marianas*, 155.

Chapter 22

1 "Survivors: The Rescue of George Tweed," 72.
2 Sherrod, "Radioman George Tweed," 47.
3 "Mrs. Roscoe Bennett to US Navy Department" (December 27, 1941) in "Tweed Service Record."
4 "Tweed, George Ray, RM1c, USN, Request for Information" (January 7, 1942) in "Tweed Service Record."
5 C. B. Hatch Letter to Mary Tweed (February 9, 1942) in "Tweed Service Record."
6 C. B. Hatch Letter to Mrs. Bennett (May 4, 1942) in "Tweed Service Record."

7   "Narrative by George Ray Tweed," 3.

8   "Yank Lives Like Hunted Prey 31 Month on Guam; Escapes." *Chicago Tribune*, August 11, 1944, 1.

9   Tweed and Clark, *Robinson Crusoe, USN*, 215.

10 Ibid., 216.

11 "Survivors: The Rescue of George Tweed," 72.

12 Horne, "Rescued after 2-1/2 Years," 7.

Chapter 23

1   Van Der Vat, *The Pacific Campaign*, 317.

2   Thomas Buell. *The Quiet Warrior: A Biography of Admiral Raymond A. Spruance*. Boston, MA: Little, Brown, 1974, 258.

3   Ian W. Toll. *The Conquering Tide: War in the Pacific Islands, 1942–1944*. New York: W.W. Norton & Company, 2015, 458.

4   Ibid., 463.

5   Morison, *New Guinea and the Marianas*, 180.

6   Crowl, *Campaign in the Marianas*, 29.

7   Morison, *New Guinea and the Marianas*, 152.

8   Toll, *The Conquering Tide*, 459.

9   Van Der Vat, *The Pacific Campaign*, 320.

10 Gailey, *The War in the Pacific*, 308.

11 "Operation Forager: The Battle of Saipan: 15 June–9 July 1944." Naval History and Heritage Command, https://www.history.navy.mil/browse-by-topic/wars-conflicts-and-operations/world-war-ii/1944/saipan.html (accessed August 24, 2021). Hereafter cited as "Operation Forager: The Battle of Saipan."

12 Buell, *The Quiet Warrior*, 258.

13 Toll, *The Conquering Tide*, 462.

14 "Operation Forager: The Battle of Saipan."

15 Gailey, *The War in the Pacific*, 324.

16 Crowl, *Campaign in the Marianas*, 265.

17 Gailey, *The War in the Pacific*, 334–35

Chapter 24

1   Symonds, *World War II at Sea*, 541.

2   Mawdsley, *The War for the Seas*, 398.

3   Ibid., 399.

4   Dull, *Imperial Japanese Navy*, 303.

5   Morison, *New Guinea and the Marianas*, 233.

6   Dull, *Imperial Japanese Navy*, 304.

7   E. B. Potter. *Nimitz*. Annapolis, MD: Naval Institute Press, 1976, 302.

8   Symonds, *World War II at Sea*, 543.

9   Dull, *Imperial Japanese Navy*, 305.

10 Symonds, *World War II at Sea*, 543.

11   Buell, *The Quiet Warrior*, 262.
12   Gailey, *The War in the Pacific*, 310; Van Der Vat, *The Pacific Campaign*, 322.
13   Symonds, *World War II at Sea*, 544.
14   Costello, *The Pacific War*, 480.
15   Mawdsley, *The War for the Seas*, 403.
16   Toll, *The Conquering Tide*, 483.
17   Ibid., 487.
18   Dull, *Imperial Japanese Navy*, 309.
19   Costello, *The Pacific War*, 483.
20   Spector, *Eagle Against the Sun*, 311.
21   Gailey, *The War in the Pacific*, 315.
22   "Battle of the Philippine Sea: June 19–20, 1944." Naval History and Heritage Command, https://www.history.navy.mil/content/history/museums/nmusn/explore/photography/wwii/wwii-pacific/mariana-islands/philippine-sea.html (accessed December 22, 2020).
23   Ibid.
24   Costello, *The Pacific War*, 482.
25   Symonds, *World War II at Sea*, 552.
26   Potter, *Nimitz*, 303.

Chapter 25

1   Horne, "Rescued after 2-1/2 Years," 7.
2   "Narrative by George Ray Tweed," 6.
3   Tweed and Clark, *Robinson Crusoe, USN*, 230.
4   "USS McCall (DD-400)." NavSource Naval History, http://www.navsource.org/archives/05/400.htm (accessed November 3, 2020).
5   Morison, *New Guinea and the Marianas*, 412.
6   CO USS *McCall* to Commander in Chief US Fleet. "Report of Operation of USS *McCall* on 10 July 1944." August 10, 1944, 1. Hereafter cited as "Report of Operation of USS *McCall*."
7   "Narrative by George Ray Tweed," 14.
8   War Diary, *McCall*, July 10, 1944.
9   "Warrant Officer George Tweed Who Survived Guam Gives Credit for Survival to 24,000 Little Brown People." *Chino Record* (CA) (November 2, 1944), 8. Hereafter cited as "Warrant Officer George Tweed."
10   Thomas E. Quinn Collection (AFC/2001/001/33869), Veterans History Project, American Folklife Center, Library of Congress. https://memory.loc.gov/diglib/vhp/bib/loc.natlib.afc2001001.33869 (accessed November 4, 2020). Hereafter cited as "Thomas E. Quinn Collection."
11   War Diary, *McCall*, July 10, 1944.
12   "McCall II (DD-400)." Naval History and Heritage Command, https://www.history.navy.mil/research/histories/ship-histories/danfs/m/mccall-ii.html (August 6, 2015).

Chapter 26

1   "Narrative by George Ray Tweed," 17.
2   "Thomas E. Quinn Collection."
3   "Report of Operation of USS *McCall*," 2.
4   "Narrative by George Ray Tweed," 19.
5   "Warrant Officer George Tweed," 8.
6   Horne, "Rescued after 2-1/2 Years," 7.
7   Sherrod, "Radioman George Tweed," 41.
8   Tweed and Clark, *Robinson Crusoe, USN*, 241.
9   War Diary, *McCall*, July 10, 1944.
10 "RDM3-C James Arthur Mills, Redland, Member of Party that Rescued Radioman Tweed." *McCurtan Gazette* (Idabel, ID), November 29, 1944, 1.
11 Ibid.
12 Ibid.
13 War Diary, *Hornet*, July 11, 1944.
14 Ibid.
15 "James R. Armstrong U.S. Navy—World War II Seaman First Class Interviewed by Herkimer Fulton County Historical Society." New York State Military History Museum, https://dmna.ny.gov/historic/veterans/transcriptions/Armstrong_James_R.pdf (accessed November 11, 2020).
16 Morison, *New Guinea and the Marianas*, 412–413.
17 Horne, "Rescued after 2-1/2 Years," 7.
18 Shirley Povich. "Protector of Tweed on Guam Tell Story to Post Writer." *Washington Post*, March 10, 1945.

Chapter 27

1   Brooks, *Hell is Upon Us*, 266.
2   Cyril J. O'Brien. and United States. Marine Corps History and Museums Division. *Liberation: Marines in the Recapture of Guam (Marines in World War II Commemorative Series)*. Washington, DC: History and Museums Division, Headquarters, US Marine Corps, 1994, 4.
3   Roy Geiger to Commander in Chief Pacific Fleet and Pacific Ocean Areas. "Operation Report—Marianas." September 3, 1944, 4.
4   Morison, *New Guinea and the Marianas*, 377.
5   Commander Task Force Fifty-Three to Commander in Chief, United States Fleet. "Report of Amphibious Operations for the Capture of Guam" (August 10, 1944), Enclosure A: Operations Chronology, 16. Hereafter cited as "Operations Chronology."
6   Commander Task Force Fifty-Three to Commander in Chief, United States Fleet. "Report of Amphibious Operations for the Capture of Guam" (August 10, 1944), 6. Hereafter cited as "Report of Amphibious Operations for the Capture of Guam."
7   "Operations Chronology," 24; Morison, *New Guinea and the Marianas*, 381.
8   "Operations Chronology," 25.
9   Denfeld, *Hold the Marianas*, 182.

10   Crowl, *Campaign in the Marianas*, 336.

11   Ibid., 322.

12   Morison, *Aleutians, Gilberts, and Marshalls*, 89.

13   "M4 Sherman Tank." The National World War II Museum, https://www.nationalww2 museum.org/visit/museum-campus/us-freedom-pavilion/vehicles-war/m4-sherman-tank (accessed March 17, 2021).

14   Rottman and Gerrard, *Guam 1941 & 1944*, 34.

15   Brooks, *Hell Is Upon Us*, 270.

16   Morison, *New Guinea and the Marianas*, 373.

17   Crowl, *Campaign in the Marianas*, 332–333.

18   Denfeld, *Hold the Marianas*, 158.

19   Gailey, *The War in the Pacific*, 325.

20   Crowl, *Campaign in the Marianas*, 322.

21   Dixon, Gilda, and Bulgrin. "The Archaeology of World War II Japanese Stragglers," 112–13.

Chapter 28

1   Geiger, Roy to Commander in Chief Pacific Fleet and Pacific Ocean Areas. "Operation Report—Marianas" (September 3, 1944), 2.

2   O'Brien, *Marines in the Recapture of Guam*, 1.

3   "Report of Amphibious Operations for the Capture of Guam," Enclosure C: Comments on Air Support, 13.

4   "Operations Chronology," 28.

5   O.R. Lodge and the United States Marine Corps. *The Recapture of Guam. Marine Corps Monograph, No. 12.* Washington, DC: Historical Branch, G-3 Division, Headquarters, US Marine Corps, 1954, 39.

6   Paul J. Borja. "In Asan, Banzai and Bravery." US National Park Service, https://www.nps.gov/parkhistory/online_books/npswapa/extContent/Lib/liberation19.htm (accessed March 17, 2021).

7   Dave Lotz and Rose S.N. Manibusan. "Liberating Guam." US National Park Service, https://www.nps.gov/parkhistory/online_books/npswapa/extContent/Lib/liberation16a.htm (accessed January 25, 2021).

8   O'Brien, *Marines in the Recapture of Guam*, 12–13.

9   Denfeld, *Hold the Marianas*, 186.

10   Bill Gulda. "Kenoshan, Hero of Guam Battle, Honored." *Kenosha News*, July 21, 1994, 1.

11   Lodge, *The Recapture of Guam*, 55.

12   Gailey, *The War in the Pacific*, 327.

13   Rottman and Gerrard, *Guam 1941 & 1944*, 49.

Chapter 29

1   Brooks, *Hell Is Upon Us*, 287.

2   Rottman and Gerrard, *Guam 1941 & 1944*, 56.

3 Frank O. Hough. *The Island War: The United States Marine Corps in the Pacific*. Philadelphia: J.B. Lippincott, 1947, 271.
4 O'Brien, *Marines in the Recapture of Guam*, 25.
5 Borja, "In Asan, Banzai and Bravery."
6 Ibid.
7 Morison, *New Guinea and the Marianas*, 388.
8 Rottman and Gerrard, *Guam 1941 & 1944*, 60.
9 Morison, *New Guinea and the Marianas*, 388.
10 Hough, *The Island War*, 274.
11 Ibid., 260.
12 O'Brien, *Marines in the Recapture of Guam*, 27.
13 Lodge, *The Recapture of Guam*, 78.
14 Hough, *The Island War*, 279.
15 O'Brien, *Marines in the Recapture of Guam*, 28.
16 Denfeld, *Hold the Marianas*, 192.
17 Crowl, *Campaign in the Marianas*, 366.
18 "Report of Amphibious Operations for the Capture of Guam," 13.

Chapter 30

1 Hough, *The Island War*, 280.
2 Center of Military History. *Guam: Operations of the 77th Division, 21 July – 10 August 1944*. Washington, DC: United States American Forces in Action Series, 1990, 42.
3 Hough, *The Island War*, 281.
4 Crowl, *Campaign in the Marianas*, 368.
5 Lodge, *The Recapture of Guam*, 95.
6 Brooks, *Hell Is Upon Us*, 291.
7 Lodge, *The Recapture of Guam*, 95.
8 Crowl, *Campaign in the Marianas*, 370.
9 Center of Military History, *Guam: Operations of the 77th Division*, 60.
10 Crowl, *Campaign in the Marianas*, 374.
11 O'Brien, *Marines in the Recapture of Guam*, 32.
12 Ibid., 31.
13 Rottman and Gerrard, *Guam 1941 & 1944*, 61.
14 Ibid., 69.
15 Crowl, *Campaign in the Marianas*, 378.

Chapter 31

1 Lodge, *The Recapture of Guam*, 123–124.
2 O'Brien, *Marines in the Recapture of Guam*, 34.
3 Lodge, *The Recapture of Guam*, 124.
4 Center of Military History, *Guam: Operations of the 77th Division*, 65.
5 Crowl, *Campaign in the Marianas*, 381.

6   Center of Military History, *Guam: Operations of the 77th Division*, 69.
7   Rottman and Gerrard, *Guam 1941 & 1944*, 73.
8   War Diary, Task Group 53.5, August 2, 1944.
9   Crowl, *Campaign in the Marianas*, 390.

Chapter 32

1   O'Brien, *Marines in the Recapture of Guam*, 36.
2   Crowl, *Campaign in the Marianas*, 409.
3   O'Brien, *Marines in the Recapture of Guam*, 36.
4   Lodge, *The Recapture of Guam*, 144.
5   Crowl, *Campaign in the Marianas*, 417.
6   O'Brien, *Marines in the Recapture of Guam*, 37.
7   Crowl, *Campaign in the Marianas*, 409.
8   Center of Military History, *Guam: Operations of the 77th Division*, 102.
9   Ibid., 104.
10 Ibid.
11 Rottman and Gerrard, *Guam 1941 & 1944*, 68.
12 Center of Military History, *Guam: Operations of the 77th Division*, 110.
13 Rottman and Gerrard, *Guam 1941 & 1944*, 68.
14 Center of Military History, *Guam: Operations of the 77th Division*, 112.
15 Crowl, *Campaign in the Marianas*, 411.
16 Center of Military History, *Guam: Operations of the 77th Division*, 116.

Chapter 33

1   Tweed and Clark, *Robinson Crusoe, USN*, 250.
2   Sherrod, "Radioman George Tweed," 42.
3   "Now Back at Home." *New York Times* (August 11, 1944), 7.
4   "Never Lost Hope." *Chicago Tribune* (August 11, 1944), 1.
5   Louis Aaron. "Fame Pursues Tweed, Who Hid from Japs on Guam for 31 Months." *Seminole Producer* (OK) (September 1, 1944), 6.
6   "Wants to Go Back." *Chicago Tribune* (August 13, 1944).
7   "Tweed, Hero of Guam Gets Quick Divorce." *New York Times* (August 17, 1944), 20.
8   "Yank Who Hid 2-1/2 years on Guam Marries." *Chicago Tribune* (July 9, 1945), 7.
9   "Tweed Service Record."
10 "Tweed Decorated for Feat at Guam: He Gets Legion of Merit." *New York Times* (September 10, 1944).
11 "Warrant Officer George Tweed," 8.
12 "Guam's Fugitive Stirred by Movie: Sailor, Who Hid for 31 Months." *New York Times* (October 26, 1944).
13 Al Chase. "Sailor Tells How He Hid Out on Guam." *Chicago Tribune* (April 29, 1945), E8.
14 Tweed and Clark, *Robinson Crusoe, USN*, 261.

Chapter 34

1   Rottman, *Pacific Island Guide*, 390.
2   Denfeld, *Hold the Marianas*, 156.
3   Palomo, *An Island in Agony*, 163.
4   Blaz, *Bisita Guam*, 86.
5   Ibid., 82.
6   Judge Joaquin V. E. Manibusan. "In Tai, a Day of Terror and Tragedy." US National Park Service, https://www.nps.gov/parkhistory/online_books/npswapa/extcontent/lib/liberation13.htm (accessed March 30, 2021).
7   Palomo, *An Island in Agony*, 175.
8   "Father Duenas' Execution Site."
9   Tony Palomo. "A Man of Courage and Conviction." US National Park Service, https://www.nps.gov/parkhistory/online_books/npswapa/extContent/Lib/liberation7.htm (accessed March 30, 2021).
10 Palomo, *An Island in Agony*, 181.
11 "Father Duenas' Execution Site."
12 Babauta, "George Tweed."
13 Blaz, *Bisita Guam*, 119.
14 Leo Babauta. "War Atrocities: Manenggon Concentration Camp." Guampedia, https://www.guampedia.com/war-atrocities-manenggon-concentration-camp/ (accessed March 30, 2021).
15 Blaz, *Bisita Guam*, 124.
16 Ricardo J. Bordallo and C. Sablan Gault. "The Journey to Manengon." National Park Service, https://www.nps.gov/parkhistory/online_books/npswapa/extContent/Lib/liberation12.htm (accessed March 30, 2021).
17 Babauta, "War Atrocities: Manenggon Concentration Camp."
18 Blaz, *Bisita Guam*, 139.
19 Bordallo and Gault, "The Journey to Manengon."
20 Paul J. Borja. "Liberators Meet the Liberated." National Park Service, https://www.nps.gov/parkhistory/online_books/npswapa/extContent/Lib/liberation26.htm (accessed March 31, 2021).

Chapter 35

1   Crowl, *Campaign in the Marianas*, 418.
2   Center of Military History, *Guam: Operations of the 77th Division*, 122.
3   Lodge, *The Recapture of Guam*, 149.
4   Center of Military History, *Guam: Operations of the 77th Division*, 123.
5   Lodge, *The Recapture of Guam*, 151.
6   Rottman and Gerrard, *Guam 1941 & 1944*, 81.
7   Denfeld, *Hold the Marianas*, 203.
8   Lodge, *The Recapture of Guam*, 157.
9   Denfeld, *Hold the Marianas*, 202.
10 Crowl, *Campaign in the Marianas*, 436.

11 Lodge, *The Recapture of Guam*, 152.
12 Denfeld, *Hold the Marianas*, 204.
13 O'Brien, *Marines in the Recapture of Guam*, 43.
14 Center of Military History, *Guam: Operations of the 77th Division*, 131.
15 Crowl, *Campaign in the Marianas*, 436.
16 Lodge, *The Recapture of Guam*, 158.
17 Lodge, *The Recapture of Guam*, 153.
18 Bruce Lloyd. "Chagui'an Massacre Marked with Memorial." Pacific Daily News, https://www.guampdn.com/story/news/local/2019/08/08/chaguian-massacre marked-memorial/1951952001/ (August 8, 2019).

Chapter 36

1 Rottman and Gerrard, *Guam 1941 & 1944*, 81.
2 "Narrative by Major General Henry L. Larsen, USMC, Island Commander, Guam." World War II Interviews. College Park, MD: National Archives. April 23, 1945, 7. Hereafter cited as "Larsen Narrative."
3 "The Bushido Code: An Overview." PBS, https://www.pbs.org/wgbh/sugihara/ readings/bushido.html (accessed August 10, 2021).
4 Tina A. Aguon. "WWII: Guam Combat Patrol Hunted Japanese Stragglers." Guampedia, https://www.guampedia.com/wwii-guam-combat-patrol-hunted-japanese- stragglers/ (accessed March 23, 2021).
5 Center of Military History, *Guam: Operations of the 77th Division*, 131.
6 "Larsen Narrative," 9.
7 Rottman and Gerrard, *Guam 1941 & 1944*, 81.
8 Lodge, *The Recapture of Guam*, 161.
9 Aguon, "WWII: Guam Combat Patrol."
10 Lodge, *The Recapture of Guam*, 162.
11 Robert Amstutz Oral History Interview Transcript. National Museum of the Pacific War, https://digitalarchive.pacificwarmuseum.org/digital/collection/p16769coll1/ id/7500 (accessed January 16, 2023), 20.
12 Denfeld, *Hold the Marianas*, 205.
13 Lodge, *The Recapture of Guam*, 162.
14 Palomo, *An Island in Agony*, 224.
15 Dixon, Gilda, and Bulgrin, "The Archaeology of World War II Japanese Stragglers," 118.
16 Aguon, "WWII: Guam Combat Patrol."
17 Denfeld, *Hold the Marianas*, 205–206.
18 Lodge, *The Recapture of Guam*, 165.
19 Masako Watanabe. "Japanese Straggler Recalls Nearly 8-Year Survival in Jungle." Pacific Daily News, https://www.guampdn.com/news/local/japanese-straggler-recalls-nearly- 8-year-survival-in-jungle/article_0fd1917f-f495-593b-a982-9a5c5f4071e3.html (July 12, 2017).
20 Ibid.
21 Dixon, Gilda, and Bulgrin, "The Archaeology of World War II Japanese Stragglers," 118.

22 Anumita Kaur. "Japanese Stragglers Remained Hidden in Guam's Jungles for Years After World War II." Pacific Daily News, https://www.guampdn.com/news/culture/japanese-stragglers-remained-hidden-in-guams-jungles-for-years-after-world-war-ii/article_0edcd81c-559e-53d5-88fe-001b63fa3a29.html (July 1, 2019).

23 Denfeld, *Hold the Marianas*, 206.

24 Omi Hatashin. *Private Yokoi's War and Life on Guam, 1944–1972: The Story of the Japanese Imperial Army's Longest WWII Survivor in the Field and Later Life*. Leiden, The Netherlands: Brill, 2009, 12–13.

25 Asahi Shimbun Tokuha Kishadan. *28 Years in the Guam Jungle: Sergeant Yokoi Home from World War II*. Tokyo: Japan Publications, 1972, 127.

26 Ronald Yates. "Veterans of Guam Revisit the Land that Time Forgot." *Chicago Tribune* (April 28, 1986).

Chapter 37

1   Van Der Vat, *The Pacific Campaign*, 330.

2   Rottman and Gerrard, *Guam 1941 & 1944*, 87.

3   Lodge, *The Recapture of Guam*, 160.

4   "Larsen Narrative," 3–4.

5   Navy Department. *Building the Navy's Bases in World War II; History of the Bureau of Yards and Docks and the Civil Engineer Corps, 1940–1946: Volume 2*. Washington: US Government Printing Office, 1947, 357.

6   Ibid., 355.

7   Crowl, *Campaign in the Marianas*, 443.

8   Navy Department, *Building the Navy's Bases*, 352.

9   Crowl, *Campaign in the Marianas*, 443.

10 Navy Department, *Building the Navy's Bases*, 354.

11 Morison, *New Guinea and the Marianas*, 220.

Chapter 38

1   Costello, *The Pacific War*, 487.

2   Amstutz Oral History, 22.

3   "77th Infantry Division: Combat Chronicle." US Army Center of Military History, https://history.army.mil/html/forcestruc/cbtchron/cc/077id.htm (accessed December 20, 2021).

4   Van Der Vat, *The Pacific Campaign*, 372.

5   Spector, *Eagle Against the Sun*, 493.

6   Gailey, *The War in the Pacific*, 449.

7   "FDR Biography." Franklin D. Roosevelt Presidential Library and Museum, https://www.fdrlibrary.org/fdr-biography (accessed May 11, 2021).

8   Carsten Fries. "Victory in the Pacific: Japan's Surrender and Aftermath: August–October 1945." Naval History and Heritage Command, https://www.history.navy.mil/content/history/nhhc/browse-by-topic/wars-conflicts-and-operations/world-war-ii/1945/victory-in-pacific.html (accessed May 11, 2021).

9 "Downfall: The Plan for the Invasion of Japan." US Army Center of Military History, https://history.army.mil/books/wwii/MacArthur%20Reports/MacArthur%20V1/ch13.htm (accessed May 11, 2021).
10 Spector, *Eagle Against the Sun*, 544.
11 Fries, "Victory in the Pacific."
12 Ibid.
13 "Potsdam Declaration." Britannica, https://www.britannica.com/topic/Potsdam-Declaration (accessed May 12, 2021).
14 Gailey, *The War in the Pacific*, 488.
15 Fries, "Victory in the Pacific."

Chapter 39

1 Mansell, *The Forgotten Men of Guam*, 82.
2 "Jackson Narrative," 10.
3 Bob Hackett and Sander Kingsepp. "Kokansen: Stories of Diplomatic Exchange and Repatriation Ships." Combined Fleet, http://www.combinedfleet.com/Kokansen.htm (June 1, 2016).
4 Smith, *Counting the Days*, 185.
5 "Marine Survives Imprisonment, Beating," 11.
6 Ibid.
7 Mansell, *The Forgotten Men of Guam*, 176.
8 Hale and Gordon, *First Captured, Last Freed*, 133.
9 Shannon J. Murphy. "WWII: Prisoners of War Sent to Japan." Guampedia, https://www.guampedia.com/wwii-prisoners-of-war-sent-to-japan/ (accessed March 31, 2021).
10 Ibid.
11 Giles, *Captive of the Rising Sun*, 156.
12 Raj Sood. "Marine Endures War in POW Camp." US National Park Service, https://www.nps.gov/parkhistory/online_books/npswapa/extContent/Lib/liberation11.htm (accessed March 30, 2021).
13 Hale and Gordon, *First Captured, Last Freed*, 137.
14 "The Liberation of POWs: Sept. 1945." Center for Research Allied POWS Under the Japanese, http://www.mansell.com/pow_resources/liberation_photos.html (accessed June 13, 2021).
15 Murphy, "WWII: Prisoners of War Sent to Japan."
16 Kim Guise. "Operation Swift Mercy and POW Supply." The National World War II Museum, https://www.nationalww2museum.org/war/articles/operation-swift-mercy-and-pow-supply (September 18, 2020).
17 "Tokyo War Crimes Trial." The National World War II Museum, https://www.nationalww2museum.org/war/topics/tokyo-war-crimes-trial (accessed June 13, 2021).
18 Donald R. Shuster. "US Navy War Crimes Trials on Guam." Guampedia, https://www.guampedia.com/u-s-navy-war-crimes-trials-on-guam/ (accessed May 23, 2021).
19 "Guam Site of Pacific War Trials." US National Park Service, https://www.nps.gov/parkhistory/online_books/npswapa/extcontent/lib/liberation30.htm (accessed May 17, 2021).

20 Ibid.
21 Shuster, "US Navy War Crimes Trials on Guam."
22 Timothy P. Maga. "Away from Tokyo: The Pacific Islands War Crimes Trials, 1945–1949." *The Journal of Pacific History*, June 2001, 50.

Chapter 40

1 Sydney Combs. "In WWII, the Japanese Invaded Guam. Now They're Welcomed as Tourists." National Geographic, https://www.nationalgeographic.com/history/article/wwii-japan-invaded-guam-now-welcomed-tourists (December 13, 2019).
2 "Larsen Narrative," 5.
3 Jerick Sablan. "Beyond Liberation: Catholic Churches Quickly Rebuilt after World War II." Pacific Daily News, https://www.guampdn.com/news/local/beyond-liberation-catholic-churches-quickly-rebuilt-after-world-war-ii/article_ee0a0d8c-2ae6-5b99-b628-6065a72ed64b.html (April 21, 2019).
4 Dominica Tolentino. "Rebuilding from the Destruction of War." Guampedia, https://www.guampedia.com/rebuilding-from-the-ashes-of-war/ (accessed May 29, 2021).
5 "Trust Territory of the Pacific Islands." Britannica, https://www.britannica.com/place/Trust-Territory-of-the-Pacific-Islands (accessed January 3, 2022).
6 Tolentino, "Rebuilding from the Destruction of War."
7 "Guam." Britannica, https://www.britannica.com/place/Guam (accessed June 21, 2021).
8 "History: Commander, Joint Region Marianas." Commander, Navy Installations Command, https://www.cnic.navy.mil/regions/jrm/installations/navbase_guam/about/history.html (accessed May 29, 2021). Hereafter cited as "History."
9 "October 2023 Monthly Arrivals Summary." Guam Visitors Bureau, https://www.guamvisitorsbureau.com/sites/default/files/october_2023_preliminary_arrival_summary.pdf(accessed December 27, 2023).
10 Ibid.
11 Frank Quimby. "Guam Commonwealth Act." Guampedia, https://www.guampedia.com/guam-commonwealth-act/ (accessed January 5, 2021).
12 "Eras of Andersen History." Andersen Air Force Base, https://www.andersen.af.mil/About-Us/History-Tour/ (accessed May 29, 2021).
13 "Andersen Air Force Base History." Andersen Air Force Base, https://www.andersen.af.mil/History/ (accessed January 5, 2022).
14 "History."

Epilogue

1 "Larsen Narrative," 8.
2 Babauta, "George Tweed."
3 "Guamanians Boo Yank Hero for Slurring Priest." *Chicago Tribune* (September 17, 1946), 16; Doug Lovelace. "Priest Leads Guam Demonstration Against George Tweed, Navy Hero." *Brownville Herald* (TX) (September 17, 1946), 3.

4   "Ghost of Guam Admits Priest Story is Untrue." *Seattle Star* (WA) (September 27, 1946), 1.
5   Mansell, *The Forgotten Men of Guam*, 156.
6   Layla Raymanova. "George Tweed Interview Pt4." YouTube, https://youtu.be/GRhJuQdRuio (September 1, 2009). Hereafter cited as "George Tweed Interview Pt4."
7   "George Tweed Interview Pt3."
8   Ibid.
9   "George Tweed Interview Pt4."
10 "Tweed Service Record."
11 Robert Anderson. "*No Man Is an Island* Fairly Good War Film." *Chicago Tribune* (October 2, 1962), A3; Bosley Crowther. "No Man Is an Island." *New York Times* (October 11, 1962), 47.
12 Weiss, "George Tweed, Controversial War Hero."
13 "Tun Artero; Hid Sailor on Guam." *Chicago Tribune* (May 3, 1984), B16.
14 Ibid.
15 "George R. Tweed, 86: Eluded Foe on Guam." *New York Times* (January 19, 1989), B16.

INDEX

Italy, 37
Ito, Masashi, 264
Iwo Jima, 170, 271

J

Jackson, Leona, 51-53,
71-72, 79-80, 276-278
Jaluit, 146
Japan, 16, 22, 32, 38, 40-41,
43, 45, 47, 108, 110,
130, 141-143, 147,
164, 198, 218, 226,
245, 265, 269, 286
American prisoners
in, 276-280
Downfall of, 272-274
Guam stragglers return
to, 263-264
Surrender of, 275
Java Sea, Battle of, 95
JN-25 (Japanese Naval
Code), 106
Johnston, Agueda, 99-101,
123, 134, 240
Johnston, Clarence, 87, 125-
127, 132, 135, 245, 291
Johnston, William, 99-100
Joint Chiefs of Staff (United
States), 103, 109, 113,
141, 147, 149, 274

Joint Region Marianas
Command, 288
Jones, Luther, 87-88,
90, 124-125
Joslin, Harold, 74
Joy, Turner, 193

K

Kaga, 112
Kako, 60
Kane, John, 232
Kauffman, John, 72
Kennedy, President John F., 285
KGEI San Francisco,
117, 119, 158
Kimmel, Husband, 104
Kimura (Unknown first
name), 124-125
King, Ernest, 102-103, 105-
107, 142-143, 150, 175
Kinugasa, 60
Kluegel, John, 88
Knox, Frank, 104-105
Kobe, Japan, 273, 276
Koga, Mineichi, 143-
144, 148, 168
Komatsu, Father Petro, 140
Korea, 36, 60, 82, 280, 286
Korean War, 287
Kramer, Dolores, 238
Krump, Michael, 87, 124-125

McMillin, George, 18, 42-44,
46, 49-50, 54, 63, 67-68,
76, 79, 85, 218, 276
McNulty, William, 44
Merizo, Guam, 63, 131
Mexico, 10
Midway Island, 23, 29,
110-112, 141
Midway, Battle of, 112-113,
150-151, 168, 171
Mili, 146
Mills, James, 186
Minagawa, Bunzo, 263-264
Mississippi, 150
Missouri, 275
Mitscher, Marc, 152, 154,
163-164, 171, 173, 178
Mitsubishi F1M2
"Pete," 48-49, 51
Moore, Charles, 210
Mount Barrigada, 228, 230
Mount Lamlam, 25, 220
Mount Macajna, 221
Mount Mataguac, 221, 254
Mount Santa Rosa, 26, 215,
222-223, 227, 230-232,
251, 253-254, 257-258
Mount Tapochau, 164
Mount Tenjo, 74
Murphy, John, 282

N

Nagoya, Japan, 273
Nagumo, Chuichi, 47-48,
111, 165-166
Nanking, China, 38
Naputi, Francisco, 246
Naval War College, 104, 150
New Caledonia, 110
New Guinea, 22, 109-110,
113-114, 142, 148
New Mexico, 200-201
New Orleans, 227
New York, NY, 212, 239
Nimitz, *Chester*, 102-109, 111-
112, 144, 150-151, 165,
174, 237, 265, 268-269
No Man Is an Island, 293
Normandy, France, 162, 274
North Airfield, 269
Northern Attack
Force, 152, 162
Northwest Airfield, 269

O

O'Brien, Cyril, 205, 280
Obata, Hideyoshi, 149, 165,
196-197, 221-222, 254-256
Ogo, Francisco, 87
Okinawa, 174, 271
Omiya Jima, 78
Operation A-Go, 149, 169

Operation Coronet, 274
Operation Forager, 148, 150, 152, 154, 162, 167, 191
Operation Olympic, 274
Operation Straggler, 263
Operation Swift Mercy, 281
Ordot, Guam, 85, 225
Organic Act of Guam, 285
Oribiletti, Bruna, 208
Orote Airfield, 268
Orote Peninsula, 11, 22-23, 27, 32, 51, 53, 63, 65, 138, 191, 194, 197-198, 209-210, 213-214, 216-219, 268, 284
Osaka, Japan, 273, 278-279
Ozawa, Jisaburo, 169-174

P

P-47 Thunderbolt, 253
Pacific Cable Station, 59
Pacific Ocean, 21-22, 36, 39, 44, 107, 109, 135, 138, 151, 236, 267, 274
Pago Bay, 25, 27, 131
Pago River, 225, 226
Pago, Guam, 27
Palaus Islands, 148, 169, 197
Pan Am Clipper, 23, 30, 33, 50-52
Panama Canal, 21

Panay, 38
Pangelinan, Ben, 118, 244
Pangelinan, Juan, 131-131, 134, 244-246
Pati Point, 269
Paul Hamilton, 23
Pearl Harbor, Hawaii, 39, 41, 86, 106-107, 111-112, 144, 147, 151, 165, 218, 236, 266
    Japanese attack on, 47-50, 52, 91-93, 102, 104, 156
Penguin, 32, 49, 52-55, 65-66, 73, 87, 125
Pensacola, 132
Perez, Frank, 126
Perez, Juan, 63, 125-126
Philadelphia, PA, 46
Philippines, 9, 22, 28-29, 32, 38, 40-41, 44-45, 59, 104, 120, 138, 165, 168, 282, 288
    American reconquest of, 142-143, 151, 271
    American surrender of, 94, 118
    Japanese attack on, 91, 93
    Spanish colony, 7, 12

Philippine Sea, 144, 149,
168, 171, 191
Philippine Sea, Battle of,
169-175, 258, 270
Piti Navy Yard, 23, 49,
52-53, 70, 79, 209
Piti, Guam, 29, 77, 244
Plaza de España, 16, 32,
51, 63-64, 77, 224
Port Moresby, New Guinea,
110, 113-114
Portland, OR, 23, 238
Potsdam Declaration, 275
Puerto Rico, 28, 150
Pugua Point, Guam, 135

Q

Queen Maria of Spain, 9
Quinn, Thomas, 181-
182, 184-185
Quitugua, Jesus, 116, 119

R

R.L. Barnes, 32, 54
Rabaul, Solomon
Islands, 108, 113
Radio Agaña, 16, 33, 50, 54, 60
Radio Libugon, 33,
54, 57, 59, 74
Rainbow 5 War Plan, 39
Redwood City, CA, 118

Reyes, Jesus, 99
Ritidian Point, 53, 230,
232, 254, 269
Robinson Crusoe, USN, 240, 290
Robsion, John M., 36
Rocky Mount, 192
Rojos, Ramon, 158-159
Roosevelt, President Franklin,
40, 94, 103, 143, 273
Roslansky, Marvin, 80
Rota, 22, 46, 62, 149, 157, 173
Russia, 45
Russian Baltic Fleet, 36
Russo-Japanese War, 36

S

Saez, Don Pascual Artero y, 132
Saipan, 12, 48, 51, 53, 99,
149-154, 163-166, 170-
171, 191, 193, 197-198,
208, 222, 237, 246,
253, 258, 270, 282
Saito, Yoshitsugu, 164, 166
San Diego, CA, 34, 237
San Francisco, 102
San Francisco, CA, 21,
23, 30, 118, 158
San Juan, Puerto Rico, 24
San Luis d' Apra Harbor
– See Apra Harbor
Santa Paula, CA, 237

ACKNOWLEDGMENTS

WRITING A STORY ABOUT WORLD War II is an enormous under-taking. The conflict occurred more than seventy-five years ago. None of the key participants were still alive when I started research for the book. The project could not have been completed without the help of many individuals. The list is often too lengthy to publish, but there are always some people worthy of special thanks. As with any naval history project, the outstanding people at the National Archives and the Naval History and Heritage Command provided abundant assistance in locating documents and photos. My agent, Ethan Ellenberg, provided great wisdom and support. The excellent team at Post Hill Press, especially Alex Novak and Caitlin Burdette. They provided expert guidance throughout the publishing process. I want to thank Philip Schwartzberg at Meridian Mapping for making the maps. Lastly, I want to thank my wife, Sandy. I am eternally grateful for her enduring support and encouragement.

ABOUT THE AUTHOR

JOHN J. DOMAGALSKI IS THE author of five books, including *Escape from Java*, *Under a Blood Red Sun*, and *Sunk in Kula Gulf*. Domagalski's fascination with history began at a young age through building model ships and reading books about World War II. His interest eventually grew into research and writing, and he has interviewed scores of veterans from the Pacific War. His articles have appeared in *WWII History*, *Naval History magazine*, and *World War II Quarterly*. He is a graduate of Northern Illinois University and lives near Chicago. For more information, visit his website at www. pacificwarauthor.com.